Northwest Greenland

NORTHWEST GREENLAND

A History

Richard Vaughan

The University of Maine Press

Published by the University of Maine Press
51 PICS Building, Orono, Maine 04469-0150 U.S.A.

First edition 1991
01 00 99 98 97 96 95 94 93 92 91   1 2 3 4 5

The paper used in this publication meets the minimum requirements of American National Standard for Information Sciences—Permanence of Paper for Printed Library Materials,
ANSI Z39.48-1984.∞

Library of Congress Cataloging-in-Publication Data

Vaughan, Richard, 1927–
    Northwest Greenland : a history / Richard Vaughan. — 1st ed.
        p.   cm.
    Includes bibliographical references and index.
    ISBN 0-89101-072-6
    1. Greenland—History.   I. Title.
G760.V38   1991   91-8114
998.2—dc20   CIP

Manufactured in the United States of America

Contents

Acknowledgments		vii
1.	Introduction	1
2.	The Inuhuit and Their Neighbors in Early Times	12
3.	A Century of Explorers and Whalers, 1817–1917	29
4.	Eskimos and Whites *An Uneasy Partnership*	48
5.	The Inuhuit Economy Transformed	63
6.	The Demands of Subsistence and Science	78
7.	The Meteorite Rush	96
8.	Archaeology and Anthropology *The Eskimo as Research Material*	111
9.	America in Greenland	132
10.	The Inuhuit in the Twentieth Century	151
11.	Epilogue	169
	Bibliography	177
	Index	195

Illustrations
Following page 88

1. Looking over Inglefield Gulf from Qaanaaq in early July
2. The North Water south of Cape Atholl
3. The mountain and former Inuhuit settlement of Uummannaq
4. Plan and elevation of an Inuhuit winter house, 1903
5. Fur clothing of an Inuhuit woman in the nineteenth century
6. The meeting of Inuhuit and Europeans on 10 August 1818

7. Inuhuit men aboard Amundsen's ship *Gjøa*
8. The Wanderer's Home
9. Josephine Peary gives away unwanted expedition utensils, 1892
10. Arctic fox at Thule Air Base
11. Dovekies or little auks at Iterlak near Cape Atholl
12. The Tent, largest of the Cape York meteorites
13. Comer's Midden at Uummannaq, 1937
14. Thule Air Base
15. Qaanaaq, capital of Avanersuaq
16. An Inuhuit dog team at Qaanaaq

Maps

1. Greenland   2
2. Avanersuaq   4

Acknowledgments

*T*he following people were kind enough to read parts of this book in manuscript or to help in one way or another in its writing: Hans Christian Gulløv, André van Holk, Andrew MacLellan, Ray Newell, Herbert Prins, L. M. J. U. van Straaten, John Vaughan, and Nellejet Zorgdrager. Special thanks go to my wife, Margaret, who, besides much else, transferred an untidy manuscript onto computer disks, and to Andy Field, who drew the maps.

Thanks are also due to the staff and authorities of the following institutions who facilitated the assembling of the material on which this book is based: the Instituut voor Taxonomische Zoölogie of the Zoological Museum, University of Amsterdam (especially Ko de Korte), the Scott Polar Research Institute, Cambridge (Terence Armstrong and Harry King), the Dundee Museum (David Henderson), the University Library, Groningen (especially interlibrary loans), the Local Studies Library, Hull (Jill Crowther), the Town Docks Museum, Hull (Arthur Credland), the American Museum of Natural History, New York (Linda Reichert), and the Kendall Whaling Museum, Sharon, Massachusetts (Stuart Frank).

Invaluable assistance in the preparation of this book was given by my colleague Renée Nip, Groningen, and by Gordon Jackson of the University of Strathclyde, Glasgow. Colleagues at the Arctic Centre, Groningen, especially Louwrens Hacquebord, have put me in their debt in many ways. I thank my son John Vaughan for spending two weeks in Dundee researching the nineteenth-century whaling industry there on my behalf. Finally, my thanks go to the authorities at Thule Air Base and the Ministry for Greenland in Copenhagen, as well as to many other people who made it possible for me to visit Avanersuaq on three occasions in 1983–85, and to the director and staff of the University of Maine Press at Orono, Maine, including copy editor Trudie Calvert, who transformed my English from British to American.

RICHARD VAUGHAN retired from the Chair of Medieval History and the Chairmanship of the Board of the Arctic Centre at the University of Groningen in Holland in 1989. He read history at the University of Cambridge, England, in 1948–51 and was awarded the degree of Ph.D. by that university in 1955 for a thesis on the English medieval chronicler Matthew Paris. His publications include books on medieval European history, on European integration, and about birds, and articles on aspects of the history of the Arctic. This book was inspired by a chance visit to northwest Greenland in 1983, followed by others in 1984 and 1985.

1

Introduction

*T*he land has always been there for the taking, and the history of human-
kind is in large part the history of that taking or of quarrels over the
spoils. Almost the entire surface of the globe has now been exploited and
transformed. The idea that nature exists for human benefit has proved extremely tenacious and will not easily be abandoned: the recently invented "nature reserve" is only a living museum of the past; it marks no reversal of
people's time-honored encroachment on nature. Just as the once impenetrable
jungle has been penetrated and is now nearly destroyed, so too the frigid Arctic
wastes of snow and ice have been a field for human interference and greed.
Whatever was there, from whales and walruses to coal and cryolite, was there
for the taking. This book attempts to portray the history of human activity in
the farthest north of all self-sustaining human settlements, Avanersuaq in
northern Greenland, hitherto known as the Thule district.

The Eskimo inhabitants of this remote part of Greenland had no name for
their land (Stein 1902a), but those living farther south in West Greenland used
the word *Avanersuaq,* literally *the place in the farthest north.* This seems the
most appropriate name for an area the local council has recently designated
Avanersuup Kommunia, *the northernmost commune,* though the whole of
northern Greenland is now sometimes called Avanersuaq. The name *Thule
district* was used from the beginning of the twentieth century. The Danish artist Harald Moltke (1964: 228), overwintering in 1903–4, first called the
Eskimo settlement Uummannaq where he was staying Thule. Later, in 1910,
two Danes set up a private trading post close by Uummannaq. One of them,
Peter Freuchen (1954: 101), claimed to have called the place Thule to prevent
his companion, Knud Rasmussen, from calling it Knudsminde—a Danish
version of Knudsville or Knudshope—on a par with Egedesminde (Aasiaat).
The name Thule, applied to the trading station, was then used for the district,
but because the trading station has disappeared and its site been abandoned, it
seems pointless to perpetuate the phrase *Thule district,* especially when fashion increasingly dictates the use of indigenous names.

1

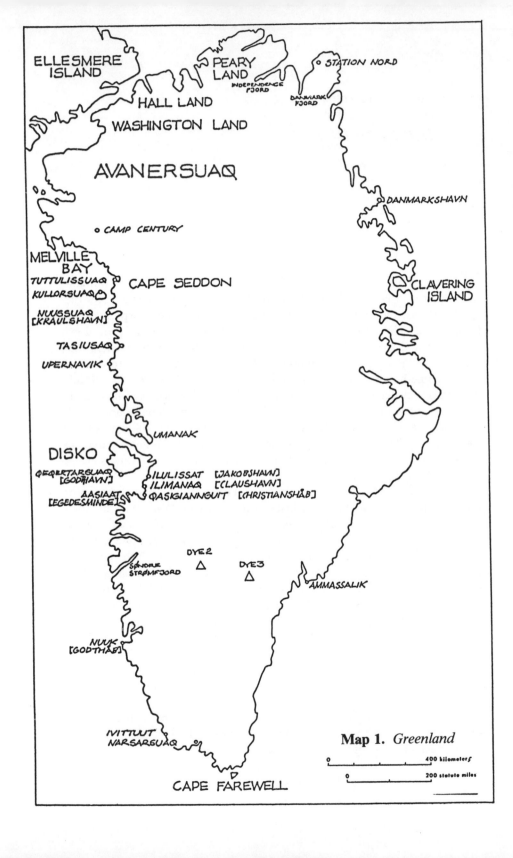

Map 1. *Greenland*

The iron laws of geography inevitably bestow an exclusive, isolated character on Avanersuaq. It consists of a series of patches of stony coastal land each seldom more than ten or twenty miles broad, stretching roughly north-south along Greenland's northwest coast for some 200 miles (300 km) as the crow (or raven) flies between the northern end of Melville Bay and Smith Sound, the entrance to Kane Basin, and the 100-mile-long coastal strip of Inglefield Land stretching northeastward along the south shore of Kane Basin. The southern part of Avanersuaq's coast is intersected by bays and fjords, most of which terminate in glaciers, which are in fact tongues or outflows of the Greenland ice sheet or Inland Ice. On one side of this fragmented, often precipitous, terrain is the sea; the other is bordered by the Inland Ice, an impenetrable barrier, an ice desert, forming a nearly level but dome-shaped plateau that can be crossed only by a specially equipped expedition. If one follows the coast northward along uninhabited though ice-free Inglefield Land, one arrives at the so-called Humboldt Glacier, which marks the northern extremity of the Avanersuaq of this book. It is not really a glacier but is similar to the Melville Bay coast at the southern extremity of Avanersuaq: it is a stretch of shore where no land or rock intervenes between the Inland Ice and the often frozen sea. The ice front or ice cliff of the Humboldt Glacier extends northward uninterrupted for 60 miles (100 km). In Melville Bay ice cliffs extend along the coast nearly continuously for a distance of 200 miles (300 km). When one remembers that much of the region's sea is covered with ice several feet thick for nine months of the year, it becomes apparent that Avanersuaq is boxed in with ice.

Although Greenland's gigantic ice sheet (Fristrup 1966) appears to be unmoving in its frozen stillness, it is nonetheless added to yearly by about 3 feet (1 m) of snow over its entire surface, which is slowly compressed into ice, while ice is lost through its numerous outflow glaciers to the sea. In summer especially the ice in these glaciers moves slowly downward and seaward, and large pieces break off noisily to form icebergs that, if not grounded, float away down the fjords and out into the sea. This process is called calving. In Avanersuaq the fjords become solidly frozen over in the late autumn, and these newly produced icebergs are frozen in and halted wherever they happen to be. Fortunately for the inhabitants of Qaanaaq, some large ones are always stranded for the winter just offshore from the town and provide the only available source of fresh water during the winter months (Fig. 1). Every now and then a truck drives out over the sea ice, blocks of ice are cut from an iceberg, and the load of ice is brought back to Qaanaaq and melted in the town's central heating plant. The edge of the Inland Ice in Avanersuaq is often bordered by an ice cliff that may be 100 feet (30 m) high, or else by steep heaped-up moraines of ice-polished boulders associated with deep snowdrifts. In summer, excursions onto the Inland Ice are impeded by the many rushing streams of ice-cold

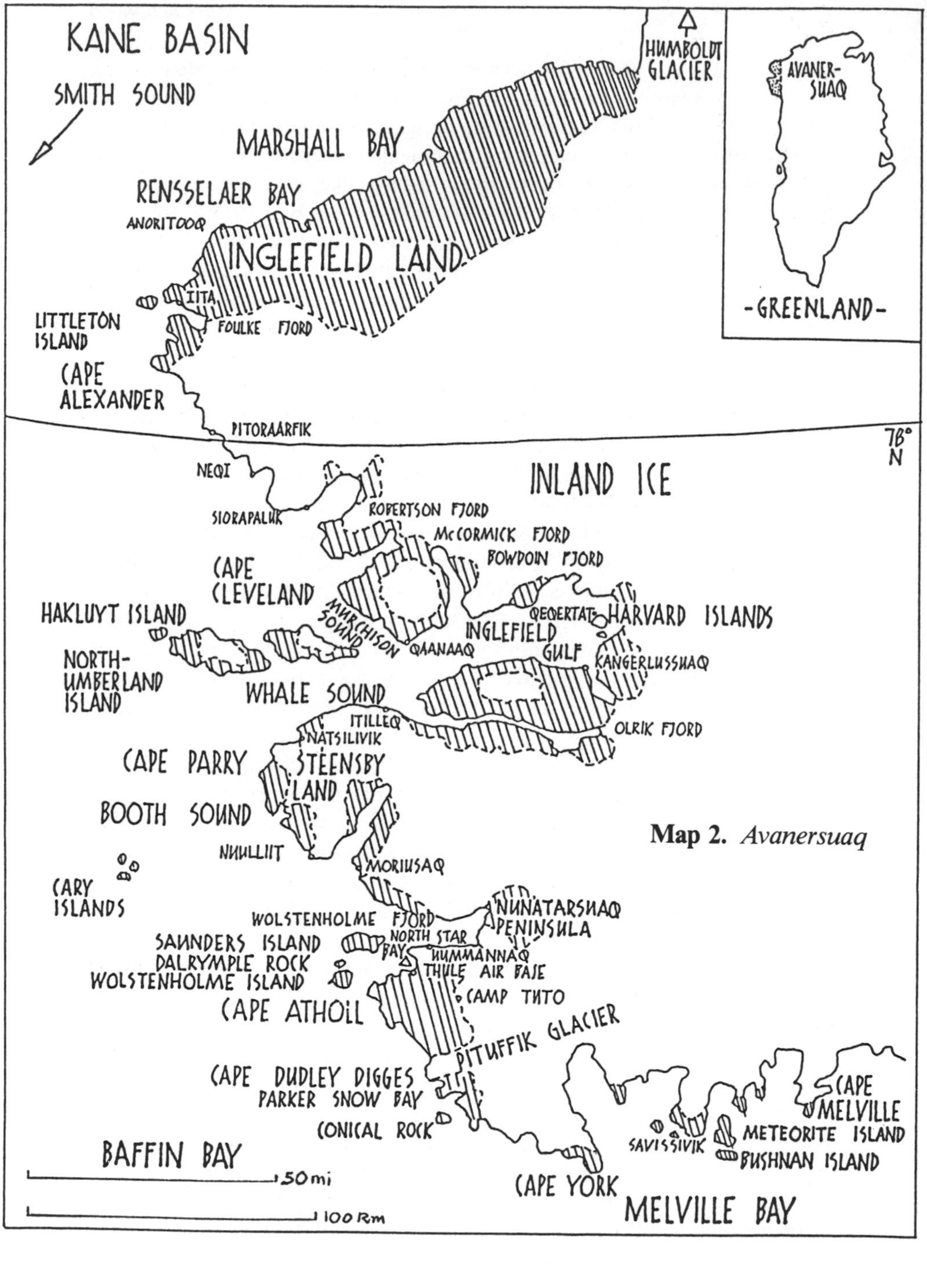

KANE BASIN

SMITH SOUND

MARSHALL BAY

RENSSELAER BAY

ANORITOOQ

INGLEFIELD LAND

IITA

LITTLETON
ISLAND

FOULKE FJORD

CAPE
ALEXANDER

HUMBOLDT
GLACIER

AVANER-
SUAQ

-GREENLAND-

PITORAARFIK

76°
N

NEQI

SIORAPALUK

INLAND ICE

ROBERTSON FJORD

McCORMICK FJORD

BOWDOIN FJORD

CAPE
CLEVELAND

HAKLUYT ISLAND

MURCHISON
SOUND

INGLEFIELD
GULF

QEQERTAT

HARVARD ISLANDS

QAANAAQ

NORTH-
UMBERLAND
ISLAND

KANGERLUSSUAQ

WHALE SOUND

OLRIK FJORD

ITILLEQ

NATSILIVIK

CAPE PARRY

STEENSBY
LAND

BOOTH SOUND

Map 2. Avanersuaq

NUULLIIT

CARY
ISLANDS

MORIUSAQ

NUNATARSUAQ
PENINSULA

WOLSTENHOLME FJORD

SAUNDERS ISLAND

NORTH STAR
BAY

DALRYMPLE ROCK

UUMMANNAQ

WOLSTENHOLME ISLAND

THULE AIR BASE

CAPE ATHOLL

CAMP TUTO

PITUFFIK GLACIER

CAPE DUDLEY DIGGES

PARKER SNOW BAY

CAPE
MELVILLE

CONICAL ROCK

METEORITE ISLAND

SAVISSIVIK

BUSHNAN ISLAND

BAFFIN BAY

50 mi

100 Rm

CAPE YORK

MELVILLE BAY

melt water and by a layer of slush or water-sodden snow on its surface. Take a step onto the Inland Ice in July or August and your foot sinks in 12 inches (30 cm) or more. The hole thus made fills rapidly with water: thigh waders are more appropriate than boots.

Most of the peninsulas of partly ice-free land in Avanersuaq that jut out westward into the northern end of Baffin Bay between the fjords have their own flat, domed ice caps, each with its own system of glaciers descending steep valleys to the sea. The same is true of Northumberland and Herbert islands, which lie between Whale and Murchison sounds. Other islands, such as those named for Richard Hakluyt and James Saunders, are snow-covered during most of the year. Herbert Island has three glaciers debouching from the northern side of its ice cap; Northumberland Island has a dozen or so glaciers descending from its dome of ice. These ice caps, which on the mainland peninsulas are usually continuous with the Inland Ice, were distinguished from it by being named Highland Ice by the Danish explorer Lauge Koch. That glaciologist and geologist, to whom we owe much of our knowledge of the physical geography of northern Greenland, enumerated 145 glaciers in Avanersuaq, which he called the Cape York district, 25 of which issue from the Inland Ice and the rest from the Highland Ice (Koch 1928). He sledged across or along many of them, watched them calving, measured them, and once narrowly escaped death by falling into a snow-covered crevasse in one of them.

The Inland Ice is a unique, extraordinary, unforgettable phenomenon. No wonder the American explorer Robert Peary called it the "Great Ice." Its pitted surface of compressed, wind-swept snow forms a flat but perceptibly convex and, in Avanersuaq, ever-present horizon. To the west, above and beyond the fjords or the coastal mountains, which are flat topped or rounded and seldom rise above 2,000 feet (700 m) in height, the Inland Ice is everywhere, usually with its accompanying iceblink: a bright streak in the sky immediately above the horizon. The Inland Ice is pale gray in color, or brilliant white, or it may have the faintest tint of bluish-green. At times it almost seems to merge with the sky; it can look like a low-lying cloud bank or even the sea. From it every now and then vicious storms sweep down the slopes and glaciers; from it, practically continuously, an icy wind blows.

Just as strange and silently impressive as the Inland Ice is the sea ice. Imagine a sea without waves, without apparent movement, inert, still; a sea you can walk on, a sea that is never blue, only shades of gray and white. This frozen sea, though it looks motionless, is always moving. The layer of ice covered with compressed snow moves up and down with the tide, frequently has cracks and leads of open water in it, and can break up in a storm. Along the shore, sticking fast to the rocks or beach, is a band of ice that may be a few yards wide or much more, known as the ice foot or land-fast ice. This does not move with the tide; there is always a narrow lead of water and often a difference of level between it and the sea ice.

In spite of the winter covering of ice on much of the sea, in the northern part of Baffin Bay there is a large, permanent polynya or area of open water, of unfrozen sea, which persists year-round. The nineteenth-century whalers called it the North Water (Fig. 2). Even in the winter, this open water is seldom far from Avanersuaq's capes and offshore islands. It is the North Water that makes it possible for humans, animals, and birds to live in Avanersuaq and for plants to grow there. Its warming effect on the surrounding land was studied in 1972–74 by the North Water Project (Müller et al. 1977, Ito 1982). It was thanks to the North Water that Peary (1898a: 443) could describe Avanersuaq as an "Arctic oasis, its abundance of vegetable and animal life being in striking contrast to the icy wastes of Melville Bay and Kane Basin north and south of it, and to the desolate barren shores of Ellesmere Land westward across Smith Sound."

The Inland Ice and the sea ice are eye-catching visual phenomena that engage one's attention for minutes at a time. Not so the invisible but ever-present underground ice called permafrost, a layer of frozen ground, which borings have shown to be about 1,600 feet (500 m) thick in northwest Greenland (Fristrup 1978). In summer, in Avanersuaq, the upper surface of the permafrost lies between 8 inches and 4 feet (20 and 120 cm) below ground level (Davies et al. 1963). Buildings have to be raised on stilts or insulated in some other way or they will sink into the ground when their warmth melts the permafrost. Only the shallowest of graves can be dug, and archaeological investigation is often very difficult. Harrison J. Hunt (Hunt and Thompson 1980: 77), who helped Captain George Comer excavate an Eskimo midden at Uummannaq in summer 1916, noticed that the permafrost thawed at the rate of a mere 2 inches (5 cm) each day.

Although vegetation in Avanersuaq is seldom luxuriant, it exists in suitable places and even thrives here and there. Flowering plants are often abundant. W. Elmer Ekblaw, in 1913–17, found 125 species of vascular plants between Melville Bay and the Humboldt Glacier (MacMillan 1918a: 397–402). Many of them are familiar to us as Alpines, but the Avanersuaq version is often slightly different. Thus the creamy-white representative of the rose family, the mountain avens, is *Dryas integrifolia,* not *octopetala* of the Alps. But some of Avanersuaq's most attractive flowers are identical to those well known farther south and in rock gardens. In June the purple saxifrage tinges the hillsides a rich deep purple in places, and the moss campion's round green cushions and tiny bright pink flowers are common. The beauty of these and other plants is enhanced because they often grow entirely by themselves on the bare, stony ground, not intermixed with other vegetation. This is especially true of the elegant Arctic poppy, the blooms of which may be yellow or white. It is one of the few Arctic plants that, like its well-known red relative in Europe, can quickly colonize an area where the surface has been disturbed by road or other construction. In June this plant gives color to the drab grays of the American air base near Uummannaq (Thule Air Base) and the surrounding terrain.

There are no trees or shrubs in Avanersuaq. The tallest plant is the Arctic willow, which spreads its gnarled branches flat over the ground and in June proudly sends its catkins straight up toward the sky to a height of 2 inches (5 cm). The nearest approach to heather is the 4-inch-high *Cassiope tetragona,* which has sweet-scented white bell-shaped blooms. It forms extensive mats in favorable terrain and comes in handy for the Eskimos' campfire and for the nest lining of oldsquaws (long-tailed ducks). The crowberry, *Empetrum nigrum,* is found hugging the ground here and there but seldom, if ever, fruits.

Avanersuaq is mostly desert—a frozen Arctic desert of ice and rock. Large, gently undulating areas of boulder-strewn country, the stones loose and sharp, support no vegetation at all. One can clamber over these boulder fields for hours and see no sign of life. Elsewhere, on the gentler slopes and less high tops of some of the bare hills, the stones may lie flat on or embedded in the clay surface. Here, a thin, patchy vegetation of sparse grass or sedge and flowering plants can form, sufficient, perhaps, to enable a few birds and mammals to survive in the summer. In a very few places veritable oases in this desert can be found, where vegetation flourishes and plants and animals are numerous. These oases occur in two very different environments. Here and there are broad, shallow valleys or low-lying flat areas, either on the coast or inland by the shore of some fjord, with shallow lakes and pools around which a dense growth of sedge and cottongrass in soft, marshy ground supports many insects and birds. Birds like the snow goose and the king eider come to these marshy flats in summer to breed, and here in days gone by the caribou grazed. The other sort of Avanersuaq oasis occurs on slopes and cliffs along the shore abutting onto the North Water and on some of the islands. Here, the droppings of countless breeding seabirds have fertilized the ground and promoted a rank growth of mosses, lichens, and grass. On parts of blizzard-swept Hakluyt Island a thick carpet of lichen and lichen peat provides the breeding kittiwakes with abundant nest material, itself the result of fertilizing droppings rained down on the island's surface by dense flocks of dovekies (little auks) that fly to and fro over it throughout the summer.

The Eskimo inhabitants of Avanersuaq traditionally divided their homeland and hunting territory into four districts, the names of which expressed the relationship of the people there to the wind (Rasmussen 1921a and b, Ulloriaq

1985: 102). The most southerly part of Avanersuaq was called Nigerliit, meaning *the people living nearest the southwest wind*. Here, between Cape York and that most exquisitely beautiful of all bays, Parker Snow Bay, its entrance guarded on either side by bold, rocky headlands, are the Crimson Cliffs, so named in 1818 by Sir John Ross (1819: 138) from the rose-tinted snow seen along them. He was lampooned for this choice of name by the cartoonist George Cruikshank, who portrayed the captain and his men processing through the streets of London on their return from the Arctic not as conquering heroes but as figures of fun, with frostbitten limbs and noses and a bucket of "RED SNOW" dangling from a pole. Peary (1910: 72–73), who tells us that the color is caused by the alga *Protococcus nivalis*, calls it a "red banner of the Arctic" and says that it greeted him on all his northern journeys. Other features along this coast are the steep and rugged island called Conical Rock, well known to nineteenth-century whalers, and the cave Paakitsoq, favorite overnight lodging place of the old-time Eskimo inhabitants (Freuchen 1961: 213).

The region around the shores of Wolstenholme Fjord makes up the next district of Avanersuaq, Akuunaarmiut, meaning *the people living in between* or *in the middle*. On the southern side of the fjord the ice-capped peninsula of Steensby Land juts out westward to culminate in Cape Parry, to the north of which is Avanersuaq's largest fjord system, penetrating nearly 60 miles (100 km) inland in the shape of Inglefield Gulf. Its shores belong to the third district of Avanersuaq, called by the Inuhuit Oqqorliit, meaning *those living in the lee of the southwest wind*.

Robert Peary, who first explored the great inlet formed by Whale Sound and Inglefield Gulf, describes this Eskimo heartland vividly (1898a: 458):

> It presents every phase of Arctic scenery, climate, and life,—is, in fact, a little Arctic world in itself. Along its shores are to be found low grassy slopes; towering cliffs, massive and solid, carved, by the Titan agencies of the savage North, into wild forms; wind-swept points where nothing can exist; sheltered nooks where never a violent breath of air penetrates; valleys where luxuriant grass is brightened by myriads of yellow, purple, blue, and white flowers; slopes and plateaus as barren as the surface of a cinder pile; huge glaciers which launch a prolific progeny of bergs into the sea; tiny glaciers which cling tenaciously in the angles of the cliffs; miles and miles of glistening blue, berg-dotted water; and everywhere a few miles back from the shore, the shore of that other silent, eternal, frozen desert sea, the "Great Ice."

Moving north along the coast from Inglefield Gulf, after rounding Cape Cleveland we cross the mouths of McCormick Fjord, at the head of which were the lush caribou pastures of Peary's Tugto Valley, and Robertson Fjord, on the north shore of which is the most northerly present-day Inuhuit settlement of Siorapaluk, and arrive at another coast of rocky headlands interrupted by glaciers. We are now in the fourth and most northerly district of Avanersuaq, Avannarliit, meaning *those that live nearest the north wind.* Here is Cape Alexander, Greenland's most westerly point, the only cape in Avanersuaq off which the sea is almost never frozen. Rasmussen (1921b: 536) stated that, even in winter, it was never possible to sledge round it; according to Freuchen and Salomonsen (1958: 53), "nobody ever drives a dog team around the famous Cape Alexander in Smith Sound." North of Cape Alexander is the country near and to the north of Iita, on the north shore of Foulke Fjord, made familiar by the overwinterings of nineteenth-century American expeditions, which was formerly inhabited by Eskimos. From Littleton Island the coast trends northeastward, and a long line of cliffs reaching to the Humboldt Glacier fringes stoney, uninhabited Inglefield Land.

A description of Avanersuaq would scarcely be complete without some mention of the group of around twelve small islands, six of which are over a mile in length, lying 40 miles (65 km) offshore, called the Cary Islands. Though long ago inhabited by Eskimos who hunted whales and used whale bones in the construction of their winter houses (Wordie 1938; Anon. 1852: 337), these islands have seldom been visited in historic times either by Eskimos or by white people. Nowadays, a Danish party flies over there annually by helicopter from Thule Air Base and hoists the Danish flag, perhaps to remind Canadians of Danish claims to ownership.

The geology of Avanersuaq, and in particular that of the immediate vicinity of Thule Air Base, has been studied intensively (Munck 1941, Troelsen 1950, Holmes and Colton 1960, Davies et al. 1963, and Nichols 1969). For nearly 300 miles (500 km) to the south of Avanersuaq down Greenland's west coast only metamorphic or igneous rocks occur. Then, in Avanersuaq, pre-Cambrian sedimentary rocks in the south are succeeded in Inglefield Land in the north of the district by Lower Paleozoic sedimentary rocks of more recent origin. The major geological event in the last few thousand years or more has been an intermittent but persistent retreat of the ice, which until soon after 9000 B.P. (before the present) covered the entire area except for the steep outlying islets of Dalrymple Rock and Conical Rock. During this recession of the ice, the land rose and littoral deposits were lifted above sea level to form the raised beaches so familiar in the north. In one of these, during the construction of Thule Air Base in August 1953, some large bones and baleen belonging to a Greenland or bowhead whale (*Balaena mysticetus*) were unearthed. The animal's remains had been buried on the shore by sand some 8,500 ± 200 years previously and were now 43 feet (13 m) above sea level (Davies et al. 1963: 58). Only in the last 2,000 years have scattered peat deposits been formed in Avanersuaq by the occasional oases of vegetation (Malaurie et al. 1972).

In Avanersuaq the long period of continuous winter darkness finally comes to an end in February, when the sun first appears above the horizon. The days lengthen rapidly thereafter until, toward the end of April, the sun begins to remain visible above the horizon throughout the night, not to set again until late in August. But its springtime reappearance by no means brings immediate warmth, and March is the coldest month (Stahlschmidt and Tommerup 1978). The winter snow cover melts in May or June, but the ice that forms in winter in Avanersuaq's fjords does not disappear easily. It is some days into July before the first ship of the year, an icebreaker of the United States Coast Guard, can penetrate Wolstenholme Fjord and tie up at the jetty of the world's most northerly deepwater port in North Star Bay, at the head of the annual supply convoy for Thule Air Base. In August, the fjords are ice-free except for the icebergs that break off from the glaciers and float out to sea at this time of year; but this is only an interlude. As Peary's colleague John M. Verhoeff noted in autumn 1891, new ice begins to form in the fjords before the end of September: he recorded a temperature of 8° F (−13° C) on the last day of that month. In October the ice in McCormick Fjord increased in thickness from 4 inches (10 cm) at the start of the month to about 17 inches (42 cm) at the end. By the close of November the ice was 26 inches (65 cm) thick, and it reached a thickness of 4 feet at the end of January 1892. In 1891 the sun had ceased to appear above the horizon at midday sometime in the second half of October (Peary 1898a: 155 and 432–35).

In spite of occasional rainstorms in summer and blizzards in winter, Avanersuaq has an extremely arid climate, rivaling that of the Sahara Desert. Annual precipitation amounts to a mere 3 to 5 inches (70 to 130 mm) (Nichols 1953, Malaurie 1982: 40n and 113n, Roby et al. 1984, Fredskild 1985). High winds are relatively frequent.

It is not yet entirely clear whether current ideas about climatic change in historic times in the general area of Greenland are true for Avanersuaq (see, for example, Dansgård et al. 1970, Malaurie 1976). If they are, then a warmer period culminating in 1000–1100 A.D. was followed by a cooling which produced the so-called Little Ice Age in the seventeenth century. Recent investigation has shown that the first half of the nineteenth century was a period of very unfavorable climate in the eastern Canadian Arctic (Alt et al. 1986). From about 1850 onward the climate steadily warmed, but the warming is thought to have been reversed around 1930. There is, however, no sign of this reversal in Avanersuaq, where ice fronts, both of glaciers and the Inland Ice, seem everywhere still to be retreating and where, as Table 1 appears to confirm, temperatures continued to rise at least until the 1980s. The climatic history of Avanersuaq remains to be written.

Table 1.

Comparison of average and lowest winter temperatures recorded by expeditions wintering in Avanersuaq, 1853–1935, with recent data

Source	Date	Place	Mean winter temperature		Minimum winter temperature
Kane 1856b: 425	1853–55	Rensselaer Bay, Inglefield Land	−35° C −31° F	Dec. to March	−56° C −69° F
Peary 1898a: 437	1891–92	Red Cliff House near Cape Cleveland	−28° C −18° F	Dec. to March	−48° C −54° F
MacMillan 1927: 273–75	1913–17	Iita	−24° C −12° F	Dec. to March	−41° C −42° F
Shackleton 1937: 342–43	1934–35	Iita	−23° C −10° F	Feb. to March	−38° C −37° F
Fredskild 1985: 6	1967–82	Qaanaaq	−22° C −8° F	Dec. to March	−28° C −18° F

Such then in brief is the land and climate of Avanersuaq. The limited areas not covered permanently by ice are mostly of stone and rock. Though somewhat ameliorated by the North Water, the climate is harsh. Even in the warmest month, July, the mean temperature does not exceed 40° F (5° C), and during most of the rest of the year it is well below the freezing point. Here, in what was justly called Thule, humans were until very recently on the margin of subsistence, their lives imperiled or severely hampered by extreme low temperatures, by Arctic winter storms, by difficulties of transport and communications, and by the long period of winter darkness. This was the stage on which the scenes described in the following pages were played out.

2

The Inuhuit and Their Neighbors in Early Times

*J*ust as the usually accepted name for Avanersuaq, the Thule district, was found to be inadequate and has not been used in this book, so too the current name for the area's inhabitants, the Polar Eskimos, is inappropriate. For many years the word *Eskimo* was out of fashion. As long ago as 1865, Clements R. Markham urged that the term *Inuit* be used, and many twentieth-century authors avoided the word *Eskimo* because they thought it derogatory, deriving from an Indian word for *eaters of raw meat*. But now the word has been rehabilitated by a new hypothesis which links it with a Montagnais Indian word meaning *speaking the language of a foreign land* (Damas 1984: 6, Kleivan and Sonne 1985). I use it freely here, as well as its synonym *Inuit* but have discarded the epithet *Polar* because the Polar Eskimos live nearly a thousand miles from the North Pole. Instead, the Eskimo inhabitants of Avanersuaq are given their own name for themselves, namely *Inuhuit* (also spelled *Inughuit;* singular *Inuhuaq*), meaning *great and beautiful human beings,* which is the equivalent of the West Greenlandic word *Inusuit, large people* (Gilberg 1984a: 593). It must be emphasized that the Inuhuit distinguish themselves clearly from the West Greenlanders or Kalaallit, that is, the Eskimos living south of Melville Bay along the west coast of Greenland. Before the Danes began calling them Polar Eskimos at the beginning of the twentieth century, they had been variously called Arctic Highlanders, Smith Sound Eskimos, Whale Sound Eskimos, and Cape York Eskimos.

What limited knowledge we have of the activities of the inhabitants of Avanersuaq in prehistoric times must be pieced together from the results of excavations of abandoned houses and middens by Danish archaeologists Erik Holtved and Eigil Knuth or inferred from discoveries in Alaska, Canada, or other parts of Greenland (Holtved 1944a and b and 1954a and b, Knuth 1977–78, Dumond 1977, Gad 1984, Damas 1984, Gulløv 1986, Schledermann 1990). Northwest Greenland has often been a high road and a gateway for successive groups of Eskimos and their predecessors, a gateway into

Greenland and also a crossroads or junction. Once in Avanersuaq, people could continue their wanderings either northward along the northern shores of Greenland or southward down the west coast of Greenland. The history of the Eskimos in Greenland is one of the slow, intermittent, and probably repeated circulation around the coasts of the country along the narrow strip of ice-free land between the Inland Ice and the sea, of successive small hunting groups following or settling in the same areas as their predominant prey. be it caribou, musk-ox, whale, or seals and other sea mammals. These groups moved around the periphery of Greenland from Avanersuaq or from Washington or Hall Land to the north of it, either via the northern tip of Greenland, the largest area of ice-free land, and then down the east coast in a clockwise direction (Gulløv 1982b), or southward counterclockwise down the west coast and then up the east coast. Traces of this perambulation survived into historic times. In August 1823 Commander Douglas Charles Clavering of the Royal Navy came across a group of twelve Eskimos on the island named after him in latitude 74° north on the east coast of Greenland (Vahl et al. 1928b: 16 and Stefansson 1943: 181–83). It is impossible to ascertain whether this group was traveling north or south; no other Eskimos have been known to be present along the east coast of Greenland north of 69° north until the resettlements of modern times.

The notion generally accepted among anthropologists and archaeologists that Eskimos migrated from west to east across the North American continent and then traveled around Greenland was first postulated on 27 February 1865 by the British geographer and historian Clements R. Markham, who was president of the Royal Geographical Society from 1893 to 1905. On that date he presented a paper to the society on the "origin and migrations of the Greenland Esquimaux." From archaeological evidence based on ten Eskimo sites scattered across the Canadian Arctic archipelago, he had become convinced that he could trace the route "taken by these ancient wanderers in search of the means of sustaining life." He envisaged them moving steadily eastward in small, straggling groups. He thought of them finally arriving in Greenland "not improbably at the 'wind-loved' point of Anoatoq [Anoritooq]"—which is exactly where a party of Eskimo immigrants probably had arrived from Canada, unknown to Markham, only three years before he spoke. He surmised that the migration across Smith Sound had taken place in the fourteenth to sixteenth centuries, and he supposed that these people, after reaching Avanersuaq, "separated in parties to the north and south, the former wandering whither we know not, the latter crossing Melville Bay . . . and eventually peopling the islets and fiords of south Greenland." On this hypothesis, Markham continued, some of these wanderers remained in the Anoritooq area, "established their hunting grounds between the Humboldt and Melville Bay glaciers, and became the ancestors of that very curious and interesting race of men, the 'Arctic Highlanders'" (1865: 97).

Recent archaeological research (summarized in Fitzhugh 1984) shows that people had reached Greenland, probably from the west, in the third millennium before Christ. Traces of their occupation have been found at "Old" Nuulliit in Avanersuaq and in Peary Land in the extreme north of Greenland, as well as elsewhere. They have been called the Independence People from the fjord of that name, and they are thought to have penetrated north Greenland in two distinct groups separated by several centuries. They used small tools made of chipped stones or bone, lived in stone dwellings roofed with musk-ox skins, and depended largely on musk-oxen for their sustenance. Instead of blubber lamps they used open wood fires. They seem to have had no kayaks, no sledges, and no dogs. These immigrants were followed by others who have been called the Dorset People from a site at Cape Dorset on Baffin Island. They may have moved across from America around 500 B.C., and Holtved unearthed unmistakable traces of their culture at Marshall Bay, Inglefield Land, and elsewhere in Avanersuaq. They used blubber lamps, lived in permanent winter houses made of turf and stones, built igloos of snow, hunted sea mammals along the ice edge, and used the bow and arrow to kill caribou and birds.

Some time around or soon after A.D. 1000 this Dorset culture was overwhelmed and replaced by a new wave of people from the west. As opposed to earlier Palaeo-Eskimos, these newcomers have been called Neo-Eskimos, but they are also known as the Thule people (Jordan 1984). They hunted the big Greenland right whale or bowhead with kayaks and umiaqs or women's boats, as well as other sea mammals. The ruins of their houses were excavated by Holtved in Avanersuaq not only in Inglefield Land but also at "New" Nuulliit (in Steensby Land) and Uummannaq on the south shore of Wolstenholme Fjord. Subsequent radiocarbon dates of Holtved's finds, some of which are now thought to be too early, range between A.D. 800 and 1070 with a possible margin of error of one hundred years either way. This so-called Thule culture seems to have been transformed quickly into the Inussuk culture, named from the place near Upernavik on the West Greenland coast where a midden was excavated by Danish archaeologist Therkel Mathiassen with Frederica de Laguna's help in 1929 (de Laguna 1977).

At much the same time the newly arrived Neo-Eskimos settled in northern Greenland, Eric the Red and his Viking followers began the history of Norse activities in southern Greenland, in A.D. 985 or 986. Up until 1938 there was no evidence that these activities ever extended farther north than the Upernavik district, where the famous rune stone was found on the island of Kingigtorssuaq in 1824 (see Vaughan 1982). In 1938 and in more detail in 1944, Holtved (1938a, 1944a and b; see also 1945) published the results of his excavations in

Avanersuaq and the astonishing fact became known that among the twelve thousand finds he had brought back to Copenhagen and donated to the National Museum's Ethnographical Department were at least a dozen of indisputably Norse origin that must have come from the Greenland Vikings. Among these objects are a small wooden box, the bronze leg of a cooking pot, part of a small wooden funnel, part of the bottom of an oaken barrel, a broken piece of an iron spearhead, "a rusty conglomeration of flat interlinked iron rings," which "can scarcely be other than a piecc of chain mail," a bone comb, a spoon box, a draftsman of bone, two turned chessmen, namely a rook of whalebone and a pawn of walrus ivory, and a piece of woolen cloth measuring 22 by 16 inches (56 by 40 cm). Every one of these objects except the chain mail, which had never previously been found in Greenland, is similar to objects excavated in the Norse settlements in south Greenland. The woolen cloth has since been dated by the carbon 14 method to A.D. 1270 (±50 years) (Gulløv 1982a; 233).

Although they could have derived from a single shipwreck, these finds were not concentrated in one place. The wooden box was found at Uummannaq in Comer's Midden; the funnel, spoon case, and pawn came from two different abandoned houses on Ruin Island; and the remaining three objects came from three different house ruins at Inuarfissuaq. The last two places are in Marshall Bay, Inglefield Land. When Holtved returned to dig in Avanersuaq after World War II, he excavated some of the sixty-two house ruins at "New" Nuulliit on the northern shore of Wolstenholme Fjord. It was said to be the largest archaeological site ever discovered in Greenland up to that time, but Holtved found no more Viking objects. Norse material similar to that found in Avanersuaq by Holtved has since been unearthed from house remains in the Buchanan Bay area of eastern Ellesmere Island, not one hundred miles from Marshall Bay on the other side of Smith Sound and dating from A.D. 1000 to 1400 (Schledermann 1980 and 1982).

We do not know the exact nature of the contacts between the Norse settlers of Greenland and their Eskimo neighbors to the north, but there are some indications of trade (McGhee 1984 and 1987). So far only Norse objects found in Eskimo settlements have been mentioned, but at least one object of probably Eskimo origin has been identified from a Norse site. At Nipaitsoq in the Western Settlement (Vesterbygd) of the Vikings, inland from Nuuk (Godthåb), an arrowhead was excavated in 1977 which analysis showed to have been made from a fragment of one of the Cape York meteorites (Andreasen 1982). Whatever all this may tell us about the Vikings in Greenland, it certainly suggests that Avanersuaq's inhabitants were by no means isolated in the years between A.D. 1000 and 1500, which was probably a relatively warm period. They must have had more than occasional contacts with the Eskimos then living in Ellesmere Island, as finds of meteoritic iron from the Cape York meteorites in various places in Canada indicate (McGhee 1984, 1987). They were undoubtedly also in contact with the Eskimos to the south, on the west coast of Greenland, whose Inussuk culture they shared, and very probably also with the Norsemen still farther south, who we know were in the habit of making prolonged hunting voyages northward at least as far as Upernavik (Vaughan 1982, McGhee 1984 and references).

After about 1500 all this may have changed, but we know nothing about what was happening in Avanersuaq in the period of supposedly deteriorating climate that climaxed elsewhere in the Little Ice Age in the seventeenth century. Perhaps the region was unoccupied for a time. Therkel Mathiassen noted in 1945 that "the Thule district has not produced finds from the 17th–18th century," and William Baffin, whose voyage incidentally betokens a warm rather than a cool climate, saw no trace of people when he sailed along the Avanersuaq coast in 1616. It is only with the beginning of the white man's historical record in Avanersuaq in 1818 that we again have information about the region's inhabitants. Even though this information was obtained with difficulty through West Greenlandic or Danish interpreters, and the Inuhuit were viewed through heavily distorting European or American spectacles, it is still possible to give some account of their way of life at the time of their initial contacts with whites in the first half of the nineteenth century. This has recently been done for their material culture in terms of artifact types and their constituent parts (Oswalt 1987). The picture has to be put together from the accounts of British naval commander John Ross and two of his officers and of the Americans Elisha Kent Kane and Isaac I. Hayes and their associates William Godfrey, Carl Petersen, and the Eskimo interpreter Hans Hendrik. In addition to these, Clements Markham read a paper to the Ethnographical Society of London in the spring of 1865 based largely on his interviews with the Inuhuaq Qalasersuaq, who learned English during his stay in England in 1850 to 1855 (Markham 1866, Bugge 1965).

In 1818 the Inuhuit were certainly distinct from their Inuit neighbors, the West Greenlanders to the south of Melville Bay. The cut of their jackets and breeches was different (Fisher 1819: 55), and their language differed in pronunciation and to some extent in vocabulary (Ross 1819: 120–23). Moreover, they had no kayak or umiaq. But they certainly could not have been so isolated as to believe "themselves to be the only inhabitants of the universe, and that all the rest of the world was a mass of ice," as Ross maintained (1819: 123–24). After all, the Tuluvaq whom Ross (pp. 121, 134) described as a king living at Pitoraarfik was actually a West Greenlandic *angakkoq* or shaman, who, fleeing from an epidemic, had left his home in the Upernavik district shortly before 1800 and emigrated north to Avanersuaq with his family in an umiaq (Lynge 1955: 17, 112; see Søby 1985: 225). His arrival in an umiaq gives the lie to the statement of one of Ross's officers, Alexander Fisher (1819: 56), that "they never saw a ship before, nor even a canoe. From this it is evident that they have not any communications with their countrymen to the southward." The statement of another officer, Edward Sabine (1819: 73), "that we found them ignorant, even by tradition, that there were other people in the world than themselves," is equally unacceptable. The Inuhuit certainly did have a tradition of people living far to the south, embodied in the story of a certain Qisuk, who narrowly escaped being murdered when on a visit to them (Hendrik 1878: 33–34; Lidegaard 1985: 48–49; Rasmussen 1925: 118–19 and 1908: 215–17; see Søby 1977–78 and 1985: 253–54). They also had a tradition of other Eskimos living north or northwest of themselves across the other side of Smith Sound in Ellesmere Island (Hayes 1867: 337). Robert Stein, after a long stay with the Inuhuit, pointed out in 1902 that they even had a name for the West Greenlanders of the Upernavik district, namely *Kawangarniten* or Qavanngarnitsat, meaning *those living to the south,* and for the Eskimos on the west side of Smith Sound, namely *Adlahsuin, the others,* or, as A. L. Kroeber (1899a) had it, *Adlet.* The same officer (Sabine 1819: 87) also made the equally absurd claim that in 1818 the Inuhuit "had never seen land over the sea, and were unacquainted with the word *akilinuk* [Akilineq] by which the people of south Greenland call the opposite coast of Davis' Strait." The first part of this statement cannot possibly be true because the Canadian coast is clearly visible across the entrance to Smith Sound from many places in Avanersuaq north of Whale Sound.

Although the Inuhuit in 1818 were certainly not cut off from and ignorant of their fellow Inuit, it seems likely that their trading and other contacts with the outside world had been irregular if not exceptional in the decades or even centuries before 1818. Devon and Ellesmere islands were perhaps no longer occupied by Eskimos after about 1500, until around the middle of the nineteenth century, and the Inuhuit themselves seem not to have crossed over to the west shore of Smith Sound in the nineteenth century until about 1870. The former contacts between the inhabitants of Avanersuaq and the eastern Canadian Arctic archipelago had thus ceased. It also seems likely that whatever earlier trade there had been with the West Greenlanders to the south of Avanersuaq had ceased long before 1800. Such is the impression given by the West Greenlander Hans Hendrik (1878: 33–35) or Suersaq, who lived with the Inuhuit for five years in 1855–60 (Laursen 1956, Lidegaard 1985, Dawes 1986). Pointing out that the ancestors of the Inuhuit had kayaks, he claimed that they had formerly obtained wood by bartering walrus ivory with the West Greenlanders. This assertion is supported by a West Greenlandic legend (Rasmussen 1908: 4) about a man who lived in the north of the Upernavik district, beyond the farthest settlement. He sledged north in three successive years while hunting bears in spring and found unfamiliar sledge tracks and even houses but no people. On his second visit he took a supply of wood with him, which he left by the strangers' houses as a gift. The following year he found the return gifts of the strangers: a large bundle of walrus tusks and a fine bitch with a litter of puppies. This seems to amount to "silent trade" and raises the possibility of regular barter in the past.

In the early nineteenth century, then, the Inuhuit supported themselves; their simple subsistence economy required no imports from outside Avanersuaq. They lived on and clothed themselves with the products of the hunt, which was concentrated on sea mammals, especially seals, walrus, and narwhals, but also included birds and hares caught with nets made with sealskin thongs and foxes caught in stone traps. At that time the Inuhuit were apparently without bows and arrows. They did not hunt caribou, and fish formed no part of their diet. But remarkably, they had a supply of meteoritic iron with which bone spear and harpoon points could be tipped and knives made.

The exact sources of the different raw materials that were essential to the existence of the Inuhuit in the first half of the nineteenth century have been identified and investigated. They obtained iron from Savissivik by breaking small flakes off the large meteorites found there or along the shore not far from Cape York (Ross 1819: 95, 112). Soapstone for cooking pots and lamps came from an exposure on the coast between Cape York and Cape Atholl. In 1966 Ivars Silis (1968) accompanied some Inuhuit to this soapstone outcrop high in the cliffs north of the Pituffik Glacier, which Hans Peder Steensby (1910: 276) had been told about in 1909. They quarried firestone, or iron pyrites, with which to make fire, south of Booth Sound, near Drown Bay (Mylius-Erichsen and Moltke 1906: 404–5), at a place called Ingnerit. Finally, the dry grass they used inside their boots, which was essential to prevent frostbitten toes, was apparently collected from the fertile cliff slopes below the dovekie (little auk) colonies of the coast southwest of Cape Atholl (Holtved 1967: 45).

The total Inuhuit population probably consisted of between one hundred and two hundred people, who pursued a nomadic existence, following their prey. James Saunders in 1851 was oversimplifying when he summarized their way of life with the statement that they followed the land-fast ice northward in summer, killing and caching seals along the coast, and then retreated south in winter eating up the contents of the caches. Families also made summer journeys to the south from Pitoraarfik to Cape York to hunt seals and procure iron (Ross 1819: 103) and to the north early in the spring for the annual walrus hunt near Cape Alexander (Kane 1856b: 107–10). Explorers encountered the same individuals, one year at Cape York, another year in Inglefield Land (Petersen 1857: 29–30 and Villarejo 1965: 82; M'Clintock 1859: 135 and Petersen 1860: 86–87).

For the period before about 1860 we know of twelve intermittently inhabited Inuhuit settlements or dwelling places, eight of which are among the nine places marked by the sixteen-year-old Qalasersuaq on a map he drew in 1850 (see Table 2). Each of these would harbor at one time between two and twenty or even fifty persons occupying at least two or three winter houses.

The early nineteenth-century Inuhuit employed three sorts of dwelling, according to circumstance and season. In winter they lived in winter houses, solidly built of stone, "the outside lined with sods" (Kane 1856a: 38), which were "situated always near the sea-side," sunk several feet below ground level, and were entered "by a long, narrow, and nearly underground passage" (Ross 1819: 129–30). The fullest early description of one of these houses is that of Hayes (1860: 124–27; compare Fig. 4):

> I embraced the opportunity to pay a visit to these huts. . . . I found them to be in shape much like an old-fashioned country clay oven, square in front, and sloping back into the hill. They were now covered with snow, and until after entering one of them, I could not discover of what material they were made. To get inside I was obliged to crawl on my hands and knees through a covered passage about twelve feet long. . . . After making two or three turns, I observed at last a bright light streaming down through a hole, into which my guide elevated his body; and then, moving to one side, he made room for his guest. I found myself in a den in which I could not stand upright, but which was crowded with human beings of both sexes, and of all ages and sizes. . . . The whole interior was about ten feet in diameter, and five and a half feet high. The walls were made of stones, moss, and the bones of whale, narwhal, and other animals. They were not arched, but drawn in gradually from the foundation, and capped by long slabs of slate-stone, stretching from side to side. The floor was covered with thin flat stones. Half of this floor at the back part of the hut was elevated a foot. This elevation . . . served both as bed and seat, being covered with dry grass, over which were spread bear and dog-skins. At the corners in front were similar elevations; under one of which lay a litter of pups, with their mother, and under the other was stowed a joint of meat. The front of the hut was square, and through it, above the passage-way, opened a window; a square sheet of strips of dried intestine, sewed together, admitted the light. The hole of entrance in the floor was close to the front wall, and was covered with a piece of seal-skin. The walls were lined with seal or fox-skins, stretched to dry. In the cracks between the stones where thrust whipstocks, and bone pegs on which hung coils of harpoon-lines.

The winter house of the Inuhuit was warmed by one or more shallow lamps made of soapstone, about 8 inches (20 cm) in diameter and clam-shaped. "The cavity was filled with oil, and on the straight edge a flame was

Table 2.

Inuhuit dwelling places known from before about 1860, numbered from south to north

Place	Date	Description	Source
1. Ivnanganeq Cape York	Aug. 1818 July–Aug. 1852	18 persons, 8 sledges 20 persons, 3 skin tents	Ross 1819, M'Dougall 1857, M'Clintock 1859
2. Narsaarsuk? (between Cape Atholl and Uummannaq)	Winter 1849–50	1 house, more than 1 family "12 miles down the sound" from North Star Bay	Saunders 1851
3. Uummannaq	Winter 1849–50	1 house, more than 1 family	Saunders 1851
	Summer 1850	3 or more houses, 3 or 4 dead Eskimos, no living inhabitants	Phillips 1851
4. Appat, Saunders Island	Autumn 1854	11, then 16 persons traveling north	Hayes 1860: 247–48, 273
5. Natsilivik	Sept.–Dec. 1854	About 20, later about 50, persons; 13 persons of 3 families in 1 house; 2 houses in all and several snow houses in Dec.	Hayes 1860: 120, 128, 299, 300
6. Itilleq	Aug. 1861	30 persons in 3 sealskin tents	Hayes 1867: 430
7. Kiatak, Northumberland Island	July 1854	3 empty houses, recently occupied	Kane 1856a: 333
8. Illuluarssuit ("Karsooit")	Dec. 1854	2 houses	Hayes 1860: 245, 309
9. Neqi	Dec. 1854	"a double hut"	Hayes 1860: 311
10. Pitoraarfik	Winter 1818	At least 1 family	Ross 1819: 103
11. Iita	Sept. 1854	12 persons from 3 families in 2 houses; 2 ruined houses	Kane 1856a: 404
	April 1855 Aug. 1855	14 persons from 4 families 30 persons in 7 tents at head of Foulke Fjord	Kane 1856b: 113 Kane 1856b: 327–28
12. Anoritooq	Sept. 1854	1 house, not occupied	Kane 1856a: 379–80

burning quite brilliantly," wrote Hayes (1860: 127–28). "The wick which supplied fuel to the flame, was of moss. The only business of the women seemed to be, to prevent the lamps from smoking, and to keep them supplied with blubber, large pieces of which were placed in them, the heat of the flame trying out the oil." The lamp was trimmed with a small stick (Ross 1819: 79), presumably of Arctic willow. Fire was made by striking two stones together. Kane (1856a: 379–80) watched an Eskimo doing this. One of the stones was "a plain piece of angular milky quartz, held in the right hand, the other apparently an oxide of iron. He struck them together after the true tinder-box fashion, throwing a scanty supply of sparks on a tinder composed of the silky down of the willow catkins . . . which he held on a lump of dried moss." The blubber lamp provided heat to boil meat in a soapstone caldron suspended above it; to dry garments hung on a drying rack made, at least in one house, "of bear-rib bones lashed together crosswise" (Hayes 1860: 128), fixed above that; and also to warm the house, which it did so effectively that the occupants often removed some or all of their clothes.

The second sort of Inuhuit dwelling was the snow house, which was used in winter either when one was caught by a blizzard en route between two settlements or to supplement the accommodation at such a settlement if too many people arrived there at the same time and could not squeeze into the existing stone and turf houses. The early explorers make no mention of Inuhuit snow houses built with snow blocks cut with a knife and arranged in a spiral but rather write of dugouts burrowed into large snowdrifts. When traveling northward with some Inuhuit toward the Humboldt Glacier at the end of April 1855, Kane (1856b: 154) and his companions slept in a burrow scooped out of a snowdrift rather than in a proper snow house. In February 1861 "Tcheitchenguak" constructed such an "artificial cave in a snow-bank" at Hayes's winter quarters near Iita (1860: 243–44). It is difficult to be sure that Qulutana was not thinking of such a dugout when he told Hayes, whose stone-built refuge was already crowded with nineteen persons, "that his party could build a snow-hut and sleep in it" (1860: 249). Perhaps the Inuhuit did not have the snow house built of blocks of snow so familiar among the Canadian Eskimos.

In summer the Inuhuit lived in a tent made of sealskins called a tupeq. No detailed description of these tents seems to have been made by any of the early explorers.

Few other people, even among Eskimos, have so perfected the art of travel with dog team and sledge as the Inuhuit. In 1818, Ross (1819: 80), who acquired two sledges from them, one of which is in the British Museum (King 1982), noticed the "amazing velocity" with which the first Inuhuit ever seen by Europeans went off on their sledges over the sea ice toward the land. Kane (1856b: 211–12) claimed that the 100-mile-long (160 km) drive from Cape

York to Saunders Island had been accomplished in a single day at a stretch. Such rapid winter and spring travel was possible only in good weather over good sea ice. In summer, or at least in July and August, when their sledges had neither snow nor ice to run on, the Inuhuit of 150 years ago, lacking boats, were virtually without means of transport. Except for one with wooden runners seen by Edward Belcher in 1852, the Inuhuit sledges described by the early explorers were entirely constructed of pieces of bone lashed together with strips of sealskin. Hayes (1860: 215–17) gives a detailed account of what he thought was "the most ingeniously contrived specimen of the mechanic art that I have ever seen":

> It was made wholly of bone and leather. The runners, which were square behind and rounded upward in front, and about five feet long, seven inches high, and three fourths of an inch thick, were slabs of bone; not solid, but composed of a number of pieces, of various shapes and sizes, cunningly fitted and tightly lashed together. Some of these were not larger than one's two fingers; some were three or four inches square; others were triangular, the size of one's hand; while others, again, were several inches long and two or three broad. These pieces were all fitted together as neatly as the blocks of a Chinese puzzle. Near their margins were rows of little holes, through which were run strings of seal-skins, by which the blocks were fastened together, making a slab almost as firm as a board.
>
> These bones are flattened and cut into the required shape with stones. The grinding needed to make a single runner must be a work of months; but the construction of an entire new sledge, I was afterwards informed, was unheard of in the present generation. Repairs are made as any part becomes broken or decayed; but a vehicle of this kind is a family heirloom, and is handed down from generation to generation. The origin of some of the Esquimau sledges dates back beyond tradition.
>
> Upon turning over the specimen before me, I found that the runners were shod with ivory from the tusk of the walrus. This also had been ground flat and its corners squared with stones; and it was fastened to the runner by a string which was looped through two counter-sunk holes. This sole was composed of a number of pieces, but the surface was uniform and as smooth as glass.
>
> The runners stood about fourteen inches apart, and were fastened together by bones, tightly lashed to them. These cross pieces were the femur of the bear, the antlers of the reindeer, and the ribs of the narwhal. Two walrus ribs were lashed, one to the after-end of each runner, for upstanders, and were braced by a piece of reindeer antler, secured across the top.

The Inuhuit dog team was not, as Alexander Fisher thought (1819: 59), "yoked in pairs," but fanwise. Again, Hayes (1860: 219) provides a detailed description:

All being ready, the dogs, seven in number, were next brought up, led by their traces. The harness on them was no less simple than the cargo they had to draw. It consisted of two doubled strips of bearskin, one of which was placed on either side of the body of the animal, the two being fastened together on the top of the neck and at the breast, thus forming a collar. Thence they passed inside of the dog's fore-legs, and up along the sides to the rump, where the four ends meeting together were fastened to a trace eighteen feet in length. This was connected with the sledge by a line four feet long, the ends of which were attached one to each runner. To the middle of this line was tied a strong string which was run through bone rings at the ends of the traces, and secured by a slipknot, easily untied. This arrangement was to ensure safety in bear-hunting. The bear is chased until the sledge is within fifty yards of the prey, when the hunter leans forward and slips the knot, and the dogs, now loose from the sledge, quickly bring the bear to bay.

About the dogs themselves the explorers have little to say. All of them, from Ross on, stopped to procure dogs in West Greenland on their way north, and some of these, at least from the time of Kane's expedition, must have interbred with the Inuhuit dogs. It is a shame that Ross (1819: 103) does not fulfill his promise of an appendix describing "the peculiarities of this variety, and the few circumstances in which it differs from the common Esquimaux dog." He says only, not very helpfully, that the Inuhuit dogs "are of various colours, but chiefly resembling that given in the plate [uniform dark grayish-brown]; they are of the size of a shepherd's dog, they have a head like a wolf, and a tail like a fox; their bark resembles the latter, but they have also a howl like the former" (p. 133; see Fig. 16).

Inuhuit dress in the first half of the nineteenth century was imperfectly described by the early explorers, who seem only to have mentioned garments that were worn by men (see Fig. 7 and, for women, Fig. 5). They were as follows:

1. An outer coat or cloak of bearskin used in winter (Ross 1819: 125).

2. A hooded outer coat of sealskin, the hair outside, terminating at the bottom in a tongue in front and behind. The hood trimmed with fox skin (Ross 1819: 125).

3. A hooded outer coat of fox skin (Kane's *kapetah* = *kapatak;* see Kane 1856b: 22–23), also with a tongue below at front and rear. One noticed by Kane (1856a: 203) was "of mixed white and blue fox pelts, arranged with something of fancy." Markham (1866: 130) records that the hood or *nessak* (*nasaq*) was "lined with bird skins and trimmed with fox fur."

4. An inner coat or shirt of bird skins, worn feathers inward. According to Kane (1856b: 23), "more than five hundred auks [dovekies or little auks] have been known to contribute to a garment of this description"; fewer

than one hundred was probably the rule. Ross (1819: 125), who thought this garment was the lining of the outer coat, asserts that it was made of eider duck or auk skins.

5. Bear or dog skin breeches reaching down to the knee but up scarcely over the hips so that the wearer's bare skin was at times exposed between their top and the bottom of the outer coat.

6. Sealskin boots, the hair inward or, more likely, removed; the soles, according to Ross (p. 125), covered with walrus hide.

7. Bearskin boots, the hair out, terminating with the bear's foot, claws to the front (Kane 1856b: 23–24), padded inside with dry grass.

8. A bird skin sock or inner boot (Kane 1856b: 23, Markham 1866).

9. Mittens of sealskin, hair out, padded inside with dry grass (Kane 1856b: 24–25).

10. "A fox's tail held between the teeth to protect the nose in a wind" (Kane 1856b: 24).

Though several families frequently shared dwellings, Inuhuit society was based on the family unit. Edward Sabine (1819) asserted that "the head of the family has control over the members, but is interfered with by no other authority," but most of the early explorers thought that the Inuhuit had chiefs of some kind. Ross's quaint notion of Tuluvaq as "a king" was not entirely shared by his brother officers (Sabine 1819; Fisher 1819: 56), and Sabine even thought that the West Greenlandic word for a chief, *naalagaq,* was unknown to the Inuhuit. But the *naalagaq,* like the shaman or *angakkoq,* certainly did exist among them; it or an equivalent term was given informally to certain experienced and influential individuals. Both Kane and Hayes reveled in the prestige they believed they acquired when addressed by the Inuhuit as *naalagaqsuaq,* the suffix -*suaq* meaning "great," but Frederick A. Cook (1911: 441) thought that the Inuhuit were likely to call any stranger *naalagaqsuaq,* "which the vanity of the early travellers interpreted as the 'great chief.'"

The Inuhuit seemed to have no knowledge of warfare and "to have no diseases among them" (Ross 1819: 134–35); their number was thought to be limited by starvation, murder, and infanticide (Kane 1856b: 64, 108). Their sense of fun did not pass unnoticed. As Markham put it (1866: 134): "The visitor who first sees a party of Arctic Highlanders will be at once struck by their merry good-natured countenances, their noisy fun and boisterous laughter." Their supposed propensity for thieving was likewise a matter for comment. "They showed a disposition to steal every portable article that came in their way," wrote Godfrey (1857: 144). "If detected in the act, they would pass it off as a joke, never showing any sign of shame or anger when the stolen article was taken from them." Another of the "natural propensities" of the Inuhuit for which the explorers had little sympathy was their lack of European standards of hygiene. Ross's statement is typical (p. 133): "The habits of this people appeared to be filthy in the extreme; their faces, hands, and bodies, are covered with oil and dirt, and they look as if they never had washed themselves since they were born. Their hair was matted with filth." The sailing master on HMS *Resolute* in 1852 thought the Inuhuit "degraded creatures," "without exception, the most disgustingly filthy race of human beings it has been my lot to encounter" (M'Dougall 1857: 72–73).

The Inuhuit buried their dead in a cairn or pile of loose stones and boulders, often somewhere near their winter houses. Fisher (1819: 62) found several such heaps on the coast near Cape York, in one of which a human skull was visible. "The space within which it was enclosed was between five and six feet long, two feet broad, and about the same in the height." On the coast near Iita, in autumn 1853, Kane (1856a: 51) found such a grave in which the corpse was enclosed in a sack of skins, the knees drawn up to the body, and the dead person's accoutrements placed around him. In another burial, at Pitoraarfik, the corpse was sewn up in skins with the limbs extended and then covered with the usual heap of stones (Kane 1856b: 118–19). Edward A. Inglefield, in 1852, almost certainly at Natsilivik, came across a winter house with the entrance blocked by a stone. Removing it, he found the corpse of a man inside. Later he learned that it was an Eskimo custom to seal up a house in this way when someone had died in it (1853: 59).

The early explorers ascertained that the Inuhuit could count only up to ten, that they derived an appreciation of the passage of time from the apparent movement of the stars, and that they had names for some constellations. According to Kane (1856b: 209–10), the Inuhuaq "measured his life by winters. . . . Winter is for him the great dominant period of the year: he calls it *okipok* [*ukiaq*], the season of fast ice." Then, in the spring, *upernasak* [*upernassaq*] follows, "the time of water-drops," and at the end of May or in June comes *upernak* [*upernaaq*], the season of snowmelt, which is followed in August by *aosak* [*aasaq*], "the season of no ice," when the fjords are free of ice. The fifth and last season begins late in September and is called *okiakut* [*ukiakkut*], the time of freeze-up (compare Gilberg 1984 for the seasons among the present-day Inuhuit).

The Inuhuit mentality was far from conservative or rigid. Sabine noticed how receptive Majaq was to new ideas. He appeared extremely interested in the abundance of wood on board ship, examined various articles in the cabin, and was particularly taken with the kayak belonging to the expedition's West Greenlandic interpreter John Sacheuse (Sabine 1819: 83):

> [He] asked many questions about the way in which it was made. He wished to buy it, and offered plenty of skins in exchange. We recommended him to

set about making one, which he seemed disposed to attempt, but remarked that some part of the frame was made of wood, of which he had none. We told him that bone would do equally well, to which he assented.

I have little doubt that, if we visit them this year, we shall find that something of the kind has been tried. I wish they could have seen the canoe in the water, as it would have made a much deeper impression on them, and they would have been the more disposed to imitate it.

Majaq was especially impressed by the height of the cabin (p. 78). "He said that he had always lived in a low house, with a low door, but that he would alter it, and that if we came again we should find that he had done so."

This account of the Inuhuit at the time of their first contacts with white men, as seen by those white men, may fittingly close with Ross's (1819: 126) description of the personal appearance of "Ervick."

> This man, who appeared to be about forty years of age, measured five feet one inch in height, his skin being of a dirty copper colour, rather darker than the generality; his face was broad, his forehead narrow and low, with some wrinkles, and the nose small and strait; the cheeks full, round, and ruddy, even through the oil and dirt which covered them; his mouth was large, generally half open, and shewing that he had lost his fore-teeth, the remainder of which were, however, white and regular; his lips were thick, particularly towards the middle; his eyes small, black, oval, and very approximate; the hair was black, coarse, long, and lank, and had certainly never been cut or combed; his beard and mustachios, which were suffered to grow, were scanty, and confined to the upper lip and chin; his body was fleshy, inclining to corpulence; the hands thick and small, fingers short, and the feet very short and thick.

In the course of the nineteenth and early twentieth centuries, against a background of increasing contacts with, and pressures from, white men, which will form much of the subject matter of the rest of this book, the Inuhuit came into renewed contact with their Eskimo neighbors to the south, both those in Greenland and in Canada.

During millennia of prehistoric times, small, wandering bands of Arctic people had from time to time crossed the ice or the sea between America and Greenland. Some returned whence they came, others moved on to be followed sometimes by a veritable migration. The last of these wanderings took place between 1850 and 1870. This dramatic and dangerous adventure, parts of the story of which have only recently been uncovered from Eskimo legend and oral tradition both in Greenland and Canada (Mary-Rousselière 1980; Petersen 1964; Gilberg 1976a; and Ulloriaq 1985), impinged at least twice on the white man's historical record.

North across the often ice-covered waters of Lancaster Sound, from the northern tip of Baffin Island, along the 800-mile-long rocky, ice-bound coasts of Devon Island and Ellesmere Island there was, in the nineteenth century, an enormous empty space where no one lived and practically no one had ever been. It was in this space, on 29 July 1853, on the south coast of Devon Island, that Commander Edward Inglefield of the supply ship HMS *Phoenix* came across a group of twenty-two Eskimos led by a certain Qitlaq. It is likely that Inglefield told Qitlaq about Smith Sound, about the proximity of Greenland to Canada, and about the Inuhuit and their dwelling places in Avanersuaq, all of which Inglefield had himself explored the previous summer in the *Isabel.*

Qitlaq was slow to act on this information. He was still on Devon Island five years later, on 11 July 1858, when Captain F. L. M'Clintock, commanding the yacht *Fox*, came across him and eleven companions on the east coast near Philpots Island. M'Clintock (1859: 144) noted that "the old chief Kal-lek is remarkable amongst Esquimaux for having a bald head. He inquired by name for his friend Captain Inglefield" and told M'Clintock that the three families represented by himself and his companions had spent the previous two years on the southeast coast of Devon Island.

Not long after this encounter Qitlaq seems to have decided to travel on northward and visit the Eskimos of whom Inglefield had told him on the far side of Smith Sound. At some stage a group of his companions, some of whom had probably been with him when he crossed Lancaster Sound, had subsequently separated but then rejoined him, turned back. Eventually, most likely in the spring of 1862, Qitlaq and thirteen or fifteen others crossed Smith Sound around the northern edge of the North Water, perhaps between Cape Sabine and Anoritooq, and settled down for the summer at Iita. In the course of that summer they blew up a depot of gunpowder and other stores which Hayes had left near Iita in the previous year, either by examining the barrel of powder too closely by the light of a blubber lamp or by cooking some birds too close to it. Soon afterward, they met up with the Inuhuit. Ten years later, in the winter of 1872–73, at Iita, Emil Bessels was given a firsthand account of some of these events by Qitlaq's son Ittukusuk, who had accompanied his father all the way from southern Baffin Island (Bessels 1879: 342).

The arrival of this tiny group of fourteen or sixteen persons, about equally divided between the sexes, from the North American continent, was a portentous event for the Inuhuit; some would even claim that this injection of new blood and new technology saved them from the extinction which Kane and Hayes had predicted but which however Clements Markham (1866) did not accept. A hundred years later Rolf Gilberg (1976a and b) reckoned that 217 out of a total Inuhuit population of 603 were direct descendants of the immigrants of 1862. He (1984a) reports that the newcomers brought with them the kayak, the bow and arrow, and the fish lure and spear, thereby facilitating and extending the Inuhuit hunt for sea mammals and adding two new items to their diet: caribou meat and fish. The immigrants also introduced new types of drum song (Hauser 1986) and an improved snow house, although the Inuhuit rejected their fashion of tattooing.

The adventures of Qitlaq and his followers had another repercussion on the Inuhuit: it encouraged them to travel across to the western or Canadian side of Smith Sound to Ellesmere Island. Qitlaq and some others returned there after a stay of some six years or so in Avanersuaq. According to Robert Stein (1902a), two Inuhuit, Utiniaq and Arrutaq, with their families, traveled extensively along the Ellesmere Island coast in about 1875. At the end of the nineteenth and early in the twentieth century, the Inuhuit crossed the frozen Smith Sound often enough to initiate a regular tradition of hunting expeditions to Ellesmere Island. They accompanied Peary and Stein there in 1898–1902 (Peary 1907), Rasmussen in 1907 (Rasmussen 1935 and Møller 1961), Cook (1911) and then Rudolph Franke (1914) in 1908, and Harry Whitney (1910) in 1909. Thereafter, trips to Ellesmere Island became commonplace, with or without white explorers.

In the nineteenth century contacts between the Inuhuit and the West Greenlanders remained as occasional as they probably had been in the eighteenth century. John Sacheuse, the interpreter for John Ross's 1818 expedition, communicated only briefly with the Inuhuit at Cape York. Hans Hendrik or Suersaq interpreted for both Kane and Hayes and lived for five years among the Inuhuit, but it was not his West Greenland kayak that served as model and inspiration for the Inuhuit but that in use on Baffin Island, introduced to them in 1862, only a year after Suersaq had left them. Frequent contacts were not inaugurated until 1903, when three West Greenlanders accompanied the first Danish expedition to Avanersuaq. They sledged north across Melville Bay in 1903, remained several months with the Inuhuit, and took five Inuhuit with them when they returned south to West Greenland in February 1904. A new era in the relationship between the Inuhuit and the West Greenlanders had begun.

In the foregoing pages the reports of early white explorers have been used to try to portray the Inuhuit way of life before it began to be transformed by pressures from British and American explorers and whalers, by the injection of new Inuit blood from Canada in 1862, and by the renewed contacts with the West Greenlandic Eskimos after 1903. Although the history of human activities in Avanersauq in the nineteenth century is reasonably well illuminated by Eskimo oral tradition (for example, Ulloriaq 1985) and the white historical record, what happened there in the centuries between the end of the archaeological record unearthed by Holtved and others around A.D. 1500, and A.D. 1800, remains wholly obscure, though is it likely that archaeologists will someday find out.

3

A Century of Explorers
and Whalers, 1817–1917

N obody in the nineteenth century voyaged expressly to northwest
Greenland; Avanersuaq was visited only incidentally, as a diversion en
route to some other goal. English and Scottish whalers stopped at Cape York
or elsewhere in Avanersuaq on their way across Smith Sound to hunt whales
in Lancaster Sound and elsewhere off the Canadian coast. Royal Navy "discovery" ships called there either on their way in search of the Northwest Passage or in search of Sir John Franklin, who was lost looking for the Northwest Passage. Then, on 7 May 1858, a letter from Dr. Isaac. I. Hayes was read
at a meeting of the American Philosophical Society "proposing to make an attempt to reach the north pole of the earth" (Hayes 1860: 358), and he and others after him were subsequently in Avanersuaq only on their way to pursue
that somewhat questionable goal. It was the last of the great North Pole enthusiasts, Robert Peary, who in 1891 initiated a thorough exploration of Avanersuaq and investigation of its Inuhuit inhabitants by taking a boatload of
scientists there with him to carry out the necessary research and to help defray
his costs. Only in the first years of the twentieth century did an expedition arrive in Avanersuaq with no intention of going anywhere else: the Danish
members of the Literary Greenland Expedition of 1903 were interested only in
studying the Inuhuit and establishing a Danish presence in Avanersuaq.

Because William Baffin, in search of the Northwest Passage, had in 1616
sailed around the shores of the bay named after him and reported categorically on his return that "there is no passage nor hope of passage in the north of
Davis Straights" (Markham 1881: 150), it was a long time before his voyage
up Greenland's west coast as far as Smith Sound and back south down the
Baffin Island coast was repeated. Eventually, however, at a time when whalers
had reported favorable ice conditions, the British admiralty resolved to try
again, and an expedition was sent in 1818 under the command of John Ross
(Dodge 1973, Berton 1988). The title of his book describes more accurately
what he did than what he was supposed to do: *A Voyage of Discovery made
under the Orders of the Admiralty in His Majesty's Ships* Isabella *and* Alexander *for the purpose of exploring Baffin's Bay and inquiring into the Proba-*

bility of a North-west Passage. The words *exploring Baffin's Bay* are printed
in bold type, but Ross's official instructions, which said nothing about exploring Baffin Bay, ordered him to "make the best of your way into Davis' Strait,
through which you will endeavour to pass to the northward, without stopping
on either of its coasts, unless you shall find it absolutely necessary." He was
urged to omit no precaution "that prudence may dictate, to avoid accidents on
an enterprise of so arduous a nature as that of conducting ships in safety
through fields of ice in unknown seas." He was reminded that "the first, and
most important, object of this voyage, is the discovery of a passage from
Davis' Strait, along the northern coast of America, and through Behring's
Strait, into the Pacific" (Ross 1819: 1–14). Fortunately for our knowledge of
the Inuhuit, Ross's way toward the Northwest Passage was blocked from 9 to
16 August 1818 off Bushnan Island and Cape York by fields of ice. Sadly for
Ross, his meticulous, though partly inaccurate, report on the hitherto unknown group of Eskimos he called Arctic Highlanders was ignored or be-
littled, but the failure of his subsequent irresolute search for the Northwest
Passage engaged the public's attention and drew on him the ridicule and criticism of many. In the already mentioned Cruikshank cartoon of him and his
men in procession through the streets of London on their return, even the
expedition's chief claim to fame in the field of natural science is made fun of,
for a red-coated marine is shown carrying aloft a bird on the tip of his bayonet
with a label inscribed with the word *sabini* dangling from its beak—a reference to the new species of gull found by the expedition and named after one of
its members, Edward Sabine (J. Sabine 1818).

The most vicious of John Ross's critics was Secretary of the Admiralty
John Barrow. Nearly twenty years later, in 1846, this peppery old gentleman,
then aged eighty-two, began his *Voyages of Discovery and Research within
the Arctic Regions, from the Year 1818 to the Present Time*, with an extraor-
dinarily derogatory account of Ross's 1818 expedition. The puntilious and ir-
ascible Barrow complains that in his book Ross refers to himself repeatedly as
"captain," though during the expedition he was a mere commander and was
promoted to captain only after his return. He claims that any two members of
the Yacht Club could have completed the trip round Baffin Bay in five months
and "run far enough up Sir Thomas Smith's Sound to ascertain the insularity,
or otherwise, of . . . Greenland" (p. 48). He concluded that Ross was unfit
to have conducted a voyage of discovery. But he went too far in his dispar-
agement of Ross's chapter on the Arctic Highlanders, which was based largely
on information obtained via the West Greenlandic interpreter John Sacheuse
(Laursen 1955, see Fig. 6). Writes Barrow (1846: 33):

> The titles of this extraordinary chapter are: "*The Situation of the Arctic
> Highlands—Nature of the Country—Produce of the Country—Language*

*of the Arctic Highlanders—Origin of the Arctic Highlanders—Dress—
Description—Subject of Religion—Mode of Living, and Customs—Habits
and Customs."* Ross, indeed, suspects that this account "may appear in some
points to be defective;" he may safely satisfy himself that it will not only *appear*, in some points, to be *defective*, but will be so pronounced in all: in
point of fact, he never set his foot on shore, and could not, by any possibility,
have known any thing of the stuff he has set down, which is of that kind of
manufacture not worth the paper on which it is printed.

The next British naval officer to visit Avanersuaq was Mr. James Saunders,
commanding the supply ship HMS *North Star.* Since Ross's unsuccessful attempt in 1818 to find the Northwest Passage, a series of British naval expeditions had sailed through Davis Strait and Baffin Bay on the same errand and
been equally unsuccessful; none of them seems to have touched on Avanersuaq. This sustained effort culminated in 1845 with the dispatch of the ill-starred expedition led by the fifty-eight-year-old Franklin. It was last heard of
on 26 or 28 July in Melville Bay, when Captain Robert Martin, commanding
the Peterhead whaleship *Enterprise,* entertained some of Sir John's officers at
dinner on board his ship. They had been shooting dovekies (little auks) and
were confident that they had provisions for up to five or perhaps six years
(Simmonds 1852: 394–96); they also had nearly three thousand books on
board the two ships to while away that time (Nanton 1971: 229n.). Three
years later, in 1848, the first relief expedition was sent out (Wright 1959,
Neatby 1970), and a series of some thirty of these followed until 1858, several
of them touching briefly at Cape York on their way across the northern end of
Baffin Bay to Lancaster Sound and the maze of islands in the Canadian Arctic where Franklin had disappeared.

HMS *North Star,* dispatched by the admiralty with a cargo of provisions
for the lost expedition, reached Melville Bay at the end of July 1849 and was
almost at once beset in the ice. Instead of forcing her way through the North
Water and then crossing to Canada, she only managed with great difficulty to
edge her way into Wolstenholme Fjord, which was providentially free of ice.
On 30 September 1849 Saunders took his ship into winter quarters in a little
bay on the south shore of the fjord, directly under the flat-topped mountain
called Uummannaq. This bay has ever since borne the name of the only English ship ever to winter in northwest Greenland. A grim monument of this
event still stands on the stony shore of the bay, now in sight of Thule Air Base.
Set in the top of a massive heap of boulders is a gravestone with the beautifully carved inscription: "SACRED to the MEMORY of Wm. Sharp of H.M.S.
North Star: who departed this life Nov, 1 1849 AGED, 26 YEARS." Three other
seamen lost their lives. One of the four, perhaps William Sharp, was killed by a
fall down a cliff; the others fell victim to scurvy, which Saunders succeeded in

staving off by broaching the stores he was carrying for Franklin. By July 1850 the crew of the *North Star* were anxiously awaiting the breakup of the ice that hemmed them in. "Mr. Leask the ice master, was sent to the top of a high hill every day, to examine its state in the offing." They got away on 1 August without troubling to tidy up after their stay, for, later that same month, when Captains Erasmus Ommanney and C. G. Phillips and party searched the surrounding terrain, they found evidence of the "recent presence of a Queen's ship in the neighbourhood"—"a couple of shirts (one marked Corporal J. Cullamore)," bits of clothing, broken bottles, crockery, "iron hoops and nails, painted wood, a washing tub and the footsteps of Europeans" (Simmonds 1852: 290–94, Saunders 1851, Phillips 1851; see also Anon. 1852).

Ommanney and Phillips were among the officers of a four-ship Royal Navy squadron under Captain H. T. Austin, which, in company with two other ships, had stopped briefly off Cape York early in August 1850. On 10 August a party from the *Lady Franklin* and the *Sophia* walked seven miles over the sea ice and climbed to the summit of Bushnan Island (Sutherland 1852a: 238–44). On 12 August, off Cape York, contact was made with five Eskimos, one of whom, "Kalli" or Qalasersuaq, was taken aboard HMS *Assistance* by Captain Ommanney. It was Qalasersuaq who piloted "her Majesty's steam-vessel *Intrepid*" into North Star Bay after Ommanney had left the *Assistance* anchored off Wolstenholme Island. He and Captain Phillips found the Inuhuit settlement of Uummannaq deserted (Simmonds 1852: 316–17).

The Royal Navy paid another fleeting visit to northwest Greenland in 1852, when two ships belonging to Sir Edward Belcher's squadron halted briefly at Cape York on 31 July. The sailing master of HMS *Resolute*, George F. M'Dougall, who published an account of his voyage in 1857, describes the Inuhuit settlement at Cape York, which he closely inspected, even entering one of the tents but, alas, giving no details of its construction. Sir Edward, on the *Assistance*, thought "he had seen quite enough of the individuals, not to care about inspecting their habitations." He continued on to Cape Dudley Digges, where he landed briefly toward midnight that same day, remarking, "About five miles north-west from it is a high-peaked unnamed island" (1855a: 67, 69). He seems to be referring to the whalers' landmark Conical Rock, which lies five miles south-southeast of the cape in question.

Another naval officer who visited northwest Greenland in that same summer of 1852, Captain Edward A. Inglefield, was in command of the schooner *Isabel* on behalf of Lady Jane Franklin, who was now playing just as active a role in the search for her lost husband as the lords of the admiralty. Inglefield (1853) had been instructed to investigate as thoroughly as possible a most improbable story then circulating that Franklin and his men might have been massacred by the Inuhuit. He ransacked the deserted winter houses at Uummannaq: "from some of the graves we turned out the filthy clothes and household goods of the natives." But they found no living natives until they reached Natsilivik, nor could they find any trace of the Franklin Expedition. Thereafter, Inglefield steamed north into Smith Sound to take what he called in his title "a peep into the Polar basin," before returning home.

In the spring of 1849 Jane Franklin had appealed to the United States to join in the search for her husband. After her petition to the president and a debate in Congress (Simmonds 1852: 325–31), New York shipping magnate Henry Grinnell helped to fit out a First, and then a Second Grinnell Expedition, the declared aim of both of which was to search for Sir John and his companions. A young U.S. Navy doctor, Elisha Kent Kane (Elder 1858, Mirsky 1954, Corner 1972), volunteered to serve on the First Grinnell Expedition under Lieutenant Edwin J. De Haven, and his "personal narrative" of it was published in 1853. After a brief contact with two Inuhuit whom they came across "upon the land ice, gesticulating in grotesque and not very decent pantomime" (Kane 1856c: 132) off Cape York on 15 August 1850, and after landing briefly once or twice on the Avanersuaq coast south of Cape Atholl, the First Grinnell Expedition crossed to Lancaster Sound, where it helped the British discovery ships to find Franklin's 1845–46 winter quarters.

Kane, doctor now turned captain, led the Second Grinnell Expedition himself in the brig *Advance,* which Grinnell had placed at his disposal. It seems that Kane genuinely believed that this expedition, which set out from New York on 30 May 1853, might succeed in finding living survivors of the Franklin Expedition. This event was, however, made extremely unlikely by the fact that any such survivors would have had to have lived through seven successive Arctic winters. Moreover, Kane was making for Smith Sound, and Franklin would have had to have ignored his instructions to search for the Northwest Passage via Lancaster Sound. Nonetheless, Kane believed that Smith Sound might lead into an "open Polar sea": after all, only the year before, Captain Inglefield had sailed well into the sound and seen no ice ahead of him. If it did, then surely he could sail westward along the southern shore of this supposedly unfrozen "Polar sea," perhaps to find Franklin.

Although he enjoyed a rapid passage across the often ice-choked Melville Bay on 27 July–3 August 1853, Kane could penetrate no farther north than the coast of Inglefield Land and there, in a cove to which he gave the name Rensselaer Bay after his family home in Philadelphia and his Dutch ancestors (van Rensselaer), the *Advance* was berthed for the winter, completely hemmed in by ice. Exploring parties were sent northeast along the Greenland coast as far as Washington Land and northwest across to Ellesmere Island, and contact was made with the Inuhuit, from whom Kane and his men obtained much needed fresh meat. Attempts to escape southward in open boats in the summer and autumn of 1854, after it became clear that the brig would not be released from the ice that year, came to grief. First, Kane himself went south in July but was forced by ice fields to return in August; then Dr. Isaac Hayes, the expedition's surgeon, led a party southward at the end of August, but they returned exhausted to the brig in December. Eventually, in the summer of 1855, Kane extricated his men, but not his ship, and led them south to safety, losing only three from a total of nineteen. At Upernavik on 11 September they fell in with the two United States vessels sent in search of them, the *Release* and the *Arctic,* under Lieutenant Henry J. Hartstene, who had been as far as Iita looking for them. There, he had been told by the Eskimos of Kane's voyage south in open boats (Kane 1856b: 326–29).

Kane's expedition had failed in its prime objective: "No traces of Sir John Franklin" ran a headline in the *New York Daily Times* for 12 October 1855 (Corner 1972: 226). But Kane was rightly welcomed home as a conquering hero and has rightly been accepted since then as one of the greatest of Arctic explorers. He traversed the coast of unexplored Inglefield Land, discovered the Humboldt Glacier and the Kennedy Channel, and opened a route to the north for subsequent explorers. Like so many Arctic voyagers, he found something that had no existence in fact, in this case an "open Polar sea" to the north of Kennedy Channel. Above all, he displayed his sparkling literary talents in that greatest of all Arctic classics, which inspired so many subsequent Arctic explorers, his two-volume *Arctic Explorations,* published in 1856 not long before his untimely death in 1857.

The fate of Sir John Franklin was finally made known in 1854 by John Rae (Richards 1985), long after all hope of finding living survivors had vanished. In 1859 Captain F. L. M'Clintock, commanding the *Fox* for Lady Franklin, brought back the first authentic relics of the expedition: twenty-six pieces of silver plate, some bearing the Franklin crest or the initials of owners, a prayer book, a copy of *The Vicar of Wakefield,* two double-barreled guns, several pairs of spectacles, five watches, a medicine chest, clothing, and many other articles. Thus was inaugurated a sort of Franklin treasure hunt, a search first for souvenirs and then for archaeological data, which continues to this day (Sutherland 1985). On his voyage to the Canadian Arctic, M'Clintock had stopped briefly near Cape York on 26 June 1858 and communicated with the Inuhuit through his Danish-born interpreter Carl Petersen (M'Clintock 1859: 135).

For nearly a decade after the wintering of the *North Star* in Wolstenholme Fjord in 1849–50 exploring ships passed northwest Greenland almost annually on their way to look for Franklin, but after M'Clintock's 1858 visit, a long pause ensued, until the early 1870s, interrupted only by Dr. Hayes (1867), who wintered at Iita in the schooner *United States* in 1860–61. He too numbered the discovery of a chimerical "open Polar sea" among the achievements of his expedition. Apart from a fifty-mile excursion onto the Inland Ice and some limited investigations in the neighborhood of Iita, Hayes's energies and attention were concentrated on exploration to the north. The next American expedition to penetrate Smith Sound, that of Charles F. Hall, was dedicated to reaching the North Pole, and he managed to force his ship, the *Polaris,* much farther north than had his predecessors (Blake 1874, Markham 1875: 183–200, Davis 1876, Bessels 1879, and Loomis 1972).

Hall's North Polar Expedition was dogged by disaster through no fault of his own. He himself died, some said by poison. On the return voyage south through Smith Sound, in the night of 15–16 October 1872, somewhere off Littleton Island, the *Polaris* was badly nipped in the ice. At a moment when eighteen persons were out on the floe and a substantial quantity of stores and equipment had been moved there too, the ship suddenly parted company from the floe and drifted away into the wild, stormy night. The people marooned on the floe, who, luckily for them all, included two Eskimo hunters and the experienced whaling captain George Tyson, managed to survive until they were rescued on 30 April 1873 by the sealer *Tigress* off the Labrador coast. They had drifted south through Baffin Bay and Davis Strait for a distance of nearly 2,000 miles in 190 days. Meanwhile, the *Polaris* had been beached near Iita, and her fourteen crew members, helped by the local Inuhuit, had soon built a substantial house ashore. On 3 June 1873 they began their voyage south in two homemade boats and were picked up 25 miles (40 km) southeast of Cape York by the Scottish whaler *Ravenscraig* on 23 June. Avanersuaq received another visit from a United States ship on 13–17 August 1873, when the *Tigress,* which had been bought by the government and fitted out as a relief vessel, commanded by J. A. Greer, called briefly at the winter quarters of the *Polaris's* crew near Iita, only to discover from the Eskimos that they had already departed for the south.

Encouraged by the success of the *Polaris* in pushing her way so far north, and no doubt inspired by a feeling of rivalry, in 1875 the admiralty dispatched the British Arctic Expedition with the aim of discovering the North Pole (Markham 1878, Moss 1878, Nares 1878). This expedition, commanded by Captain George Nares, halted off Cape York, landed briefly on one of the Cary Islands, and visited Iita and Littleton Island on its way north in July 1875. On its way home it landed at Cape Isabella and then anchored for five hours off Natsilivik on 12 September 1876.

Allen Young, a gentleman of private means, was already a veteran merchant navy captain when he served as sailing master under M'Clintock in the *Fox* in 1857–59. He later purchased the British naval gunboat *Pandora* from the admiralty, fitted it out for ice navigation, and in 1875 followed in the footsteps of Sir John Franklin in hope of finding the Northwest Passage. On his way to and from this unachieved goal he halted at the Cary Islands (Beynen

1876, Lillingston 1876, MacGahan 1876, Young 1879). In the following year he undertook another Arctic voyage, agreeing, at the request of the Royal Geographical Society and the admiralty, to allow the *Pandora* to act as a relief or support ship for the British Arctic Expedition. In the course of his activities, which included delivering mail to Nares and his men, Young made a thorough investigation of Avanersuaq. He landed once more at the Cary Islands, but also at Littleton Island, Sutherland Island south of Cape Alexander, and Natsilivik. On Sutherland Island his landing party found a cairn and record within it placed there by Lieutenant Hartstene on 16 August 1855: "The Arctic postal service is thus susceptible to improvement," comments Lieutenant Koolemans Beynen, the Dutch naval officer serving on the *Pandora* (Beynen 1877: 216n.).

After the departure in September 1876 of the *Pandora* and the two ships of the British Arctic Expedition, HMS *Alert* and *Discovery,* northwest Greenland was ignored by exploring expeditions for four successive summers. This pause was followed by a flurry of activity in the four summers beginning in 1881, when, in August, the ill-starred Greely expedition—officially called the Lady Franklin Bay Expedition from the place on Ellesmere Island where it was to set up a station under the auspices of the 1882–83 International Polar Year (Barr 1985)—made brief halts at the Cary Islands and at Littleton Island and neighboring Lifeboat Cove on its way north (Lanman 1885: 81–82, Greely 1886a: 60–66). Subsequently the inevitable relief ships also visited Avanersuaq (Schley 1887, Schley and Soley 1889, Powell 1961). The *Neptune* was at various places on the coast near Iita and Littleton Island in August 1882; the *Proteus* called at the Cary Islands and at Pandora Harbour between Cape Alexander and Foulke Fjord on 20–22 July 1883, and after she had been wrecked by the ice off Ellesmere Island, her crew returned in open boats south along the Avanersuaq coast, just missing the *Yantic,* which was at Littleton Island briefly on 3 August, and the Swedish expedition ship *Sofia,* which was in Parker Snow Bay on 26–29 July (Nordenskiöld 1885: 319–35). Finally, in 1884, the *Thetis* and the *Bear* passed north along the coast of northwest Greenland with only brief halts on their way to rescue Adolphus W. Greely and his surviving companions.

In 1891 the history of Avanersuaq took an important turn with the first appearance there of the American explorer Robert E. Peary (Green 1926, Hobbs 1936, Weems 1967). It would be wrong to consider Peary merely in terms of his preoccupation to "nail the Stars and Stripes to the North Pole," though from 1897 on, if not from earlier, he was obsessed by that ambition (Herbert 1989). Mainly as a by-product of his earlier goal of crossing the Inland Ice to explore northeast Greenland and of his tenaciously pursued plan of taking the Cape York meteorites to the United States of America, Peary was responsible for the sudden opening up of Avanersuaq and for greatly increasing knowledge of its geography, natural history, and Inuhuit inhabitants.

Having wintered in 1891–92 at Red Cliff House near Cape Cleveland on the south shore of McCormick Fjord, Peary set out in May 1892 with the Norwegian Eivind Astrup on what he called "the great white journey" across the Inland Ice from the head of McCormick Fjord to the head of Independence Fjord in northeast Greenland. Among the other members of his North Greenland Expedition was his wife, Josephine (Peary 1893), whose principal role seems to have been that of expedition cook: "I at once set to work to get the boys a square meal" (p. 36) is a typical entry in her journal. Then there was Langdon Gibson, an ornithologist, who in 1922 published a valuable paper on the birds encountered by the expedition; Frederick A. Cook, surgeon and anthropologist; and John M. Verhoeff, mineralogist and meteorologist, who lost his life in circumstances that were never properly explained because his body was never recovered. Apparently he fell into a crevasse while crossing the glacier now named after him.

The North Greenland Expedition was accompanied by a party of nine academics and others led by Professor Angelo Heilprin, executive curator of the Academy of Natural Sciences of Philadelphia (Keely and Davis 1893, Peary 1898a). These enthusiasts, forming the West Greenland Expedition, devoted several days in the late summer of 1891 to investigating the surroundings of McCormick Fjord while Red Cliff House and the expedition's stores were being unloaded, and they also studied the dress and hunting equipment of the Inuhuit.

When, in the following year, 1892, the Academy of Natural Sciences fitted out the *Kite* to bring Peary home, the venture was again under Heilprin's leadership, its members this time including a botanist, an artist, a journalist, a photographer, and a taxidermist (Heilprin 1893). They made excursions onto glaciers, visited Eskimo settlements, deserted and otherwise, and hunted big game, namely walrus and caribou. On 5 August the professorial party ascended onto the featureless expanse of the Inland Ice above the head of McCormick Fjord. They had only just planted a pole in the snow with a board nailed to it on which was painted a pointing finger and the words "To McCormick Bay. Kite in port, August 5" when, incredibly, they descried two black dots in the distance, which soon resolved themselves into the figures of Peary and Astrup. The explorers had completed the most arduous sledge journey so far undertaken by white men, without any assistance from Eskimos, and Peary was returning, after covering over 500 miles of featureless white waste, on a precisely correct course. No wonder he was acclaimed by Clements Markham, the president of the Royal Geographical Society, when he introduced Peary to the society in December 1897 as "without exception, the greatest glacial traveller in the world. He is also far and away the greatest dog-sledge traveller in the world as regards rapidity and distance" (Hobbs 1936: 112).

The base for Peary's further exploration in north Greenland in 1893–95 was a prefabricated wooden building he called Anniversary Lodge, which was erected in August 1893 at the head of Bowdoin Fjord (Peary 1898b). Peary, Astrup, and their companions were taken there along with this accommodation by the St. John's whaler *Falcon,* and the same ship was chartered in 1894 for the Peary Auxiliary Relief Expedition, which was organized by the Geographical Club of Philadelphia to bring the explorers back (Bryant 1895, Ohlin 1895a and b). Among the "gentlemen adventurers" who made up this expedition were the geologist Professor T. C. Chamberlin (1895–97) of the University of Chicago, whose work on the local glaciers was widely acclaimed, the journalist H. L. Bridgman, who went as historian, and the Swedish zoologist Axel Ohlin. The expedition returned without Peary, who insisted on remaining at Anniversary Lodge for another winter, but brought back Eivind Astrup, whose exploration and mapping of the northern end of Melville Bay had been carried out in April 1894 (Astrup 1895: 289–319 and Peary 1898b: 159–74). Peary himself returned in the *Kite* in 1895 after having twice sledged from Bowdoin Fjord to Cape York and back. On the first of these trips he was shown some of the famous Cape York meteorites, the removal of which to the United States in 1896 and 1897 will be described in a later chapter.

In the years 1891–95 Peary had sledged and boated along the shores of Avanersuaq's islands, capes, and fjords, had penetrated the inner recesses of Inglefield Gulf, and had brought scientists and other visitors from the United States into the area. These activities were readily linked with his Inland Ice explorations and his quest for the meteorites, but after their successful recovery in 1897 he turned his attention to reaching the North Pole. With that goal now exclusively in view, Peary spent most of his time on his longest single trip to the Arctic in 1898–1902 (Peary 1904a, 1907: 295–352) in Ellesmere Island, though between August 1899 and March 1900 he was at Iita. There was the usual coming and going of relief ships: the *Diana* in August 1899, the *Erik* in August 1901, both of which made a tour of Inuhuit villages in Avanersuaq, and finally the *Windward* took Peary back to America in August 1902.

During Peary's protracted stay in Ellesmere Island and the pause in his attempts to reach the Pole in 1902–5, other people moved into the area he had come to regard as his. Two Norwegian expeditions stopped briefly in Avanersuaq on their way to explore the Canadian Arctic archipelago. The first, under Otto Sverdrup (1903), visited Foulke Fjord in August 1898; the second, under Roald Amundsen (1907) in the *Gjøa,* stopped at Dalrymple Rock and Saunders Island in August 1903. A new epoch in the history of Avanersuaq began with the arrival there of the Danish so-called Literary Greenland Expedition of 1903 (Mylius-Erichsen and Moltke 1906). For the Danes had come to stay. First, in 1903, explorer-anthropologist Knud Rasmussen, journalist Ludvig Mylius-Erichsen, and artist Harald Moltke, insisting on the literary rather than scientific nature of their expedition, sledged north to Avanersuaq from the Upernavik district and back again at the end of the year after living much of the time with the Inuhuit. Then, in 1905, a Danish ship anchored in North Star Bay bringing gifts for the Inuhuit as a token of gratitude for their hospitality to the Literary Expedition, and in 1906–8 Rasmussen lived with the Inuhuit for two years. Further Danish activities in Avanersuaq form the subject of much of the rest of this book.

The story of Peary's two last visits to northwest Greenland may be briefly told. He was still exclusively interested in reaching the North Pole and touched on Avanersuaq only to recruit Inuhuit guides and porters on his way north and disembark them on his return. In August 1905 he was there with the *Erik* (Senn 1907) and the *Roosevelt,* returning in September 1906 (Peary 1907). In 1908 he was back in the *Roosevelt,* again accompanied by the *Erik,* reaching Cape York on 1 August on his way north and returning there at the close of his last visit to Avanersuaq on 17 August 1909, after his final sledge journey across the pack ice of the Arctic Ocean to what he believed to have been the North Pole (Peary 1910, Davies 1990).

It was between these two Peary North Pole expeditions that his former colleague of 1891–92, Dr. F. A. Cook (1911, Freeman 1961), arrived at Iita on his own account in the renamed fishing schooner *John R. Bradley,* owned by the wealthy American casino owner John R. Bradley. This was in August 1907. Cook resolved to winter at Anoritooq, north of Iita, and then try to reach the North Pole early in 1908. He persuaded the twenty-nine-year-old Rudolph Franke (1914), a German who had worked for North German Lloyd's Hamburg-American Line and volunteered to join Bradley on a hunting trip after reading his advertisement for a traveling companion in the *New York Herald,* to stay behind at Anoritooq with him. Cook started off from Anoritooq with Franke and a group of Inuhuit but sent Franke and some of the Eskimos back before continuing the lengthy journey, which he claimed took him to the North Pole on 21 April 1908. He spent most of the winter of 1908–9 with his two Inuhuit companions at Cape Sparbo on the north coast of Devon Island.

For once in its history, Iita was a busy place in mid-August 1908. Three ships called there: Peary's supply ship the *Erik,* his expedition ship the *Roosevelt,* and the Canadian Dominion Government Ship (DGS) *Arctic,* Captain J. E. Bernier (1910), which steamed into Foulke Fjord on 19 August 1908. He was following up the earlier Canadian visit to Avanersuaq of Commander A. P. Low (1906), who had gone ashore in Parker Snow Bay and visited Iita during the cruise of the DGS *Neptune* in 1904. With some difficulty Franke secured a passage home from Peary on the *Erik*, and the big game hunter Harry Payne Whitney (1910) was disembarked from that ship on 21 August 1908. At Iita and at neighboring Anoritooq Whitney spent the winter with some Inuhuit and two of Peary's people who had been left to look after that explorer's reserve depot of supplies, the boatswain John Murphy and the cabin boy Billy Pritchard. It was at Anoritooq that Whitney welcomed Cook back from his epic circuit round the northern part of the Canadian Arctic archipelago perhaps via the North Pole. While Cook then sledged south to Upernavik and continued home on a Danish steamer via Copenhagen, Whitney remained at Iita to welcome Peary back from his North Pole journey. He boarded the returning *Roosevelt* but transferred at North Star Bay on 23 August 1909 or soon afterward to the *Jeanie*, which had come north to fetch him.

After Whitney's departure, Iita was left in peace for a time. There were no more overwinterers there until 1913, and no ships called there in 1910–12 except the sealer *Beothic*. Chartered in 1910 by Whitney and a friend for a hunting trip to the Canadian Arctic, she put in briefly to North Star Bay. There, the newly installed manager of the Thule Trading Station, the Dane Peter Freuchen, was invited aboard. He calls the vessel the *Beautic,* was evidently impressed by the five young walruses, the young musk-ox, and the full-grown polar bear, all alive, that were being shipped to the United States, but complained that his conversation with Whitney was interrupted by the loud-mouthed captain, Bob Bartlett, who "told me to get the hell into my miserable boat because he was going to sail out of this God-damned hole" (Freuchen 1936: 31–32). An account of this expedition by one of the participants appeared in the *Cosmopolitan Magazine* for December 1910 under the title "Bagging Arctic Monsters with Rope, Gun, and Camera" (Freeman 1961: 215).

American and Canadian activities in Avanersuaq were continued intermittently for many years after Peary's 1908–9 North Pole Expedition by two of the participants, both of them sailors and owners of their own schooner. Donald B. MacMillan (1918a, 1930) led the Crocker Land Expedition to northwest Greenland in 1913–17. The aim of this expedition was to establish whether the land supposedly sighted by Peary north of Ellesmere Island really existed (it did not). The expedition was based at Iita, and some of its members wintered there for four successive years. MacMillan had decided not to be relieved when the first relief ship sent north by the American Museum of Natural History in New York, part sponsor of the expedition, the auxiliary schooner *George B. Cluett,* was forced to spend the winter of 1915–16 beset in the ice of Parker Snow Bay (*Annual Report* of the American Museum of Natural History, 1916). Eventually the Crocker Land Expedition, which gathered much valuable information about the natural history of Avanersuaq, was taken home by Captain Bartlett in the *Neptune* after a second relief ship, the *Danmark,* had been locked in the ice in North Star Bay throughout the winter of 1916–17. MacMillan (1927, and Allen 1962) was back near Iita again in 1923, when he wintered in Refuge Harbour in his specially constructed wooden schooner the *Bowdoin;* in August 1925, when he led a National Geographic Society expedition to attempt aviation in the Arctic (Rawson 1927); in about 1936; and again in 1947.

The other companion of Peary who continued to visit Avanersuaq after 1909 was the Newfoundlander Robert Bartlett (Putnam 1947, Horwood 1977), captain of Peary's ship the *Roosevelt* in 1905–6 and 1908–9, the *Beothic* in 1910, and the *Neptune* in 1917, all of which called in at Iita. In 1926 Bartlett took his own schooner, the *Effie M. Morrissey,* to northwest Greenland with an expedition organized by the American Museum and led by George Palmer Putnam (Putnam 1926, Raven 1927, Bartlett 1928: 320-8, and Streeter 1929). He was there again with the same ship in 1932 to erect a memorial to Peary at Cape York (Bartlett 1934: 251–80), and in 1935, 1940 (Beck 1946: 77), 1941 (Beck 1946: 118–19), and finally in 1945, always in the *Morrissey* and usually with a group of tourists, adventurers, or eccentrics, who paid their way to hunt walruses, film the natives, study magnetism, or whatever.

Much less well documented than the exploring voyages of the pioneers Ross, Kane, and Hayes and the more systematic expeditions under Peary and MacMillan (see especially Laursen 1972) were the voyages of English and Scots captains in search of whales (Lubbock 1937, Vaughan 1986).

When the whalers eventually arrived in northwest Greenland, two centuries had elapsed since William Baffin had expressed the hope in a letter to Sir John Wolstenholme in 1616 that "ships the next yeare would be sent for the killing of whales" (Markham 1881: 153). The whales he had seen and named Whale Sound for had gone; the whalers arrived there, like the other nineteenth-century voyagers to Avanersuaq, on their way elsewhere—in their case to make their way west through the North Water to the coasts and islands of the North American continent. There, they found whales enough.

Though the whalers had slowly extended their catching grounds north up the west coast of Greenland from the late seventeenth century on, no one followed Baffin through the dangerous fields of pack ice in Melville Bay, which for a long time formed a barrier and northern limit to the whalers' activities. Then, in 1817, the year before John Ross's expedition, a whaleship sailed north into Melville Bay and almost certainly reached the North Water. This ship was the *Larkins* of Leith in Scotland. Alexander Fisher describes how, on 16 June 1818 near Disko, Mr. Muirhead, her master, came aboard the discovery ship *Alexander* and informed him that he had "proceeded last year as far north in this country as 75° 30', and found the sea there quite clear of ice"

(1819: 24–25). The *Elizabeth* of Aberdeen followed the *Larkins* north in that same year (Markham 1875: 105, Nordenskiöld 1885: 306). According to Basil Lubbock (1937: 204), the two ships sailed north up the Greenland coast to 77° north and "crossed to the west side of Baffin Bay, where they came upon tremendous runs of fish." In 1819, at least six Hull whalers and one each from Aberdeen, Leith, and London gained the North Water and, early in August, the *Everthorpe, Thomas,* and *Ariel* of Hull all reached beyond 77° north latitude, getting as far north as Whale Sound though apparently keeping well offshore (Lubbock 1937: 211–12). In 1820 some of the whalers that reached the North Water, among them the *Friendship* and *Truelove* of Hull, which, according to Lubbock (p. 217), sailed north to 77° 40', crossed over to the "West Land," the Canadian coast, and were successful in killing whales there. There is independent confirmation of this. On 5 September 1820, when his ship was sailing south along the Baffin Island coast under the command of Lieutenant W. E. Parry, the same Alexander Fisher, now assistant surgeon on *HMS Hecla,* recorded in his journal (1821: 271) that they spoke the *Friendship* of Hull and were informed that the *Friendship* and *Truelove* of Hull "were, this summer, at the top of Baffin's Bay, and looked into Sir Thomas Smith's Sound . . . they informed us also, that some of the whaleships entered Lancaster's Sound this summer."

Thus in 1817–20, whalers from English and Scottish east coast ports developed a new whale fishery in Lancaster Sound and along the coast of Baffin Island. Exploitation of this fishery involved a counter-clockwise circuit of Baffin Bay, part of which consisted of sailing northward past Disko up the west coast of Greenland and struggling through the ice in Melville Bay. At some point on the northwest Greenland coast between Capes York and Atholl the whalers broke through into the North Water, altered course from northwest to southwest, and headed across to the Lancaster Sound whaling grounds (Vaughan 1986). Logbooks preserved in Hull (Local Studies Library, Town Docks Museum) and Cambridge (Scott Polar Research Institute) make it clear that the whalers usually tried to squeeze through Melville Bay along the narrow lead between the floating pack ice on the sea and the land-fast ice, always close inshore. The logbooks also support Albert Markham's assertion that between 1817 and 1849, "there were only four years in which attempts to reach the North Water were totally unsuccessful" (1875: 105). Thus from 1817–20 until at least the mid-nineteenth century large fleets of ships passed by annually within sight of Capes York and Dudley Digges and elsewhere in the south of Avanersuaq (see Vaughan 1987: 100). In 1827, fourteen whalers sailed north of the Cary Islands (Anon. 1852: 335–36).

In the 1850s the Hull whaling fleet began to decline and the number of whalers penetrating the North Water diminished. In 1851 eight whaleships that tried to get through to the North Water all gave up and returned south

(Snow 1851: 127–28). In 1852 about twelve ships tried for the North Water but only one, the *Alexander* of Dundee, was successful (Barron 1890: 36, 39). We know of three whalers off the Avanersuaq coast in 1858: two steam whalers seen by the Eskimos (Petersen 1860: 85–87) and the sailer *Emma* of Hull (Barron 1895).

In the second half of the nineteenth century a small fleet of steam whaleships from Scottish ports began to make regular voyages through the North Water and to linger in Avanersuaq waters or go ashore there. Captain W. F. Milne's logbooks of his voyages in the Dundee whaler *Esquimaux* in the 1880s (Wordie Collection of whaling logs, MS.1159, Scott Polar Research Institute, Cambridge, England) show that he made a habit of traveling via the Avanersuaq coast and often stopped there. On 29 June 1883 he passed close to Cape York in "loose floes." In 1885 he stopped at Conical Rock on 13 June, steamed past the Pituffik Glacier on 14 June, and stopped for two hours at Dalrymple Rock, no doubt to lay in a supply of fresh eider duck eggs. In 1886 he "hooked into the ice" at the Pituffik Glacier on 16 June and "hooked onto a floe" off Wolstenholme Island on 18 June. On 19–20 June, in company with the *Polynia,* another Dundee whaler, he stopped again near Dalrymple Rock and then sailed past Cape Parry and the mouth of Whale Sound before turning southwest for Lancaster Sound. In 1887 he was off the Avanersuaq coast from 19 June to 11 July in company with two other Dundee whalers, the *Terra Nova* and the *Nova Zembla*. In 1888 Captain Milne seems to have steamed past Conical Rock on 6 June and the Cary Islands on 7 June without stopping in Avanersuaq; but he certainly stopped there in 1894 (Savours 1960), 1903, 1905, and 1906, when he sailed in his own ship the *Eclipse.*

By the close of the nineteenth century the annual calls of the Scots whalers had become so regular that the Inuhuit had coined a special word for them— *upernallit,* meaning *those that come in the spring* (Freuchen 1936: 137), and it is hardly surprising that the whalers' help was sought in relief and rescue operations and collecting and delivering mail in Avanersuaq.

In 1892 Captain Jeffrey Phillips, who had taken the *Esquimaux* over from Milne, agreed at St. John's, Newfoundland, to convey a letter from Heilprin informing Robert Peary of the coming relief expedition. This letter was to be deposited in a small barrel at the western end of Wolstenholme Island so that, should Peary have made his way southward, he would find it. Captain Phillips performed his duties as postman on 13 June at about the time when the Inuhuaq Aleqatsiaq gave him a letter from Peary addressed from Red Cliff House to the Philadelphia Academy, which he subsequently posted in Dundee (Peary 1898a: 240–41). When the relief ship *Kite* was passing Wolstenholme Island at 5:30 A.M. on 23 July a pole was seen set up on shore. A landing party easily found the letter in a gaudily painted barrel with a covering note from Phillips. Both letter and barrel were left in place when the *Kite* continued on her way (Keely and Davis 1893: 235–36, 322–23). Another whaling captain who did duty as postman was Captain William Adams, Jr., of the *Morning* of Dundee, who left Peary's mail for him at Cape York on 17 June 1909. The three boxes containing it had been placed "on the extreme end of the cape, about fifty feet above sea-level," writes George Borup (1911: 314), who comments further: "The Eskimos had regarded the boxes as sacred and had not dreamed of molesting them, though for all they knew their contents might have been extremely valuable to them."

The Dundee whalers also took part in the efforts to rescue or trace the fate of a now almost forgotten Swedish expedition that had set out north from Godhavn (Qeqertarsuaq) on 3 August 1892 but never returned (Nordenskiöld 1894, Ohlin 1895a, Laursen 1965, 1972, Kallstenius 1967). The leader was Alfred Björling, a twenty-one-year-old Swedish botanist of adventurous disposition, who, at age seventeen, had been the first Swede to climb Sweden's highest mountain, Kebnekaise, in the far north of the country. He had already gained considerable Arctic experience as botanist on the Swedish expedition to Spitsbergen in 1890 (Thorén 1979: 187–206), as well as on his own, on a daring expedition north from Godhavn toward Melville Bay in a four-man Greenlandic rowing boat in summer 1891. His companion in 1892, when he planned to investigate the flora of Ellesmere Island, was a twenty-four-year-old zoologist from Uppsala, Evald G. Kallstenius. The two Swedes traveled to St. John's, bought a thirty-seven-ton local-built schooner, the *Ripple,* for $665, and hired for crew the twenty-one-year-old Dane Karl Kann as captain or sailing master, who had been at sea since he was fourteen, and two English-speaking hands, Gilbert Dunn and Herbert McDonald. This youthful group proved their worth as sailors and the seaworthiness of their craft by taking her from St. John's to Godhavn through some bad ice in less than a month. Though Björling hoped to return from his voyage north to Ellesmere Island that autumn, he bought furs and other equipment at Godhavn against a possible overwintering, planning in that eventuality to use the cache of provisions that had been left on the easternmost of the Cary Islands on 27 July 1875 by the British Arctic Expedition.

According to Nares, this depot consisted of 3,600 rations (1878a: 45). In 1882, when it was examined by Private William M. Beebe of the first of the Greely relief expeditions, it contained "one barrel of canned beef, two tins (40 lbs each) of bacon, one barrel (110 lbs) dog biscuit, two barrels (120 rations each) biscuit, all in good condition; 240 rations, consisting of chocolate and sugar, tea and sugar, potatoes, wicks, tobacco, salt, stearine, onion powder, and matches, in fairly good condition" (Schley and Soley 1889: 43). Lieutenant E. A. Garlington checked it in the following year and reported that there were 1,800 rations, 60 percent of which he pronounced sound, and it was still good in 1884, when the last of the Greely relief expeditions inspected it (pp. 67, 210). Whatever was left would surely still in 1892 have served to keep the five members of the Björling expedition alive through the winter.

In the summer of 1893 Captain McKay of the Dundee whaleship *Aurora,* acting on an appeal for help from the Danish foreign office, landed a party on the most easterly of the Cary Islands after his lookout had sighted a wreck there. It was the *Ripple,* almost buried under the winter's snow and ice and beached not far from Captain Nares's cairn. Near it a man's body was buried under a heap of stones. McKay gathered up all the clothes, books, and other relics he could find, including several letters from Björling, and sent them to Professor Gustaf Nordenskiöld, son of A. E. Nordenskiöld of Northeast Passage fame, who had been Björling's leader on Spitsbergen in 1890. The letters showed that Björling and his companions were loading supplies from the English cache into the *Ripple* on or soon after 16 August 1892 when the boat was wrecked. After an abortive attempt to voyage north in a small boat to Foulke Fjord, they had returned to the Cary Islands and then set out on 12 October for uninhabited Ellesmere Island instead of making for the mainland of Avanersuaq, which was much nearer and where the Inuhuit would surely have helped them through the winter. Björling seems to have been determined to carry out his botanical research on Ellesmere Island; he may have considered any move back towards inhabited Greenland too much like withdrawal and defeat.

The rest of the history of the Björling expedition will almost certainly never be written. The Scottish whalers were called into service in summer 1894, when the *Eclipse* of Dundee landed the Swede Elias Nilsson to make a further search of the wrecked *Ripple.* Unfortunately, threatening weather made Captain Milne's situation dangerous and he was forced to leave in a hurry before Nilsson had had time to do more than pick up a few more relics. A more thorough examination of what is now called Björling's Island was made on 16 December 1916 by Peter Freuchen and Lauge Koch. It is hardly surprising that by that date little new information was obtained. They did ascertain that the man who died and was buried there was not Kallstenius, who did not smoke, for the skeleton was that of a pipe-smoker who held his pipe in the left side of his mouth. Among the relics, they found twelve empty boiled beef tins, nine empty and corkless champagne bottles, the remains of a pair of pants, a white handkerchief marked "E.K.," and some pages of the book about that other disastrous Arctic expedition a decade before Björling's venture—*Three Years of Arctic Service* by A. W. Greely.

Besides assisting in the Björling search and supporting Peary, the Scots whalers played a supporting role in the two expeditions that were in Avanersuaq in 1903. The Dundee whaleship owners had been asked to establish a depot of supplies on Dalrymple Rock which could be picked up by the Norwegian explorer Roald Amundsen on his way to penetrate the Northwest Passage in the *Gjøa*. Captains Milne and William Adams, Jr., of the *Eclipse* and *Diana* respectively, carried out this task on 27 June 1903 and the stores were duly collected by Amundsen on the following 15 August, together with a letter from the two captains wishing him and his companions bon voyage (Amundsen 1907: 27–29).

The Danes, as well as the Norwegians, had been in contact with the Dundee shippers in 1902–3, requesting them to ask their captains to look out for the Literary Expedition while they were off the northwest Greenland coast in summer 1903 and render it any necessary assistance. It so happened that on 27 June 1903 the Literary Expedition *was* in need of help: one of its members, artist Harald Moltke, was lying seriously ill in a tent at the expedition's camp on Saunders Island. His two companions, Knud Rasmussen and Ludvig Mylius-Erichsen, along with some Eskimos, paddled out toward the Scottish ships in kayaks. They saw a boat lowered from one of them and rowed toward the Eider Duck Islands (Edderfugleøer), where they soon found a party of Scottish sailors looking for eider duck eggs. The sailors took them on board the *Eclipse*. "Up on the bridge of the *Eclipse*," wrote Mylius-Erichsen, "stood a rustic-looking figure with a brown hat pulled down over his head and hands in his pockets." It was Captain Milne, well liked on the West Greenland coast for his affability but now giving the two unkempt Danes, who were dressed in furs, a distinctly cool, if not downright frosty, reception. They soon discovered why. At Godhavn earlier that summer a newly appointed, somewhat earnest Danish official, Jens Daugaard-Jensen, subsequently famous as the head of the Greenland administration from 1912 to 1938 (Sørensen 1983), had refused to allow the Scots captains to remain in the roads there on the grounds that the real purpose of their stay was not to refill the ships' freshwater tanks but to trade with the local inhabitants. This objection seemed unreasonable because the Scots whalers regularly brought the Danish inhabitants of West Greenland their first post of the year. But as soon as Mylius-Erichsen diplomatically concurred with Milne that Daugaard-Jensen was "a stuck-up fellow with too much gold braid and too little brains," the Scots captain relented and entertained the two Danes and their Eskimo companion Majaq in his cabin, where Captain William Adams, Jr., of the *Diana* soon joined them. Rasmussen acted as Danish-Greenlandic interpreter, and Mylius served for Danish-English. The Scots could do absolutely nothing for the sick Moltke: they had had serious difficulties getting through the Melville Bay pack ice; they had two very sick men on board already and no doctor; they had no facilities for passengers; and they could not, even for £10 000, return to Upernavik. In no event would they be returning via West Greenland, and they might have to winter on the Canadian coast. The best they could do for the beleaguered Danes was

to give them a sack of biscuits and some sugar, tea, coffee, medicine, and potatoes. They also gave them a supply of timber with which they might be able to
construct a boat for their return journey across Melville Bay in August, by
which time it should be free of ice. Captain Adams found time to visit Moltke
in his sick bay, where the Inuhuit, many of whom knew the captain, crowded
round. Then the two ships proceeded on their way (Mylius-Erichsen and
Moltke 1906: 388–97, Andreassen 1984: 106–8).

There is a postscript to this story. Fortunately, Moltke's health slowly improved. The two other Dundee ships whose arrival shortly had been announced by Adams and Milne never appeared. The *Balaena* had been beset in
Melville Bay, and the *Vega,* which had borne A. E. Nordenskiöld and his expedition safely through the Northeast Passage in 1878–79 before being refit-
ted as a whaler, had been crushed by the ice and lost there. The Danes began
to wonder how they could survive the approaching winter. The depot left on
Dalrymple Rock for the Norwegians sorely tempted Mylius-Erichsen, who, as
his account of the expedition shows, was constantly preoccupied with food.
On 13 August he went out to Dalrymple Rock, purportedly to inspect the
cache. Three of the hundred or so cases of provisions had been broken into,
perhaps by Eskimos, and a drum of paraffin was leaking. Surely it was now
too late in the season for a ship to arrive? Mylius-Erichsen could not resist the
temptation to fill one of his jerry cans with paraffin and to remove a few tins
of meat and jam from one of the opened cases. But before the Danes could
purloin any more provisions to form the "small" winter "reserve" store they
now planned to make, the *Gjøa* was sighted. In the nick of time, Amundsen
was able to collect his provisions, less some forty tins of meat, which he gave
to Mylius and his companions (Mylius-Erichsen and Moltke 1906: 443–46;
Andreassen 1984: 123–28; see Fig. 7).

Ten years after these events took place in the approaches to Wolstenholme
Fjord the history of the Dundee whale fishery drew to a close: the last whaler
to visit Avanersuaq seems to have been the *Morning* of Dundee, commanded
by the same William Adams, in the year 1913 (Schultz-Lorenzen 1913;
Gilberg 1977a).

4

Eskimos and Whites
An Uneasy Partnership

*J*ust as the land was there for the taking, in the eyes of explorers and em-
pire builders, so were the people who inhabited it there to be used. The
Inuhuit were put to work by the exploring expeditions for minimal remun-
eration or no payment at all in almost every conceivable way. Mostly, the
men became guides, porters, hunters, and unskilled laborers for the white
men, while the women became their maidservants, seamstresses, and concubines. The explorers who made use of the Inuhuit most successfully were able
to bring them under their leadership or control and to exercise a profound influence over them, although the Inuhuit recognized no authority among themselves. To judge from their own writings, these white people claimed for
themselves a possessory right over their Eskimo auxiliaries and appear to have
thought of the Inuhuit as a whole as in some sense theirs. Hayes, Peary, and
Freuchen all used the phrase "my Eskimos."

The value, indeed necessity, of Eskimo assistance was never in doubt among
explorers. Kane (1856a: 18) had counted from the start on "the co-operation
of the Esquimaux." In 1873 Emil Bessels told A. H. Markham that "no expedition should go north without some Esquimaux for hunting and dog driving"
(Markham 1875: 199–200). MacMillan (1934: 96) writes of the Inuhuit who
assisted Peary on his North Pole expeditions: "Without their help the North
Pole would never have been attained by dog team." Cook (1911: ix) was
equally generous, acknowledging his debt to the Eskimos on his 1908 "Polar
dash" with his usual verbal flourishes: "The band of little people of the Farthest North furnished without pay the vital force and the primitive ingenuity
without which the quest of the Pole would be a hopeless task. These boreal
pigmies with golden skins, with muscles of steel, and hearts as finely human as
those of the highest order of man, performed a task that cannot be too highly
commended."

Cook's demands for labor from the Inuhuit were modest in the extreme
compared to Peary's. At Cape Hecla, at the northern tip of Ellesmere Island,

early in 1906, twenty-one Inuhuit hunters assembled with Peary's North Pole expedition, which was organized in six or seven sledge parties, each with at least one person who had accompanied him from the United States and at least two Eskimos (Peary 1907: 97). In 1908–9 the expedition consisted of twenty-two Eskimo men besides the seven original expedition members (Peary 1910: 77), providing manpower for five supporting parties, each of which would haul rations to sustain the party that reached the farthest north, consisting of Peary himself, Matthew Henson, and four Eskimos, for five days, and then return to base. With the hunters traveled their families. In 1905–6 Peary took "over half a hundred" Eskimos with him (1907: 33); in 1908–9 the number was forty-nine—twenty-two men, seventeen women, and ten children (1910; 76–77; Horwood 1977 makes it seventy-six by counting the women and children twice). In September 1906 Ross G. Marvin made as complete a census as possible of the Inuhuit population and found it to be 253: 140 males and 113 females (Peary 1907: 393). Thus, on each of his last two expeditions Peary took about one-fifth of that population with him.

All the Eskimos who accompanied Peary received full board and lodging for the duration of the expedition, and he also made sure that a supply of walrus meat was secured for the coming winter before he set course for home. Thus Henson (1912: 170–73) describes how, in August 1909 at the end of the last expedition, sixty-one walrus carcasses were delivered by the *Roosevelt* to the Inuhuit at Qaanaaq, and John W. Goodsell (1983: 153, 157) gives a grand total of seventy-two carcasses. Peary further states that "once enrolled as members of my expedition" the Eskimos knew that "at the end of the journey, when we brought them back to their homes, I would turn over to them the remaining supplies and equipment of the expedition," and he claimed that this "would ensure [their] living for another year in absolute plenty, that, in comparison with the other members of their tribe they would indeed be multimillionaires." They also "well understood that each was to receive for the services of himself and wife and dogs, for one year, a new .44 Winchester rifle" (MacMillan 1934: 61). Undoubtedly, Peary's transport and other requirements enormously affected the Inuhuit ecomony, but perhaps not in the negative way sometimes implied (Gilberg 1984a).

Peary was the first explorer to make systematic use of Inuhuit dogsled transport to penetrate from Avanersuaq either westward into Ellesmere Island and beyond or farther north in Greenland. His successors, the Danes, followed his example. Their famed Thule expeditions would have been inconceivable without the Inuhuit and their dogs. The First Thule Expedition set out from Neqi on 14 April 1912 with some 35 sledges and 350 dogs and ascended onto the Inland Ice via the Clements Markham Glacier. Most of the Inuhuit returned on 19 April after fulfilling their task of ensuring sufficient food for the exploring party's dogs at the start of the journey. Rasmussen, Freuchen, Ulloriaq, and Inukitsoq, with heavily laden sledges pulled by exceptionally large teams of twelve or fifteen dogs, then continued over the Inland Ice with Freuchen navigating (Rasmussen 1915, 1957, Freuchen 1959). The Inuhuit were soon serving as expert professional guides for exploring expeditions. At the age of twenty Ittukusuk had been one of Cook's two Inuhuit companions on his trek round the eastern Canadian Arctic islands in 1908–9. He was back there in 1914 and 1916 with the Crocker Land Expedition—"faithful E-took-a-shoo, our best man," writes MacMillan (1918a: 128). The Crocker Land Expedition also used the Inuhuit transport system to maintain winter communications between members: it was with Ittukusuk that MacMillan (1918: 138, 257), in the bright winter moonlight of January 1915, sledged 100 miles (160 km) over smooth sea ice at a single stretch, in eighteen hours, from Cape York to Uummannaq.

Next only in importance to the role of Inuhuit men and dogs in expedition transport was the service of their women as seamstresses. Again, it was Peary who pointed the way. Describing the preparations for his first Arctic overwintering at Red Cliff House on the eve of his expedition across the Inland Ice to northeast Greenland, he wrote (1898a: 159–60):

> I regarded the deerskins we had secured as of the highest value. Before I left home I had said that nothing but the impervious integument of animal skin would keep out the searching wind of the Inland Ice, and every day spent here only strengthened me in my belief, and made me prize more highly the exquisitely soft, light, velvety autumn pelts of the reindeer, the best of all furs for clothing and sleeping-bags.
>
> It was a part of my plan to obtain this material from the Whale-Sound region, and my hopes were fully realised. My men shot all the deer we needed, the skins were stretched and dried at Red Cliff, I devised and cut the patterns for the suits and sleeping-bags, and the native women sewed them.
>
> The work of preparing the skins for clothing involved a great deal of chewing on the part of my native seamstresses.
>
> The skin is folded once with the hair inside and then the operator chews back and forth along the edge until the fold is thoroughly soft and pliable, when another fold is made and the process repeated until the whole skin has been carefully chewed; after this it is scraped and worked with a blunt instrument and then, if necessary, chewed again. It took two of my workers about a day to chew a big buckskin.

A photograph in Peary's *Northward over the "Great Ice"* (1898b: 359) shows that, during the overwintering of 1894–95, he employed Eskimo women on other domestic tasks besides sewing fur garments. The illustration shows a topless young woman bending over a washing tub. It is captioned "An Arctic laundress."

Peary was not the only person sailing on the *Kite* in 1891 to exploit the sartorial skill of the Inuhuit women. When the ship halted at Cape York on its way south, the expedition's surgeon, Robert N. Keely, Jr., badly in want of a new pair of trousers, called at a tent in which an Eskimo woman was "diligently employed in cutting and sewing skins" and persuaded her, in return for a knife and some needles, to make him a pair of sealskin breeches. These were only half finished when he had to return on board the *Kite*, but the work was completed by other Inuhuit women who had boarded the ship. Even so, Dr. Keely was dissatisfied: his new breeches were not pliable but as stiff and ungainly as stovepipes. Fortunately, there was time when the *Kite* stopped at Godhavn in West Greenland for the breeches to be taken ashore and given a thorough chewing by an Eskimo woman, which was all they needed to make them supple. She added a couple of buttons for good measure (Keely and Davis 1893: 153–54, 207–8).

With his usual hyperbole, Cook (1911: xii, 85–86) describes how "an entire tribe" was "breathlessly and feverishly at work" in the autumn of 1907 preparing fur clothing for his proposed "dash" for the Pole. Each man must have two complete suits of furs: foxes were required for coats, seals for boots, hares for stockings, and caribou for sleeping bags. More prosaic is Rasmussen's incidental mention in the diary of his spring 1903 sledge journey from Saunders Island to Melville Bay and back: "Mayark's wife is making me a pair of bearskin breeches" (Mylius-Erichsen and Moltke 1906: 259).

Inuhuit labor was exploited in many other ways. As unskilled workers their services could often be obtained gratis. In July 1909, when a Danish mission society put up two wooden houses on the shore of North Star Bay, the inhabitants of neighboring Uummannaq were reportedly astonished and delighted. "Every morning, when the ship's whistle sounded, the men" walked over the shingle ridge from Uummannaq to help erect the new mission station (Steensby 1909). As postmen, the Inuhuit apparently discharged their duties conscientiously and reliably. On 13 August 1851 an Eskimo came over the ice from Cape York carrying a letter carefully "wrapped in a fold of seal-skin." It was delivered to Captain Ommanney of HMS *Assistance,* who quickly ascertained that it had been posted at Cape York the day before by Captain William Penny, who reported that he had gleaned no intelligence either of Sir John Franklin or of the *North Star.* According to W. Parker Snow (1851: 193–94), the deliverer of this letter was called "Cheepchow." "He evidently seemed conscious of the important position he there held, as Her Majesty's Arctic postman."

One can scarcely pretend that the explorers made use of the Inuhuit medical services. Indeed, it was usually the other way round. For example, in 1850 the surgeon of HMS *North Star,* Dr. James Rae, made a wooden leg for "Ootinah," whose leg had been crushed by a boulder, and looked after "Aniutark," who had suffered severe frostbite (Hayes 1867: 229, Simmonds 1852: 291, 293, Mylius-Erichsen and Moltke 1906: 377). But on at least one occasion a sick white man underwent medical treatment at the hands of an Eskimo. The 1903 Literary Expedition's artist, Harald Moltke, fell seriously ill soon after their arrival in Avanersuaq (Mylius-Erichsen and Moltke 1906: 201, 226–27). Satdloq, the Inuhuit's most powerful *angakkoq,* offered to go down into the sea on Moltke's behalf to obtain advice on the curing of his sickness from the spirits there. This proposal was turned down, but a few days later, on 25 April 1903, Mylius permitted Kale and Soqqaq to hold a seance over the unconscious Moltke. The procedure lasted a couple of hours, during much of which time Soqqaq performed a drum song. Holding the drum in one hand and the drumstick in the other, he sang in a monotone while raising and lowering himself on his knees and swaying to left and right in time to the drum and grimacing with half-closed eyes. At the close he gave ten prescriptions that had to be meticulously carried out if Moltke was to get better:

1. The patient may eat plenty of seal and walrus meat but only of male animals.
2. He may not cut meat with a knife but may use his teeth to remove it from the bones.
3. Visiting women may not sit on the bunk but only at the side.
4. He may eat caribou meat between eating the meat already mentioned.
5. He must not inhale smoke, so the lamps must be properly looked after.
6. He must never cook his own food.
7. He must not have sexual intercourse.
8. He must be grateful in every way to the angakkoq.
9. He must give the angakkoq a large dog.
10. He must give him a good gun.

Mylius-Erichsen was cynical about this advice. The last three instructions were transparent, and the others could be carried out with ease. Only male walruses were available around Saunders Island where they were camped; there was no room for anyone to sit on Moltke's bunk; and Moltke was in no fit state either to cook for himself or to have sexual intercourse. Mylius suspected that the caution against smoke might be a hint that they should employ Soqqaq's wife Arnaaluk to trim the lamps—for payment of course.

It is not easy to ascertain the extent to which the sexual services of Inuhuit women were exploited by white visitors to Avanersuaq. They may have become accustomed to promiscuity through the Inuhuit custom of wife exchange. Although it has often been maintained that the whalers made use of Inuhuit women visitors on their ships as prostitutes, evidence is hard to come by. What self-respecting whaleship captain would allow mention of such a practice in his logbook? In 1894 a seaman called Redgrave, crew member of the Dundee whaler *Eclipse,* kept a private journal (Savours 1960) which indicates that Inuhuit women at Cape York did not usually offer themselves on board as prostitutes, even if other Eskimo women did. He gives a detailed and vivid description of the Eskimos, both men and women, who swarmed over the ship at Cape York; of their clothes, their special instrument for delousing themselves, and their lack of cleanliness, but without the least hint of prostitution. Yet when the *Eclipse* reached Cumberland Sound in southern Baffin Island he was quick to notice, and deplore, this practice: "We were at once boarded by a cargo of Female Yaks called koonies and for the whole time every man had his Squaw. It was positively sikening. If people call that whaling the sooner it is stopped the better" (p. 136, Redgrave's spelling).

The investigations of the French explorer Jean Malaurie also speak strongly against prostitution on board Scottish whaleships. He discusses sexual behavior among the Inuhuit in some detail but makes no mention of prostitution. He reports (1982: 434) what the sixty-year-old Ivalo told him in 1950 about her visits to Scottish whaleships. Once she went out to two ships near Saunders Island in spite of her parents' prohibition. "Another time, she climbed aboard a whaling ship and traded little auks, a bearskin, leather straps and sealskins for a rifle, a knife, tobacco, and matches. It made her happy for a whole year." There is no hint here that Ivalo was indulging in anything other than bartering.

All of the very few references to prostitution or promiscuity by Inuhuit women on board Scottish whaleships that have come to my notice have been reiterations by Danes of statements made to them by Eskimos. It is noteworthy that the members of the Literary Expedition, some of whom boarded the *Eclipse* off Saunders Island in the summer of 1903, and who were in contact with both the *Eclipse* and the *Diana* of Dundee and their captains, make no mention whatever of any sexual contacts between Inuhuit women and Scottish sailors on that occasion; again, barter was the main topic of business. When two Scottish sailors found Oodaaq's wife alone in her tent, what did they do? They removed three fox tails without offering anything in exchange (Mylius-Erichsen and Moltke 1906: 398). In place of actual observation or hard fact, all we have in the journals of the expedition's members is a report of some gossip from the elderly Arnaaluk referring to the past. She complained about the Scottish sailors' "shameless treatment of Eskimo women," which, whatever it was, Mylius judged "unsuitable for elaboration in a book" (p. 214). This same Arnaaluk also told the Danes that "in my younger days . . . my husband on one occasion made me become a Scottish sailor's woman."

Explorers have usually been somewhat reticent about their relationships with native women—except those who were tempted but resisted. Malaurie (1982: 224–25) describes in a rather self-righteous tone how he rejected the advances of the attractive Aamma. Rudolph Franke performed what he evidently hopes the reader will accept as remarkable feats of sexual abnegation when staying at Anoritooq and sledging in Smith Sound with some Inuhuit in spring 1908. Torngi borrowed his rifle and asked him if, in return, he would like to borrow his wife for a few days. He declined (Franke 1914: 119), as he did when Tornginnguaq, left alone by her husband Qulutannguaq, asked if she could move in with him (p. 101). Finally, in March, when he was the only male at Anoritooq because all the Eskimo men were away hunting, he was visited by nine Eskimo women, all of whom, he would have us believe, wanted his body. His original diary entry in imperfect English is not, however, completely intelligible: "Presently here 9 women and only one man, this speaks for itself. To keep women away is harder then two work hard." In a similar situation, which he describes as "somewhat embarrassing," on 10 November 1894, Peary (1898b: 394, 404) was "left alone and unprotected, with five buxom and oleaginous ladies, of a race of naive children of nature, who are hampered by no feelings of false modesty or bashfulness in expressing their tender feelings." One of them later became his mistress (Rawlins 1973: 200–210). Other explorers with "Arctic concubines," as Cook called them with reference to Peary (Hunt 1981: 147), were Peary's black assistant Matthew Henson, descendants of whose son Anaakkaq still live in Avanersuaq (Ulloriaq 1984, Gilberg 1948: 60–61, Counter 1988), and Donald MacMillan, if one believes Harrison J. Hunt (Hunt and Thompson 1980: 21). According to Hunt, who claimed not to be attracted to Eskimo women—"they smell something awful"—not all members of the Crocker Land Expedition felt about them as he did. One of them told him that "when he had asked to sleep with one woman, she said, 'No, it is taught us that two men are enough for one woman and I have my husband and Mr. Mac.'"

Individual relationships between white men and Eskimos, in Avanersuaq as elsewhere, could occasionally become close, approaching real friendship, especially on hunting trips or in bed. But what was the nature of the relationship in general? In his report to the secretary of the navy of 11 October 1855 Kane wrote: "With these Esquimaux—a race of the highest interest—we formed a valuable alliance, sharing our resources, and mutually depending upon each other. They were never thoroughly to be trusted; but by a mixed course of intimidation and kindness, became an essential service" (Villarejo 1965: 192). This distrust and use of intimidation, accompanied by violence and suspicion, dogged the relationships of explorers and Inuhuit throughout the nineteenth century and into the twentieth. In this respect Kane and his associate and successor Hayes inaugurated a most unhappy tradition of the use of force which John Ross in 1818 had done his best to avoid. There is a strong contrast between the pacific behavior toward the Inuhuit of Ross (1819: 135), who "gave strict and positive orders that no fire-arms, or other warlike weapons, should be shewn them, or given to them on any account, and when they were with us all shooting-parties were called in," and the attitude of Kane, who allowed James McGary to fire a charge of small shot at some Eskimos who had purloined a barrel of coal (Kane 1856a: 211). Kane then imprisoned in the hold a lad called Miuk, who had voluntarily and on his own visited the *Advance,* and even threatened to shoot him (Hendrik 1878: 25–26, Lidegaard 1985: 22–23) unless he told him who had cut Kane's rubber boat to pieces. Besides violence or the threat of it, both Kane and Hayes made use of trickery in the course of intimidating the Eskimos. Kane (1856b: 251) used "some simple exploits of natural magic" such as burning Qisuk's hand with a lens made of ice, and Hayes (1867: 261) used "some simple sleight-of-hand tricks" to the same end. This deliberate employment of force and trickery by the white men to manipulate the Inuhuit became more dangerous and damaging because they convinced themselves that the Eskimos would use force and trickery against them. Perhaps the Eskimos would have done so, but there is little evidence to support such a belief. In this context, the alleged Eskimo plot against the lives of the members of the withdrawal party from Kane's expedition led by Dr. Hayes (1860) is relevant.

Before the start of Kane's second winter in the far north, Hayes and eight others insisted on being given the opportunity to make their way south to the Danish settlements in West Greenland. Leaving the brig *Advance* on 26 August 1854, they struggled southward in two boats as far as a low-lying but rocky stretch of coast south of Cape Parry, near Booth Sound. There, at the beginning of October, impenetrable ice on the sea halted their boat journey, and they built a hut with stones found with difficulty under deep snow, using a natural cleft in the rocks for two of the walls and the oars, masts, and sails of the now useless boats for a roof. Hayes called this refuge Fort Desolation, but his companion, the seaman William Godfrey (1857), more optimistically called it the Wanderers' Home and referred to its "pleasant location" (Fig. 8).

Eskimos visited this hut several times on their journeys between settlements north and south of it, Natsilivik and Saunders Island respectively, nearly always bringing supplies of raw meat and blubber that very probably saved the Americans' lives. The German "astronomer" in the party, August Sonntag, noted these valuable deliveries of meat in his journal (Villarejo 1965). For example, on 21 October four Eskimos arrived with a shoulder of bear, walrus meat and skin, some blubber, and eight thick-billed murres (Brünnich's guillemots). Godfrey traveled on to Natsilivik with these Eskimos and returned a week later with 11 pounds (5 kg) of walrus meat, 9 pounds (4 kg) of walrus fat, and two weeks' supply of old blubber to fuel the lamp he had bought from the

Eskimos. More deliveries of fresh meat and blubber arrived in early November, when the decision was made to send two members of the party, Godfrey and the Dane Carl Petersen, to Natsilivik to seek assistance in a proposed sledge journey back to the *Advance* to obtain more supplies for the winter. Petersen and Godfrey found Natsilivik deserted of able-bodied men; they were all away on a hunting expedition, and the Eskimos were "almost as badly provided with food as we ourselves were." They returned at once to the Wanderers' Home. According to Godfrey (p. 164), "the benevolent savages took pity on our wretched condition, and spared us a little food from their scanty stores. . . . We carried a small stock of walrus-meat we had obtained from the Esquimaux, strapped on our backs."

According to Hayes (pp. 224–35), who says nothing about the meat, on his return Petersen related over a cup of coffee that "they had walked all the way from Netlik, where an attempt had been made to murder them. The Esquimaux were in pursuit, and if not watched would attack our hut." "A watch was accordingly set and kept up during the night," continues Hayes, who gives a vivid description of that night of suspense, during the middle hours of which "noises were distinctly heard in the direction of FitzClarence Rock" in Booth Sound. "It was evident that we were closely watched. The savages were hovering around us . . . awaiting their opportunity." Hayes then gives a detailed account, which he got from Petersen, of how at Natsilivik Petersen thought he overheard the Eskimos plotting to murder him and all his companions and of how he thought the Eskimos were pursuing him and Godfrey on their return trip.

Petersen's reminiscences say nothing of all this, for at this point he replaces his own recollections with a translation of the diary of his German companion August Sonntag, and Sonntag simply writes that on 7 November they prepared to resist an Eskimo attack without explaining why. He adds later that on 12 November, "an Esquimau from Northumberland Island brought us a splendid piece of walrus meat with kidneys and liver, besides about fifty rotges [dovekies or little auks], some fresh seal blubber," and a quantity of old blubber. According to Hayes, they gathered from this "Kingiktok" that a certain "Sipsu" was plotting to kill them, though one of the Eskimos who had already befriended them, Qulutana, was loath to join him in this venture. In his diary, as transcribed by Petersen, Sonntag again gives no details and reports the situation much more coolly than Hayes. He says only: "It seemed to Petersen, judging from single words and questions, in the manner of reception of Petersen and William [Godfrey] lately at Netlik, and from some remarks of the Esquimau Kingiktok from Northumberland Island that there might be some suspicion of a hostile disposition against us among the Esquimaux" (Villarejo 1965: 134, 136, 139–40).

At the end of November Hayes was still fully persuaded that the Eskimos, even including the apparently friendly Qulutana, were planning to abandon him and his companions to a certain death from cold and starvation; he interpreted their repeated refusal to take them back to the *Advance* as evidence of this intention. But the true reason why Qulutana and others refused to take the withdrawal party back to the brig in Rensselaer Bay is revealed by Godfrey (1857: 171–72): they were afraid of Kane. They had pilfered various small articles while visiting the brig, including some of Kane's knives, spoons, and forks, and would not risk his ire by returning there. Kane was, after all, already known to them as a man of violence, who, in the previous winter, had had no scruples in using guns against them in threat and in reality and had detained one of their number against his will.

The shabby trick now played on Qulutana and his two companions by Hayes and his party, when the three Eskimos were staying with them one night in the Wanderers' Home, was certainly not justified by Hayes's absurd fears that the Inuhuit "had made up their minds, with a unanimity which at an earlier period seemed improbable, to abandon us to our fate and to profit by it" (1860: 288). After drugging them with what Hayes (p. 290) described as "a small vial of laudanum" and Godfrey (1857: 172), who claimed credit for the idea, referred to as an opiate fortuitously labeled "Godfrey's Cordial," they removed the Eskimos' clothes and absconded with their dogs and sledges. Qulutana and his friends easily caught up with the Americans but were taken prisoner at gunpoint and compelled to accompany Hayes and his companions first to Natsilivik and then back to the *Advance* in a gratuitous display of coercion.

Through the 1850s and 1860s the high-handed attitude of Kane and the irrational fears of Hayes, exhibited in such episodes as these, were passed on to the American public through the published narratives of their Arctic adventures. In his account of his 1860–61 expedition, Hayes (1867: 230–34) suggests that August Sonntag may have been murdered by his West Greenlandic colleague Hans Hendrik (Suersaq) when they were sledging together in December 1860, an idea to which subsequent inquiry has lent no support whatever (MacMillan 1918a: 124, Shackleton 1937: 137). The explorers' suspicion of the Eskimos' intentions and readiness to use force or threats of force against them were evidently reinforced if not caused by their attribution of their own modes of thought and practices to the Eskimos. The tradition thus established appears again and again in the history of Avanersuaq and indeed of the rest of the Arctic.

The inclination to use force against the Eskimos so evident in Kane's and Hayes's behavior toward them was shared by Emil Bessels, the German scientist in Charles F. Hall's 1871–73 North Polar Expedition. In the spring of 1873, while sledging northward over difficult sea ice from Polaris House, near Iita, he repeatedly had problems with his two Inuhuit companions, who were unwilling to struggle with their sledges and dog teams across areas of hummocky ice that confronted the party. In spite of bribes and promises, such as the gift of a knife, an ax, or a gun, or the promise of the entire contents of the depot of supplies left in the observatory at Polaris Bay far to the north of them, if they could get there, Bessels's guides were adamant. They wished to travel south, not north into the unknown. Bessels had to agree to return to Polaris House but insisted that the trip be made in forced marches. When Arrutaq wanted to make camp instead of pressing on, Bessels aimed a loaded rifle at him and threatened to shoot him if he did not obey. Fortunately, Bessels's tendency toward violence or threats did not end in tragedy. Understandably, the expedition's Inuhuit assistants refused to accompany him on any further sledge trips (Bessels 1879: 378–92, Davis 1876: 478–82).

The same suspicion or misapprehension of the Eskimos' intentions that had been so melodramatically felt by Hayes and some of his contemporaries was shared by Americans of the Peary epoch a generation later. On one occasion disaster might have intervened had it not been for the fortunate presence in the summer of 1892 at Red Cliff House, while Dr. Cook and Matt Henson were awaiting the return of Peary and Astrup from their exploration of the Inland Ice, of a cool-headed, sensible woman, the explorer's wife, Josephine Peary (1893: 165–66; see too Gilberg 1990). The entry for 11 July 1892 in her diary begins:

> When I awoke this morning I heard Matt and the doctor talking very earnestly, but could not hear what they were saying; from their tone I judged it was something serious. Finally I called to the doctor and asked him what the trouble was. He told me that Matt had overheard Kyo and Kulutingwah planning to make away with one of us. I could not help laughing at this recital, which provoked the doctor a little; we had laughed at similar stories related by Arctic explorers, and had agreed that these natives were not at all inclined to be warlike or vindictive. I tried to reason with the boys. In the first place, if the natives had any such design, would they not have kept the three men here who left for Karnah [Qaanaaq] yesterday? Secondly, would they be likely to come over to our house and discuss their plans? And thirdly, do any of us know enough of their language to understand a conversation in which the participants are not even to be seen? The whole thing seemed very amusing to me, but both boys were evidently frightened, and wanted to be armed and ready for any emergency; consequently I gave the doctor Mr. Peary's pistol to carry and Matt my large one, and they have worn them all day.

She remained persuaded that "Kyo" and his friends had entertained no such evil intentions and commented further: "I am sorry for this episode, which has brought about an unpleasantness with the natives" (p. 169).

Cook and Henson were not the only Americans at that time to be easily scared by the supposed murderous intentions of the Inuhuit. When the relief ship *Kite* approached McCormick Fjord toward the end of July 1892 to take

Peary's expedition back to America, a small boat with several persons in it became visible in the distance. The lookout in the crow's nest suddenly "sent a spasm of terror into the breasts of the party by shouting in an excited tone: 'By God, sir, they're all huskies in that whale boat! They've killed the Peary party,' but he almost instantly set all right by crying joyfully, 'No they're not, sir; they're waving their arms; they're all right!'" (Keely and Davis 1893: 327).

It was not only Americans who were seized with occasional panic because of fear of the Eskimos. The same thing happened to the Danes on the Literary Expedition of 1903 (Mylius-Erichsen and Moltke 1906: 485–86) at the close of September, when Mylius-Erichsen, Moltke, and Jørgen Brønlund were living on Saunders Island. Fed up with the petty pilfering by Majaq and members of his family of raisins, matches, and other things, Mylius remonstrated forcefully with the Eskimo, who replied tauntingly. Mylius thereupon banned Majaq from further visits to their hut. That night and those following, fearful that Majaq might try to take revenge or force his way in, the Danes loaded their Winchester carbines and Mylius slept with his revolver at the head of his bed. Nothing happened, and the crisis passed on the return shortly afterward of Knud Rasmussen.

The precarious relationship between explorers and Inuhuit eventually brought about at least one tragic killing, which was surely a product of exactly the same suspicion and misapprehension, the same irrational fears, discussed above. It happened somewhere along the coast of Axel Heiberg Island in the spring of 1914, when two members of the Crocker Land Expedition, Donald MacMillan and Fitzhugh Green, were returning from their unsuccessful attempt to find Crocker Land. They were accompanied by two Inuhuit, Ittukusuk and Piuaatsoq. The group split for a time when the expedition's leader, MacMillan, sent Green with Piuaatsoq, who had served Peary loyally for over two years and whom MacMillan regarded as "one of the best" of traveling companions (1918a: 92), to explore the coast south of Cape Thomas Hubbard. Six days later Green returned alone and informed MacMillan that he had shot and killed Piuaatsoq.

The entry in Green's diary for 1 May 1914 (Preston 1986: 56) speaks for itself:

> We tried twice before we got away. A lull in the storm was always followed by more wind and snow as before.
>
> P. refused to go south or stay here. I was forced to follow as I had no dogs or sledge.
>
> We got away finally at seven A.M. In a little while it was as bad as ever. I could not ride as my feet were very wet and several toes seemed to be frosted.
>
> We were both going over the glare ice and P. kept whipping up his dogs. I told him I could not keep up and he advised me to follow his trail. This was

impossible. I then snatched the rifle from the load and warned him to keep behind me. A few minutes later I turned and saw him whipping up the dogs away from me.

I shot once in the air. He did not stop. I then killed him with a shot through the shoulder and another through the head.

Although MacMillan at first put out a story that Piuaatsoq had died accidentally after becoming buried by snow, he and others fully accepted Green's version of the killing. In *Four Years in the White North* (p. 92), published in 1918, MacMillan explained, "Green, inexperienced in the handling of Eskimos, and failing to understand their motives and temperament, had felt it necessary to shoot his companion."

There was certainly nothing vague or improbable about Green's story. The panic that assailed Green is easily experienced in bad weather in the lonely Arctic wastes. It was the same feeling that had gripped Hayes in 1854 and convinced him that he was about to be murdered. It seems, too, that pretending to leave a companion behind was a favorite Inuhuit trick. They did it to each other (Hayes 1867: 262), and it has happened to modern explorers. Frenchman Jean Malaurie describes such an experience (1982: 177–78), and the German explorer Christian Adler (1979: 427) relates how, on a trip to Ellesmere Island with two Inuhuit, he overheard (or did he only *think* he overheard?) them discussing ways of lightening their loads by getting rid of the white man's gear. Then one of them forged ahead and disappeared into the mist, while the other made it clear that it would be all up with Adler if he too went on ahead, leaving Adler alone. Adler explains significantly that he did not have to reach for his gun because, in the end, his Eskimo companions stayed with him.

Were the fears and suspicions of the explorers about Inuhuit intentions toward them, exemplified by the story of Piuaatsoq's death, ever justified? Does the death of Ross Gilmore Marvin, a twenty-nine-year-old lecturer in mathematics at Cornell University, Ithaca, New York, on Peary's 1908–9 North Polar Expedition, help to answer this question? Unfortunately, Marvin's tragic disappearance has still not been satisfactorily explained (see Lithner 1973 and Rockwell 1984). Veteran of Peary's 1905–6 expedition, Marvin commanded one of the supporting parties in 1909 and was sent back, some distance short of the North Pole, with two Inuhuit. These two, Qilluttooq and Inukitsupaluk, known to the Americans as Kudlooktoo and Inighito or Harrigan, arrived back at the *Roosevelt* without their leader and sorrowfully explained that Marvin had gone on ahead, broken through the thin ice of a freshly frozen-over lead, and drowned before they could reach him. Their story was repeated without question or comment by every member of the expedition (Borup 1911: 201–3, Henson 1912: 151, Bartlett 1928: 197, MacMillan 1934: 198–200, and Goodsell 1983: 135–36). The commander of such a supporting party would normally move on ahead of the rest of his team while they packed up and struck camp, and there was dangerously thin ice enough around to have drowned them all (Peary 1910: 318–20, Weems 1967: 274–75). The expedition's surgeon John W. Goodsell recorded the Eskimos' explanation of Marvin's death in his journal written at the time and only years later and probably after the subsequent developments about to be described, added (1983: 41): "We knew that if we had threatened an Eskimo with a rifle while in the field, he might have retaliated at the first opportunity with a knife or gun. On his return to the ship he would have regretfully reported how we had fallen through thin ice or down a deep crevice."

The only questioning voice in the years immediately after the expedition's return in 1909 was that of the controversial and in part discredited Frederick Cook. In his *My Attainment of the Pole* (pp. 485–86), published in 1911, Cook flatly refused to accept that Marvin had died a natural, accidental death: he would never have flouted the normal practice of his day by going alone onto thin ice without a lifeline, claimed Cook. "The death of this man points to something more than a tragedy," he wrote. According to Hunt (1981: 149) Cook even insinuated that Peary himself might have ordered Ross Marvin's murder.

No more was heard about Marvin's supposed accidental death by drowning until 1923 or 1924 when, during divine worship on Herbert Island, in the presence of many Inuhuit and the catechist Knud Kristiansen, Qilluttooq, who had just been baptized, confessed that he had killed Marvin by shooting him because Marvin had proposed leaving his companion Inukitsupaluk behind. That is, he shot Marvin because he believed Marvin was about to murder Inukitsupaluk.

Qilluttooq's confession of murder caused a stir. Knud Rasmussen, in Copenhagen at the time, learned of it in a letter from the Thule Trading Station manager Hans Nielsen. In May 1925 Rasmussen was in Washington, where he gave the news to officials of the National Geographic Society, and at the end of June 1925 he wrote to Nielsen and asked him to question Qilluttooq and Inukitsupaluk with the help of the Avanersuaq pastor Jens Olsen. This examination took place on 30 November 1925; it was followed by further investigations in Avanersuaq in the summer of 1926 by Rasmussen, accompanied by George Putnam (1947), leader of the 1926 American Museum Expedition to Avanersuaq. Though Rasmussen was unable to interview Qilluttooq satisfactorily, Inukitsupaluk supported his story, claiming that Marvin had become angry and had thrown Inukitsupaluk's clothes and gear off the sledge and driven on without leaving him any provisions. Soon afterwards Qilluttooq called to Inukitsupaluk to bring him the gun, which he did. Returning to his sledge, Inukitsupaluk heard a shot, and Qilluttooq then told him he had killed Marvin to save his friend's life.

This account of the killing, confirmed by the answers of the two Eskimos to the fourteen questions put to them the previous November, which were said to be "based on the presumption that Marvin had been guilty of provoking the Eskimos" (Freeman 1961: 250), was published that autumn in the *New York Times* and by Rasmussen. It was totally unacceptable to MacMillan, who had known both of the Eskimos and Marvin and was sure Marvin would never have lost his temper with or behaved badly to an Eskimo, nor would Qilluttooq have done anything to help Inukitsupaluk, whom he had always "despised and hated" (MacMillan 1934: 200). In spite of this skepticism, several sources (Freuchen 1954: 149, Hunt and Thompson 1980: 57, Ulloriaq 1984) claim that there were plans in 1926 to seek Qilluttooq's extradition to the United States to make him stand trial for Marvin's murder but that these were dropped when the Danes suggested that they might in that event request Green's extradition to stand trial for Piuaatsoq's murder.

Qilluttooq died in 1932. Long afterward his companion Inukitsupaluk, when an old man, told a Danish reporter that "there was bad feeling the whole way because he [Marvin] ate our rations behind our backs" (Erngaard 1973: 131). This was a new slant on the story, not confirmed by Inuutersuaq's speculation that the two Eskimos with Marvin had perhaps annoyed him by raiding the depots of supplies laid down for the larger Peary party or main division returning behind them along the trial (Ulloriaq 1984).

All these versions of the killing reflect the mistrust and follow the pattern so far outlined in this chapter, except that now it is the Eskimo who is frightened into a violent deed. But one cannot help wondering if there was more to the killing of Marvin than has been revealed. Could Peary himself have been involved in some way, not so directly as Cook insinuated? Qilluttooq was a favorite of his: his mother had sewed for the Pearys at Red Cliff House in 1891–92, but when they returned in 1893 they found that she had died and the little boy was orphaned (Peary 1904b: 27–37). Perhaps Qilluttooq felt especially close to Peary. One wonders too if Marvin might have become persona non grata with Peary (see Thomas F. Hall in Lewin 1935). His cryptic letters (Eames 1973: 79–80) written to his friend L. C. Bement from Iita in 1908 betray some sympathy with Cook, and Cook (1911: 488) seems to imply that Marvin might have been in a position to question Peary's evidence that he had reached the North Pole. Could Qilluttooq have witnessed an angry exchange between Peary and Marvin and subsequently taken the law into his own hands? But this is far too speculative, and we shall probably never know the truth.

5

The Inuhuit Economy Transformed

W hile the incidents described in the previous chapter were taking place, the Inuhuit economy, self-sufficient in 1818, came increasingly into contact with and was eventually penetrated by the economic system of Europe and America. This was essentially based on the export or distribution of manufactured products, including firearms, around the world, in exchange for valuable raw materials. It was only at the close of the nineteenth century that a regular systematic bartering of Inuhuit furs and ivory for Western products developed, and only in the second decade of the twentieth century that barter was transformed into trade by the establishment of a trading post in Avanersuaq and the introduction of money.

There is abundant evidence of wood and iron objects in Inuhuit possession in the nineteenth century. By the 1850s they were using pieces of oak barrels in sledge construction and possessed knife blades of manufactured iron and other metal objects. On 29 August 1876, when Allen Young (1879: 156–58) was on his way home in the *Pandora,* he called at the settlement of Natsilivik and noticed a piece of a wooden box marked "Limejuice, Leith," a ship's bucket, part of a mahogany table with brass studs, fragments of an iron harpoon, and pieces of a saw. The inhabitants told him that their wood came ashore from the sea and "the iron had been amongst them a long time." The Inuhuit had also begun to acquire firearms. A passenger on a whaleship noticed that two Eskimos who came aboard at Dalrymple Rock in 1873 each carried a United States government rifle stamped with the date 1864, presumably deriving from the U.S. Polar Expedition of 1871–73 (Vaughan 1987: 102–3). In 1884 "a dilapidated gun of German manufacture" and "an old United States Springfield musket, stamped 1862," were in the possession of the Inuhuit on Saunders Island (Melville 1896: 446). In 1891, just before Peary began distributing rifles to the Eskimos, those at Cape York possessed an "old and rusty gun, stamped with the name of a whale-ship to which it had belonged" (Keely and Davis 1893: 181).

The possible sources of wood and iron objects in Inuhuit possession are worth examining. One that leaps to mind, shipwrecks, was probably unimportant. Many whalers came to grief in the ice of Melville Bay in the nineteenth century but nearly always well to the south of Cape York. Kane's ship the *Advance* was abandoned in the ice in Rensselaer Bay in June 1855, but, instead of being systematically dismantled for her wood and iron, she was set on fire and burned by the Eskimos, though whether by accident or on purpose is unclear (Hayes 1867: 288–89, Mylius-Erichsen and Moltke 1906: 377, MacMillan 1918a: 156–57). The hurried departures often required in navigation through icy seas caused expeditions to leave equipment and materials ashore, as was the case with Corporal Cullamore's shirt and varous pieces of wood and iron left on the shore of North Star Bay in 1850. The few huts and other structures left in Avanersuaq by explorers may also have provided the Inuhuit with wood and other items. The wooden house built at Lifeboat Cove by some of the crew of the *Polaris*, which they called Polaris House and in which they wintered in 1872–73, had disappeared when Captain Nares (Markham 1878: 61) landed there in July 1875, though "trunks, boxes, stoves, pieces of wood, gunbarrels and odds and ends of all descriptions lay strewed about." If the Eskimos demolished it for its wood, it is surprising that they left so much apparently useful material behind. Peary's winter house, Red Cliff House, was deliberately destroyed by "a few of the natives led on by the famous angekok, Kyoahpadu" (Peary 1893: 216). Anniversary Lodge consisted of two separate buildings. One was inadvertently burned down by two Eskimos and the other torn down (Hoppin 1897: 27, Harper 1986: 17, 243).

A more important source of manufactured objects for the nineteenth-century Inuhuit may have been the donation to them from time to time of unwanted expedition equipment (Fig. 9) and the occasional distribution of free gifts by explorers or their patrons. The tradition was inaugurated by John Ross in 1818, who gives the following inventory of articles that "were intended for presents to the natives on the West coast of Greenland and coast of America":

Brass kettles	24	No.
Knives, forks and cases	300	
Axes, felling, wedge	20	
Butchers' knives	150	
Flannel, red	150	Yards.
yellow	100	
blue	100	
Felling axes	10	No.
Looking-glasses	200	
Needles, Whitechapel	2000	
Vermilion	15	Pounds.
Cutlasses	36	No.

```
Gun-flints .............................................. 1500
Scarlet-milled caps ...................................... 100
Swords ................................................. 14
Thread, Red ............................................ 20  Pounds.
Pistols ................................................. 16  No.
Scissors ............................................... 30  Pairs.
Razors.................................................. 40  No.
Coarse handkerchiefs. .................................. 50
Awls, shoemakers' ...................................... 100
Rifles ................................................. 35
Balls for ditto ........................................ 2500
Snuff .................................................. 102  Pounds.
Earthen-ware............................................ 4  Cases
Soap .................................................. 150  Pounds.
Pikes ................................................. 250  No.
Iron hoops ............................................. 2  Cwt.
Gin (English) .......................................... 129  Gallons.
Brandy ................................................ 129½
Various beads & Cowrie shells .......................... 13  Cases
Umbrellas.............................................. 40  No.
```

Although some of the knives, looking glasses and beads mentioned here were subsequently recorded as distributed to the Inuhuit, along with various articles of clothing, no weapons were given to them.

Forty years later, in June 1858, Leopold M'Clintock (1859: 137) stopped the *Fox* briefly at Cape York when he sighted Eskimos on the ice and "distributed presents of knives and needles, and explained to them that we did so because they had behaved well to the white people (as we learn from Dr. Kane's narrative of their treatment of him and his crew)."

The practice of doling out charity to the Eskimos, begun by the British, was subsequently elaborated by the Americans. In the course of the winter of 1891–92 many Americans were concerned about the fate of Peary and his companions. He had been left on the desolate shore of McCormick Fjord the previous 30 July with a broken leg, in company with his wife, Josephine. In March 1892 the Academy of Natural Sciences of Philadelphia decided to send a relief expedition that summer to bring him and his party safely home (Keely and Davis 1893: 267–73). William E. Meeham, associate editor of the *Philadelphia Public Ledger,* who joined the expedition as botanist, describes the spontaneous display of generosity:

> In the meantime Dr. Joseph T. Rothrock, of West Chester, who is prominently known in Philadelphia as a lecturer on botanical topics, conceived the happy and philanthropic idea of sending a quantity of wood for sledges,

kajaks and harpoons; of iron spearheads and household utensils, to be distributed as gifts among the Eskimos, whose settlements are on the west coast of Greenland, at Cape York and above. As trees are unknown so far north and as the people have no facilities for smelting what little iron the country yields, these articles would be invaluable to them in their struggle for existence; besides, their good-will and friendly disposition might be of incalculable service to the relief party in furthering the object of their setting out. It is, therefore, little wonder that Dr. Rothrock's benevolent scheme met with immediate and cordial support. From well-known residents of his home, in West Chester, came generous contributions. In Philadelphia, Professor Edwin J. Houston, head of the Department of Physical Geography and Natural Philosophy at the Central High School, was perhaps the most interested in this proposed good work, and through him a large quantity of articles and considerable money was contributed. Professor Heilprin, on the part of the members of the relief expedition, cheerfully promised to faithfully carry out the wishes of the donors. Into his charge were given six Arctic sleds, twenty-five spears made from files donated by Hoopes, Brother & Darlington, 100 hickory spear handles, forty-eight spools of copper wire, 120 butcher knives, thirty-two pounds of hoop iron, 108 thimbles, 1000 assorted needles, a great number of files of various sizes and patterns, about two dozen iron kettles, a dozen cleavers, two dozen saws, many scissors, thimbles, hammers, braces and bits, planes, and a large quantity of cut lumber.

The distribution of these gifts at Cape York, Itilleq, and Red Cliff House in McCormick Fjord delighted but puzzled the recipients, some of whom "ran around the deck howling and singing for very joy" and repeatedly asked Daniel Broberg, the expedition's Greenlandic interpreter, "why it was they were given such precious things for nothing." What explanation was given them or how it was understood does not emerge, only Daniel's Pidgin English report of his conversation with them: "I speakem American man good."

Similar distributions of gifts continued into the twentieth century. After the return of the Literary Expedition in 1904, the Danes sent a cargo of gifts to the Inuhuit in appreciation for the invaluable assistance they had given the expedition. These gifts, which were taken to Uummannaq on M'Clintock's old ship the *Fox,* which had been purchased in the meanwhile by the Royal Greenland Trade Department (KGH, Den Kongelige Grønlandske Handel), included guns and ammunition as well as timber and were paid for by private subscription (Steensby 1909, Sand 1935, 1936, Holtved 1960).

Gifts of manufactured goods may have been of importance in the first half of the nineteenth century, but they were soon overtaken in significance by barter. At first, this was more in the nature of occasional gift exchange than regular barter, though the distinction between the two is fine. The narratives of Ross's encounter with the Inuhuit show that when distributing gifts he expected something in return. Was this gift exchange or barter? Alexander Fisher, the assistant surgeon of HMS *Alexander,* wrote in his journal (1819: 57) that "the natives gave us some of their spears, made of the horns of the narwhal, in exchange for what they received," but a little futher on (p. 61) wrote of a group that had arrived some time later: "These natives were, as usual, provided with narwhals' horns, which they disposed of for their favourite articles, wood and iron." Probably the second group brought a few extra narwhal tusks as a result of what they had learned from the first. Ross (1819: 88) describes how the first natives they encountered "advanced, offering in return for our knives, glasses and beads, their knives, sea unicorns' horns, and sea-horse teeth." He notes that the second group "were very much delighted with the presents that were now given to them." "In return," continues Ross, "I received a spear . . . with a sledge" (p. 102). But the owner of the sledge, Majaq, prepared to return home with it, "appearing to have forgotten that he had sold it to me," "However," adds Ross, "we explained to his satisfaction that he had sold us the sledge" (p. 105). Even if appearing satisfied, Majaq seems to have had a raw deal: of this transaction, Sabine (1819: 78) records that "a bargain was made with him for a sledge and dog, for which he received a small spar, and the gunnel-streak, and one of the thwarts of a boat which had been squeezed by the ice." These Inuhuit were evidently neither used to bartering nor at first prepared for it.

Subsequent nineteenth-century explorers, up to the time of Peary, seem to have bartered only sporadically, with little prior intent, for particular coveted objects, especially dogs. In July 1852 Captain Sir Edward Belcher of the Royal Navy (1855a: 66) acquired "three very fine and handsome native dogs" at Cape York in return for "our presents, but more particularly in exchange for a boat hook and a broken oar." This sounds like another swindle. The United States Navy was also interested in dogs: on 26 June 1884, when the *Thetis* and the *Bear*, taking the survivors of the Greely expedition home, stopped at Saunders Island, Ensign Charles H. Harlow of the *Thetis* acquired a fine-looking dog, apparently in exchange for needles, buttons, clothing, and some food (Schley and Soley 1889: 244–45). Another purchase of dogs had been made in 1876 by Allen Young (1879) at Natsilivik, when he obtained three of the Inuhuit's "fine dogs" in exchange for five of his own. The eight persons who inhabited Natsilivik at that time—a chief, two lads, an old woman, a young woman, a girl, and two small children— bartered four narwhal tusks and "a stone cooking pot, made of soapstone, beautifully cut out" with him for "six large knives, a large saw, some packets of needles and threads," a fifteen-foot oar, and an ash plank. The narwhal tusks were all they had, and this perhaps shows that at Natsilivik in the 1870s barter was only occasional and on a small scale.

Fifteen years later, in 1891, when Peary's ship the *Kite* called at Natsilivik, barter seems to have intensified: the landing party found only six adults and five children living there, but "these people had quantities of sealskins and narwhal tusks, many of which were obtained in exchange for knives, saws, files and tools in general" (Peary 1893: 30). Later, at Red Cliff House during the winter, when two men arrived from Cape York, Mrs. Peary noted, "They have quite a number of narwhal tusks to trade, and are determined to have a rifle for them, but I hardly think they will get it" (p. 100). She may have been wrong here. Years later, in 1903, Taateraaq told members of the Literary Expedition that "at Cape York when Peary's first ship came up here"—the *Kite* in 1891—he acquired a repeating Winchester carbine in exchange for three large narwhal tusks. Surely, "while he was living at Cape York" was meant, and surely he was one of the two men referred to (Mylius-Erichsen and Moltke 1906: 208).

Among whalers, too, barter with the Inuhuit was only occasional until toward the close of the nineteenth century. In his pioneering study of the trading partnership between whalers and Eskimos that developed on the American side of Baffin Bay, and especially in Hudson Bay, in the second half of the nineteenth century, W. Gillies Ross (1975) has shown how this trade arose from the overwintering of the whalers there. But in Avanersuaq the whalers did not even catch whales, let alone overwinter, and were usually in a hurry to cross over to the west side of Baffin Bay. There, and especially in Cumberland Sound and Hudson Bay, they had far more contacts with the Eskimo inhabitants. Along the Avanersuaq coast contacts occurred between whalers and Inuhuit when bartering was reported not to have taken place in 1884, 1894, and 1895 (Vaughan 1987). In 1866, when it did occur, the Eskimos concerned had to use clothing they were wearing and weapons in use, showing that they did not have bartering in mind when they took the trouble to sledge out over the sea ice to board the ships. Bartering between whalers and Inuhuit is again recorded in 1878. Dr. MacKintosh (1884: 35, 40, 41) of the whaleship *Active* out of Dundee reported that at Cape York on 14 June three Eskimos came aboard and the captain gave "our visitors a good knife, and a pair of green spectacles each, with both of which they were highly delighted." On 22 June, in Whale Sound, the captain again distributed spectacles and knives to the Eskimos, this time receiving in return two narwhal tusks that had to be fetched from their winter houses. Further bartering ensued, which may not have been to the Eskimos' advantage: "The last natives had spectacles of wood and skin, with slits to look through. The skipper gave them a pair of the green goggles each, and got theirs instead and kindly gave them to me. I have quite a museum of Arctic curiosities now." Apparently, a rather innocuous barter for curios was taking place alongside a more serious barter for narwhal ivory. One narwhal had already been shot from the ship, and the barter for narwhal tusks was surely for commercial purposes. This bartering did not yet occur annually; the captain told MacKintosh that in some years they never saw Eskimos along the Avanersuaq coast.

Not until detailed research is undertaken at Dundee and elsewhere will it be possible to know how much of a trade the Scottish whaling captains developed with the Inuhuit in ivory and furs, especially fox skins, at the close of the nineteenth century. In 1903 Eskimos told members of the Literary Expedition that they gave the Scottish whalers bear and fox skins in exchange for a range of manufactured articles (Vaughan 1987), and in 1908 Rudolph Franke (1914: 171) complained, when he arrived at Uummannaq in July, that the whalers had taken the Eskimos' most valuable products and that there was little left for trading or an emergency. Whatever this trade amounted to it came to an end in 1913 with the final cessation of Scottish Arctic whaling.

At just the time when the Scottish whalers seem to have been extending their activities to include commercial bartering for ivory and furs, the explorers began to do the same thing. Like the whaleship captains, the explorers, who may well have been tempted to profit from the proceeds of private barter or to help defray their expenses in that way, would be unlikely to proclaim the fact abroad. It seems virtually certain that when the *Kite* returned home in autumn 1891 and when it took the Pearys and their companions home in 1892, its cargo included a quantity of furs and ivory, as well as "ethnological material." On his subsequent expeditions, too, Peary certainly bartered for furs and ivory to sell on his return home. There is at least one hint of this in his own published writings: he records incidentally that on his way north in 1905 he was detained at one Eskimo village by the need to take on board "the goodly supply of skins which these people have" (Peary 1907: 26). Other people mentioned it too. In 1908 a member of the crew of the *Erik,* Joseph G. White, claimed that Peary and Matt Henson "were busy trading with Eskimos and making big profit on the furs and ivory" (Eames 1973: 244n). Whitney is candid enough to give away a secret or two. He explains that the duties of Peary's boatswain John Murphy at Iita and Anoritooq in winter 1908–9 included "trading with the Eskimos, collecting furs and ivory." He also mentions that the *Erik* stopped at an Eskimo village in 1908 "to get the ivory tusks secured by natives in a recent successful narwhal hunt" (1910: 33, 62) and that, at Uummannaq on about 2 August, nearly all the inhabitants had fox skins, walrus tusks, and narwhal tusks "to trade with Mr. Peary" (pp. 23–24). Perhaps the retired rear admiral Colby M. Chester, who was said by Cook (1911: 544) to have belonged to "a coterie that divided the profits of fleecing the Eskimos" and to have been "related to Mr. Peary's fur trade," acted as Peary's agent for the sale of his furs, skins, and walrus and narwhal tusks. The Peary

Arctic Club was evidently also involved, and so may have been its president, who was also president of the American Museum of Natural History, Peary's patron and supporter Morris K. Jesup (Harper 1986: 75). One can provisionally conclude that Peary not only depended on the Inuhuit as guides and assistants for his North Pole expeditions but also that their surplus produce in furs and ivory helped to finance those expeditions, if not to line Peary's own pocket.

Peary's colleague of 1891–93 and subsequent rival in the quest for the North Pole, Frederick A. Cook, never made a secret of his own trading activities with the Inuhuit. On board the yacht *John R. Bradley* in North Star Bay in August 1907 it was a free-for-all in which everyone took part and astronomical profits were to be had (Cook 1911: 49):

> On board the yacht were busy days of barter. Furs and ivory were gathered in heaps in exchange for guns, knives and needles. Every seaman, from cabin boy to captain, suddenly got rich in the gamble of trade for prized blue-fox skins and narwhal tusks.
>
> The Eskimos were equally elated with their part of the bargain. For a beautiful fox skin, of less use to a native than a dog pelt, he could secure a pocket knife that would serve him half a lifetime!
>
> A woman exchanged her fur pants, worth a hundred dollars, for a red pocket handkerchief with which she would decorate her head or her igloo for years to come.
>
> Another gave her bearskin mits for a few needles, and she conveyed the idea that she had the long end of the trade! A fat youth with a fatuous smile displayed with glee two bright tin cups, one for himself and one for his prospective bride. He was positively happy in having obtained nine cents' worth of tin for only an ivory tusk worth ninety dollars!

Later in 1907 Cook traveled south from Iita to Cape York, partly to get into training for his proposed "Polar dash" the following spring and partly for purposes of trade (Franke 1914: 48–49). He returned with sledges loaded with fox skins and ivory for which he had bartered tobacco, gunpowder, lead, gun caps, coffee, tea, and timber. His companion Franke, who was left at Anoritooq while Cook went off on his polar travels, found life there extremely lonely. He yearned for company and hoped that Knud Rasmussen would visit him, though he feared that he and Cook had spoiled Rasmussen's trade in fox skins (pp. 101–2). A few weeks later Franke received a letter from Cook dated 17 March 1908 on the "Polar Sea north of Cape Hubbard" (pp. 127–28). "Gather all the blue fox skins you can," wrote Cook. "These must be our money for the return trip. If you can get a few bear skins take them, also Narwhale and Walross tusks, but do not give too much for them." The story of how Peary later robbed Cook and Franke of what Cook described as "$10,000 worth of furs and ivory" need not be recounted here.

By the time Donald B. MacMillan's Crocker Land Expedition established itself at Iita in the last days of August 1913, the Thule Trading Station was in full swing and it seemed unlikely that the American explorers would be able to compete effectively in the fox skin trade with Knud Rasmussen and Peter Freuchen. Yet the expedition's doctor, Harrison J. Hunt, in his diary for 29 January 1914, alleged that "MacMillan is trading for fox skins to take home for himself, giving in exchange tea, sugar, biscuit, tobacco, matches and other articles" (Hunt and Thompson 1980: 46). Later he describes how members of the expedition complained to their leader about this trading, with goods provided by the American Museum for the expedition's use, for furs which MacMillan would then sell privately in the United States, and more or less put a stop to it (p. 56). Whether MacMillan or the museum as represented by its curator of geology and extinct vertebrates, Edmund Otis Hovey, who was in Avanersuaq in 1915–17 and who had 211 fox skins at Iita in January 1917 to use for clothing and for payments to Freuchen for his help and supplies did bring back fox skins to the United States and sell them there remains an open question (Hovey to Freuchen, 3 Jan. 1917, File 1016/20, American Museum of Natural History, New York). The Crocker Land Expedition awaits its historian.

In the middle of the Peary epoch, before his last two big North Pole expeditions of 1905–6 and 1908–9 and at a time when a lively annual barter was taking place between Eskimos and whalers, the Danes arrived in Avanersuaq. Their Literary Expedition of 1903–4, on which there was no trading, substantially extended the Inuhuit's trading connections by reopening communications between Avanersuaq and the Upernavik district. The early spring sledge route the expedition pioneered across Melville Bay was used in 1905 and 1906 by Inuhuit to travel to the Upernavik district to obtain guns, ammunition, and other necessities in return for their fox and bear skins (Mylius-Erichsen and Moltke 1906: 591n, Senn 1907: 229). It must have been at this time or very soon afterward that the Inuhuit Silluk arrived at Tasiusaq from Avanersuaq with his sledge loaded with seventy-five narwhal tusks, all acquired in a single year (Lund-Drosvad 1961: 172). This bartering was cut short within a very few years by the establishment of a permanent trading station in Avanersuaq.

It seems to have been Isaac Hayes who first suggested establishing a permanent post. In July 1861, as he sailed out of the little harbor of Port Foulke near the mouth of Foulke Fjord, where he had wintered in the schooner *United States,* he was full of plans for the future (1867: 419–20). He would return to Port Foulke and found a colony that would serve as a base for further explorations to the north. He would collect the Eskimos together so as to provide "a productive source of food and furs." Dogs would be reared at the colony. If adequate funds were not available, "a sufficient profit may be made out of the colony in oils, furs, walrus ivory, eider down, etc., to pay at least a very considerable proportion of the wages of the employés, besides subsisting them." Five years later, he still hoped to found this colony at Port Foulke "and, with a corps of scientific associates, to make that the centre of a widely extended system of exploration" (p. 452). The implementation of this fancy was prevented by the American Civil War; it was eventually realized by Knud Rasmussen on the shore of North Star Bay in August 1910.

As early as 3 May 1905 journalist Ludvig Mylius-Erichsen had urged the establishment of a Danish mission and trading station at Uummannaq to bring the benefits of civilization to the Inuhuit. He and his colleagues had already discussed such a venture on the Literary Expedition; even the name Thule and the best site for the post had been settled. Alleging that this was the Eskimos' wish, he thought they could easily provide a few hundred fox and bearskins annually without depriving themselves, and that it was the Danes' moral duty to ensure them a continued supply of iron and wood, as well as ammunition and other things, to which Peary and the whalers had accustomed them. Mylius-Erichsen went on to suggest that this station could form the basis for much Arctic research, that it would make an excellent center for Inland Ice studies, and that a permanent meteorological station there would be useful. The physical practicability of this plan, that is, an annual ship to take supplies and bring back fox skins, was demonstrated when, in August 1905, the *Fox* anchored in North Star Bay with a cargo of gifts for the Inuhuit. Its commercial viability was demonstrated in 1908, when Rasmussen returned to Denmark after two years in Avanersuaq with a quantity of furs he is said to have sold for the substantial sum of 12,000 crowns (Freuchen 1954: 94).

The notion that the Inuhuit wanted the Danes to set up a permanent mission and trading station in Avanersuaq was either naive or equivocal. Mylius-Erichsen (1905) described a conversation he had with Asiajuk, using Rasmussen as interpreter. Perhaps it would be better described as an interrogation. Asked if he and his people would like to be resettled in the south, where they could more easily obtain the things they needed, Asiajuk demurred. Suppose they undertook an annual trading expedition south of Melville Bay to exchange skins for the much needed equipment and ammunition? No, that would take them away from home too long and their families might suffer want. In that case, why don't we send you an annual ship with the supplies you need? That would be better but by no means ideal because we could not all be at the same place in summer to meet it. And now the crucial question: suppose some white men settle with you permanently and receive goods from an annual ship which they then trade with you during the course of the year for your fox skins? Ah, yes, exclaims Asiajuk, that would be excellent! We hear that other Eskimos have white men living among them with whom they can trade to obtain necessary materials and equipment, so why not us? But, continues Mylius-Erichsen, in that event you will have to be taught the white mans' customs and beliefs. Fine, says Asiajuk, we want to learn. So the Inuhuit, purportedly of their own free will, received permanent trading facilities with Denmark, not to mention the Christian religion, the introduction of which to them is one of the themes of chapter 10.

Mylius-Erichsen was not only an enthusiastic supporter of a trading station among the Inuhuit; he was also a protagonist of the Danish annexation of Avanersuaq. After his death in northeast Greenland on the *Danmark* expedition of 1907, Rasmussen pursued this aim. But the Danish government would not intervene. It was unmoved, or perhaps deterred, by the story that Peary planned to set up a trading post in Avanersuaq with his assistant Matt Henson as manager. If Peary did not do this, then it was alleged that another American, Cook, would do it, with his German assistant Rudolph Franke as manager. Other Danish sources averred that the Norwegian explorer Otto Sverdrup would move in if the Danish government did not and establish a sealing station on Saunders Island (Sand 1936, Gilberg 1977a, Freuchen 1954: 94). In spite of their fears of non-Danish intervention in Greenland, which they regarded as Danish, the Danish government continued to lack interest.

Whether or not he was intent on "saving" northwest Greenland for Danish colonization as later legend had it (Birket-Smith 1936: 39, Sand 1936: 51, Holtved 1960), Rasmussen went ahead with the planned trading post on his own initiative. In the summer of 1909 he helped establish a mission station on the shore of North Star Bay called Nordstjernen or the North Star Mission, and some trade was begun. He then turned his attention to raising funds and enlisting support for a separate, permanent trading station. He persuaded a tough and adaptable young medical student with Arctic experience, Peter Freuchen, to accompany him and then act as the post's manager; he engaged the energy of an enthusiastic engineer, Ib Nyeboe, who headed a committee charged with the supply and management of the station from the beginning until 1926; and he contrived to raise the 40,000 crowns needed to set up the station by means of loans from his wife, Dagmar, and businessman Adam Biering, who had made a fortune drilling for oil at Baku on the Caspian Sea (Sand 1935, 1936, Birket-Smith 1936, Erichsen 1943, Holtved 1960, Gilberg 1977a, 1988).

In 1910 Rasmussen and Freuchen succeeded in finding a small ship which, said Freuchen, with tongue in cheek as usual, "was cheap but otherwise totally unsuited for any excursion to the Arctic" (1954: 95). In spite of a collision with an iceberg en route, she made the trip from Denmark to North Star Bay in a month, and within a few days of her arrival there Rasmussen, Freuchen, and the crew, helped by the local Eskimos, had unloaded the prefabricated wooden house they had brought with them and erected it not far above the tideline. Before the ship sailed back to Denmark she took on a cargo of walrus and narwhal ivory and 311 fox skins, which had accumulated at the mission station during the previous year (Wamberg 1961). Then, after unfurling the Danish flag on the flat summit of the hill Uummannaq, Rasmussen set off on a walrus hunt, which was one of his favorite pastimes, to procure a supply of meat for the winter. Kap York Stationen Thule, or the Thule Trading Station, was open.

Rasmussen never concealed the commercial element in the establishment of the Thule Trading Station. In the first annual report he drafted for his committee in 1911 he recognized that the station must do business and make profits if it was going to spread culture in the farthest north and help the Inuhuit to survive (Rasmussen 1961). In later years he readily admitted that the Thule Trading Station was a money-making concern: its profits had been used to pay for administrative expenses and for social services and to finance a series of expeditions he led, which became known as the Thule expeditions (Mathiassen 1934, Oldendow 1960). In 1930, in a letter to Minister of State for Greenland Thorvald Stauning, he enumerated some of the activities the station—that is, the Inuhuit—had funded or helped to fund (Gilberg 1977a: 251):

1912.   The First Thule Expedition, to northeast Greenland.
1913.   The ship *Kap York* purchased.
1916.   The Second Thule Expedition, to northeast Greenland.
1919.   The ship *Søkongen* purchased.
1919.   The Fourth Thule Expedition, to Ammassalik.
1921–24.   The Fifth Thule Expedition, to Canada and Alaska. Total cost 750,000 crowns less 132,000 crowns in government subsidies.
1929.   New parsonage and shop built; hospital built and doctor provided for.

Riding high on the booming international fur trade, the Thule station's profits were based from its foundation on the fox pelts, both white and blue, supplied to it by the Inuhuit. A varying proportion of Avanersuaq's Arctic foxes belong to the white, tundra, form and the rest are blue, or rather dark gray, coastal foxes (Bræstrup 1941, Vibe 1967) (Fig. 10). The animals were trapped in stone or (later) steel traps between October and May, and the skins were brought by the trapper to the trading station where they were exchanged for goods. According to Malaurie, in the year before the foundation of the Thule Trading Station, 1909–10, 347 blue and 64 white fox skins were brought in to the mission station, and in Freuchen's first year as manager (1910–11), 514 blue and 114 white foxes were caught (Malaurie 1982: 42). In the summer of 1914 W. Elmer Ekblaw, geologist and botanist of the Crocker Land Expedition, who was then staying at the Thule Trading Station with his colleague M. C. Tanquary, took a look at the furs stored there, waiting to be sent to Denmark on the annual supply ship in August (MacMillan 1918a: 331): "One of the most interesting sights at North Star Bay was the station fur-storehouse. The summer Tank and I were there it was hung with about 3,000 blue-fox skins in bunches of fifty, graded according to color, and 300 white in bunches of fifty, too. The collection of furs was beautiful. The soft, glossy, fluffy furs ready for market were wealth and luxury that a queen might have desired to add to her wardrobe."

Malaurie (1982: 442) took the trouble to question Inuutersuaq, who had worked in the trading station under Freuchen, about prices there in 1910–25. It seems to have been somewhat ungenerous in its dealings with the Eskimos.

1 blue fox skin brought the trapper 10 crowns (the equivalent of $1.60)
1 white fox skin brought him 5 crowns ($.80)
1 walrus rifle, 1889 model, cost 7–10 blue or 20 white fox skins
1 Mauser rifle cost 10 blue fox skins
1 seal rifle cost 2 blue fox skins
10 walrus rifle bullets cost 1 blue fox or 5 crowns
1 large knife cost 1 blue fox
1 steel fox trap cost 2 crowns
100 grams tea, 1 kilo sugar, and 5 kilos oats cost 10 white fox skins or 50 crowns ($8.00)

Compare the eighty cents paid for a white fox skin with the "more than 30 dollars apiece" paid for white fox skins to Eskimo trappers in Alaska in 1924 (Brandt 1943: 305).

Peter Freuchen, who seems to have been paying the Eskimos less than two dollars for a pelt that would be sold in Copenhagen for more than ten times that sum, has provided a vivid picture of trading at the Thule station in the early years (Freuchen 1961: 70–80). Each man traded his fox skins for goods twice a year, once in the fall and again in the spring. He would bring his wife and family and accept Freuchen's hospitality for several days. At first, they would eat, dance, and talk about everything except fox skins. When eventually Freuchen casually inquired if the man happened to have caught any foxes lately, the reply would be negative, the man insisting on his inadequacy as a trapper. Freuchen had to inquire about the contents of the packages on his sledge and remind him of the excellent skins he brought in on former occasions before he would admit that he might possibly have a fox skin or two with him. Only on the following day, and after all the Eskimos in the place had gathered around, would the man open the bags and spread out the hundred or so superb skins they contained. Then it was Freuchen's turn to expostulate his inadequacy. How can he possibly have goods valuable enough to pay for such fantastic skins? But the man now exclaims that payment is the last thing he is thinking of; Freuchen is welcome to such poor quality skins for nothing! Having accepted the skins as a gift, Freuchen asks the man if he has seen anything in his store he would like. At first he can think of nothing, but when Freuchen suggests a rifle he gladly accepts it. He and his family are invited into the store and allowed to inspect the contents. They go through everything, taking the best part of the day, and at last select what they want, while Freuchen has figured out what he can offer for the skins and written it down on a piece of paper so that his assistant can issue the goods to the buyer. The following day, after a deal has been made, when the man has his sledge and dogs ready to depart, he remembers that he would like some tobacco or something else. Freuchen explains that the experienced trader has already allowed for such last-minute extras and even for a parting gift of tea and sugar for the man's wife.

This bartering was gradually replaced after 1914 by a monetary system based on a special Thule Trading Station coinage (Freuchen 1959: 220). The coins were designed by Ib Nyeboe and were of aluminum; the first issue was of thirty thousand. Each coin had a hole in the center so it could easily be attached with string or gut to a sledge upstander or hung on a nail in the shop.

During Freuchen's ten years as manager, 1910 to 1919, the picturesque and rather random conduct of business at the Thule Trading Station produced handsome profits for Knud Rasmussen. The station was a combination of engrosser of furs and, to a lesser extent, ivory, and a retail shop. It was profitable for the most part because it had entirely cornered the market. The Inuhuit could sell their products and make their purchases only at the Thule Trading Station, which, like the Royal Greenland Trade Department in the rest of Greenland, had no competitors.

In the hundred years following 1818 the self-sufficient and isolated Inuhuit subsistence hunting economy was changed in significant ways by the activities of whalers and explorers. Subsistence hunting continued, but self-sufficiency came to an end. The Inuhuit were introduced to a range of manufactured goods, many of which directly served the subsistence hunt and therefore rapidly became necessities, among them rifles and ammunition, steel knives, and wood for sledges and kayaks, as well as alcoholic beverages, tea and coffee, sugar, and other food items. From 1910, as a result of Knud Rasmussen's initiative, all these for the first time became available on a permanent, year-round basis, except for wartime or other interruptions to supply. Likewise, in the hundred years after 1818 the Inuhuit were persuaded to create a supply of hunting and trapping products over and above those required for subsistence to be used in barter with annual visitors to Avanersuaq and later for purchases at the Thule Trading Station. The demand for furs on the world market ensured the predominance of Arctic fox pelts in the export inventory. By 1910 the Inuhuit, whose womenfolk had hitherto trapped foxes for making fox skin coats, had become trappers of foxes on a large scale for the fur trade, and the trapping was now done largely by men. To a significant extent, the hunter had become a trapper.

It would be futile to try to apportion the blame or credit for these developments, which were brought about by two great men, Robert Peary and Knud Rasmussen, and a host of lesser ones, including whaling captains such as the two Captains William Adams, father and son, of Dundee. The further severance of Inuhuit society from its nomadic, sea-mammal hunting past and its further involvement in imports and exports, which linked it more and more indissolubly with the outside world, will be described in chapter 10.

6

The Demands of Subsistence
and Science

*I*n this chapter the impact of both Eskimos and whites on the wildlife of Avanersuaq will be considered. The Eskimos formed part of the Arctic ecosystem, adapted as they were to life in these harsh and hostile surroundings, although they could survive only at the expense of animals. To the large demands for food and clothing their subsistence needs made on the local wildlife were added, in the nineteenth century, the smaller ones of white explorers and whalers. Then the naturalist collectors took their toll both of animals and birds. The motives and activities of these people are relatively easy to analyze and describe; it is harder to measure the effect of their depredations on animal populations.

This discussion will be confined to the mammals and birds of present-day Avanersuaq and to those that have become extinct in historic times. Evidence for the former existence here of the woolly mammoth or *kiliffak* is fragmentary, and it became extinct long before the start of the historical record, though an Inuhuit string figure of a *kiliffak* has been described in the literature, and the remains of one is said to have been found near Qaanaaq (Hansen 1988). Three large mammals, formerly abundant in Avanersuaq, have become extinct or rare in historic times, but in no case is it possible to prove that this was solely the result of hunting and shooting. These are the bowhead or Greenland right whale (*Balaena mysticetus*), the musk-ox (*Ovibos muschatus*), and the caribou (*Rangifer tarandus*).

Off the West Greenland coast south of Avanersuaq, and all along the opposite shore of Baffin Bay, European whalers had hunted the bowhead to virtual extinction by the early years of the twentieth century. It was in vain that, on 12 May 1927, American Museum of Natural History President Henry Fairfield Osborn, referring to a proposed expedition to Baffin Island, approved a "tentative arrangement with Mr. Putnam, that if he secures a complete skeleton of a Bowhead not less than fifty feet in length and delivers it at New York, we would be willing to pay $5,000 for it" (Reference Library, No. 1216, American Museum of Natural History, New York). In Avanersuaq, on the other hand, it certainly was not the whalers who caused the disappearance of the whales that had been so numerous in 1616 that William Baffin, pilot of "the good ship called the *Discouerie*" (Markham 1881: 138), named Whale Sound after them. When they eventually began to visit Avanersuaq waters in the years after 1817, the whalers did so only to make use of the North Water to cross over to the Canadian side of Baffin Bay.

The last time that bowheads were recorded as present in number in or near Avanersuaq was in 1818. When John Ross was forcing the *Isabella* and *Alexander* through the ice on 31 July, accompanied by the *Bon Accord* of Aberdeen, the *Everthorpe* of Hull, and other whalers, they broke through into "a large sheet of clear water, in which we saw an immense number of whales," one of which they killed. This was in 75° 33' north latitude, not far from the Sabine Islands, fairly in the center of Melville Bay. On 1 August in the same place there were still plenty of whales to be seen, but on 3 August, farther northwest, only a few. Thereafter, it seems that only a single whale was sighted, on 26 August near Cape York (Fisher 1819, Ross 1819). During the rest of the nineteenth century whales were seldom sighted in Melville Bay and almost never off the shores of Avanersuaq. The nineteenth-century whalers probably never once killed a bowhead in Greenland waters north of Melville Bay. There seem to be only two records of bowheads in Avanersuaq waters since 1818: Malaurie (1982: 52) in 1950 or 1951 interviewed an old Eskimo who mentioned 1909 as, among other things, "the last year we saw a big baleen whale spouting near Qaanaaq"; and five were seen swimming north off Saunders Island on 25 July 1903 by members of the Danish Literary Expedition (Mylius-Erichsen and Moltke 1906: 424–25).

If the whalers did not exterminate the bowhead in Avanersuaq, could this have been done by its Inuhuit inhabitants? At Cape York in 1818 Edward Sabine (1819: 83) understood from them that "their fathers could kill whales, which they cannot do now, but by what means they were unable to explain." He inferred, correctly, that the kayak and umiaq, which they lacked in 1818, must have been used by their ancestors. Peary (1898b: 380) regarded the bowhead as extinct in Avanersuaq, though he noticed whale bones built into the walls of nearly all the Inuhuit winter houses. It seems inconceivable that the Inuhuit could have killed all the whales, abandoned the kayak and umiaq, and almost forgotten about them between 1616 and 1818. More probably, it was the choking of the fjords with ice virtually year-round by a deteriorating climate that, perhaps around 1700, caused the migratory bowheads to forsake their most northerly summer haunts in Baffin Bay and at the same time rendered the kayak and umiaq unnecessary to the local Eskimos: the ice would now serve as a platform from which to hunt narwhals and seals.

John Ross (1819: 132) was puzzled to learn in 1818 from the Inuhuit he met off Cape York of an animal called *humminick,* which "had a horn on its back" and was too large for them to kill. His companion, the naturalist Edward Sabine (1819: 88), wrote of this same report: "It appears, however, that there actually is a large land animal (and horned, for so they describe it) inhabiting Greenland, and called *umimuk* by the Esquimaux who have never had any communication with Danes." He correctly surmised that this was the same animal a skull of which had been found on an ice floe off the West Greenland coast in about 1770 by the Danish missionary at Frederikshåb (Paamiut), Otto Fabricius (1929: 70–71), namely the *umimmak* or musk-ox, the first living examples of which in Greenland were not seen by white people until 1869. These long-haired dark brown grazing animals with their curved horns usually lived in small groups, often in isolated grassy valleys, and had lived and grazed in such Arctic oases for hundreds, perhaps thousands, of years. They had no natural enemies but the wolf and no defense against humans, once dogs had caused them to form a tight group with all its members facing their massive horns outward. Then they were either shot down at point-blank range by the explorers, usually after being photographed, or killed by the Eskimos, who certainly did not find them too big, with spears.

Musk-oxen were still living in Avanersuaq in 1818 and later in the nineteenth century. Kane found numerous not very ancient skulls and other skeletal remains of them in 1853–55 in Inglefield Land. He states: "None of us saw a living specimen; but the great number of skeletons, their state of preservation and probable foot-tracks, when taken in conjunction with the information of the Esquimaux, leave me no room to doubt that these animals have been recent visitors" (Kane 1856a: 456). And he was able to report that "the last of these animals seen by the Esquimaux was in the late spring of 1850, near Cape George Russell" on the coast of Inglefield Land (p. 459). "Here Metek saw a group of six." By that time the musk-ox was evidently a rarity because Hayes (1860: 55), who had collected twelve skulls in 1853–54 while serving as surgeon on Kane's expedition, mentions that some Eskimos who purloined a buffalo skin in autumn 1854 believed they had acquired "the skin of an umingmak (musk-ox), an animal of which they had heard, but which they had never seen."

In the winter of 1857–58, while the *Fox* was drifting helplessly in the Baffin Bay ice pack, M'Clintock whiled away the time listening to his interpreter Carl Petersen recounting his experiences on the Kane expedition. He writes (1859: 76):

> I have been questioning Petersen about the bones of the musk oxen found in Smith's Sound; he says the decayed skulls of about twenty were found, all of them to the north of the 79th parallel. As they were all without lower jaws, he says they were killed by Esquimaux, who leave upon the spot

the skulls of large animals, but the weight of the lower jaw being so trifling it is allowed to remain attached to the flesh and tongue. The skull of a musk ox with its massive horns cannot weigh less than 30 lbs.

On his second visit to Avanersuaq in 1860–61 in command of his own expedition, Hayes (1867: 370) was told by Qulutana that "the musk-ox was supposed to have been once numerous along the entire coast, and that they are still occasionally seen. No longer ago than the previous winter, a hunter of Wolstenholme Sound, near a place called Oomeak [Uummannaq], had come upon two animals and killed one of them." This reference to them in winter 1859–60 is the last record of living musk-oxen in Avanersuaq.

The musk-ox, then, formerly existed in Avanersuaq as it still does in neighboring Ellesmere Island and farther north in Greenland. It was hunted by the Inuhuit in the nineteenth century. But was it ever a dietary staple of theirs? And could the musk-ox hunt, as Steensby (1910: 400–401) speculated, ever have induced them to abandon those traditional Eskimo means of livelihood in the summer months, the kayak for hunting sea mammals and the bow and arrow for hunting caribou? Probably the musk-ox never provided a major part of the Inuhuit diet, nor is it likely that they made any significant contribution to its disappearance from Avanersuaq. The claim (Vibe 1986) that their extinction was caused by a combination of "Eskimo spears" and "American and English guns" is unacceptable. No American or English gun was ever fired at a musk-ox in Avanersuaq. A more likely explanation is that of Inuutersuaq, that heavy rain one winter in Inglefield Land, where he thought musk-oxen remained years after they had disappeared from the rest of Avanersuaq in the first half of the nineteenth century, led to the ground becoming coated with a layer of ice so that the animals could no longer reach the vegetation they lived on, and many starved to death. Soon afterward, the musk-ox disappeared altogether from Avanersuaq (Ulloriaq 1984).

The history of the musk-ox in Avanersuaq was reopened in 1986, when the government of Greenland reintroduced it with Danish and American help. Twenty-seven were airlifted from Søndre Strømfjord Air Base and released in three different places in Avanersuaq: seven at Cape Atholl, six on the shores of McCormick Fjord, and the remainder at Rensselaer Bay in Inglefield Land (Vibe 1986). These animals were descendants of those transferred from East to West Greenland in 1962 and 1965, which had flourished and multiplied since then in the Søndre Strømfjord area (Vibe 1981).

The third large mammal to become extinct or nearly extinct in Avanersuaq was the caribou, to use the North American name derived from the Cree Indian word, rather than reindeer, with its connotation of domestic herding (Vibe 1967, 1981; Roby et al. 1984; Meldgaard 1986). Although caribou (*tuttu* or *tugto* in Greenlandic) apparently were common and widespread in Avanersuaq in the first half of the nineteenth century, the Inuhuit, according to Qalasersuaq in 1850, "occasionally, but very rarely succeeded in killing" one (Markham 1866: 131). The reason was their lack of suitable weapons: they had no bows and arrows until after the introduction of this weapon from Canada in 1862, and the caribou could not be brought to bay with dogs as could the musk-ox. Both Taateraaq and Torngi told the Danes in 1903 how they had formerly killed caribou with bows and arrows (Mylius-Erichsen and Moltke 1906: 208–9, 542–45), and Steensby (1910: 303–4 confirmed by Holtved 1967: 108) was told in 1909 that caribou had been hunted with bows and arrows on either side of Olrik Fjord. Long lines of sealskin ropes were stretched between cairns across the routes used by the animals when migrating between their low-lying grassy summer pastures and their more upland and inland winter lichen pastures. The caribou, loath to cross these lines, followed along them to where the hunter was waiting in concealment.

Before the Inuhuit began to kill caribou with bows and arrows after 1862, both Kane and Hayes had shot them in Inglefield Land for food. In the first two months of his overwintering near Iita in western Inglefield Land in 1860–61, Hayes's (1867: 152) game list was headed by 74 caribou. In spite of his fearsome reputation as a game slaughterer, Peary's game list on 15 April 1892 after the overwintering at Red Cliff House included only 41 caribou (1898a: 242); later Josephine Peary shot 2 (1893: 193). At Anniversary Lodge on the shore of Bowdoin Fjord in autumn-winter 1893–94 he did better: at least 128 were bagged; but only 21 are mentioned in autumn 1894 (Peary 1898b). By this time caribou were also being shot in Avanersuaq by passing whalers, though probably not in large numbers and as much for sport as for the pot. On 17 June 1877 a party from the Dundee whaler *Active* went ashore at Cape Dudley Digges and shot four caribou out of seven seen (MacKintosh 1884). Ten years later, Captain Milne touched on Avanersuaq at several places in the Dundee ship *Esquimaux*. On 26 June 1887 he "hooked onto the land floe near Cape Dudley Digges" and reported, "Reindeer very numerous here." On 5 July he made fast to the land ice at Cape Parry and noted, "a good many reindeer here; got four" (Wordie Collection of whaling logs, MS. 1159, Scott Polar Research Institute, Cambridge, England).

Caribou were still common in much of Avanersuaq up to the early years of the twentieth century. In the south, the Danes reported them in 1903 on Wolstenholme Island, in the hills behind Uummannaq, and around Booth Sound on the grassy flats along the coast southeast of Cape Parry, where Milne had shot them. More than ten years after Peary had ceased shooting them in the Inglefield Gulf area, a hunting expedition into their Olrik Fjord stronghold in the autumn of 1907 by Knud Rasmussen and a group of Inuhuit bagged around seventy animals (Møller 1961). A year later, in 1908, big game hunter Harry Whitney's party shot seven caribou and a fawn in this same place.

In western Inglefield Land, where in 1860 Hayes (1867: 107) watched "several herds, amounting in the aggregate to something like a hundred animals . . . browsing upon the dead grass of the late summer" around the shores of Lake Alida at the head of Foulke Fjord, caribou were still abundant during the Crocker Land Expedition's stay at Iita in 1913–17. The expedition's doctor, Harrison Hunt, recorded bagging forty-two animals in September 1914 (Hunt and Thompson 1980: 58–60). In seldom-visited eastern Inglefield Land caribou were also abundant. When Torngi wintered at Inuarfissuaq in Marshall Bay in 1915 there were still plenty inland from there, though the famished members of the Second Thule Expedition, returning through Inglefield Land in August and September 1917, managed to shoot only three (Rasmussen 1928: 28–31, 174–75).

Sometime between about 1915 and 1930 caribou became extremely scarce in Avanersuaq. None has been reported from the south of the area since the Danes recorded them there in 1903. Further north, around Olrik Fjord, the caribou had apparently been absent for many years before one was sighted in 1936 (Vibe 1948: 21–27). Three, three, and five were shot there respectively in 1937, 1938, and 1939. In 1965, when it was thought that this Olrik Fjord population had completely died out, "nine semi-domesticated reindeer were introduced" there "from central Southwest Greenland" (Roby et al. 1984). In July 1978 three feral caribou bucks were seen on the shore of Lake Taserssuaq, between Inglefield Gulf and Olrik Fjord, but whether descendants of these introduced animals still survive around Olrik Fjord is doubtful.

In the north of Avanersuaq the caribou seem to have fared better. In 1937 Shackleton (p. 104) claimed, presumably on the strength of information from the Eskimos with whom he overwintered at Iita with the Oxford University Ellesmere Land Expedition in 1934–35, that "the last reindeer to be seen in Etah was killed by Dr. Hunt of MacMillan's 1914–17 Expedition." He had not read *Etah and Beyond,* published in 1927, in which MacMillan reported shooting four caribou not far from Iita in 1923–24. Still, we can be fairly sure that there were no caribou in western Inglefield Land in 1937. The Eskimos with Erik Holtved (1942: 160–63, 173, 181) at Inuarfissuaq in eastern Inglefield Land in summer 1936 could find very few caribou inland from there; after days of hunting they were lucky to kill six, two of them fawns. Jean Malaurie, who explored Inglefield Land more thoroughly than any other white man, mentions only one caribou seen alive by his party in 1951 (1982: 322). A young buck was photographed there, near Dallas Bay, by a geologist in 1973. Though in 1978 no caribou were seen during two aerial surveys totaling six hours of flight over Inglefield Land (Roby et al. 1984), Morten Meldgaard (1986) was told that the Eskimos "have successfully hunted caribou in Inglefield Land," mainly in the center and east, "in recent years." Evidently a few have survived there throughout the present century.

Was the Avanersuaq caribou nearly wiped out by the pressure of hunting by man? That seems unlikely. The caribou was "never an important food resource" for the Inuhuit, as one of them told Malaurie (1982: 440), and shooting by white men was never persistent over the years. Though Inuhuit hunting may have caused local and sometimes only temporary extinctions in restricted areas, such as Wolstenholme Island and the peninsula of Tuttulis-suaq in Melville Bay, it must surely have been unusual or changing climatic conditions that caused the decline in caribou numbers in Avanersuaq as a whole. Heavy precipitation combined with periods of thaw in the winter cause the formation of ice crusts which prevent the caribou from reaching their food just as they did the musk-oxen in the previous century. This happened in Avanersuaq at the beginning of the twentieth century. In the spring of 1900, for instance, dead caribou were found scattered about over the hills (Meldgaard 1986). Probably the reasons for the disappearance of both musk-ox and caribou were similar, and overkill by humans was not one of them.

A fourth large mammal, which was probably never very common in Avanersuaq, is the polar bear (*Ursus maritimus*), *nanoq* or *nanook* in Greenlandic (Vibe 1967, 1981). Unlike the caribou, it has always been an essential element of Inuhuit subsistence, not for food, though bear meat was welcome, but for clothing. The Inuhuit men and boys invariably wore bearskin breeches or trousers, reaching to just below the knees, both in summer and winter, and some wear them still (Malaurie 1982: 331) (Fig. 7). "There are three pairs of trousers in a bearskin," claimed Peter Freuchen (1961: 53) categorically. One pair per person was the norm, and though a pair might last several years, annual replacement was preferred (Holtved 1967: 105). Vibe in 1968 estimated the annual kill at fifteen to twenty bears, providing around fifty pairs of bearskin breeches, which would have been sufficient up to the 1920s at least to provide every male with a new pair every other year or so. Special expeditions had to be made by the Inuhuit to hunt bears, either south into Melville Bay, north toward the Humboldt Glacier, or west across to Ellesmere Island where in 1960 two Inuhuit hunters were fined by the Canadian authorities for shooting a mother bear with her cub (Vibe 1968). Polar bears were brought to bay with dogs and killed with lances made of narwhal tusks or bones lashed together and tipped with iron (Kane 1856a: 205) or, later, rifles. Only a small proportion of bearskins obtained by the Inuhuit were traded in.

Instead of cutting it up for trousers, the white man preferred his bearskin whole, complete with head and claws. A polar bear unlucky enough to be seen by an explorer or whaler was invariably shot, unless it was taken alive. On board the Hull whaleship *Diana* in 1866 the surgeon, C. E. Smith (1923: 31), recorded "Captain Gravill's chat about bears," part of which went as follows:

> We took that young bear home and sold him for £12. I've known good ones fetch £20. I suppose they are bought for Zoölogical Gardens.
>
> When we want to catch bears alive, we "snickle" them with a rope round the neck when they are swimming in the water. We prefer to "snickle" young bears, as it is difficult to find a cask large enough to hold a full-grown one. We cover the head of the cask with a grating of iron hooping riveted together. We feed the bears with crang if we have any, but they'll eat almost anything; I've fed 'em with soup. Sometimes I've given them a little whale-oil, but that makes them dainty. We heave buckets of salt water over them daily, and play upon them with a hose to keep them clean. If the weather is calm we hoist them up, cask and all, with a tackle and drop them overboard, or else set the cask on end and half fill it with water.

On board the *Falcon* in August 1894, somewhere off Cape York, the two Scandinavians Eivind Astrup and Axel Ohlin calmly and somewhat supercil-iously continued their game of whist in the cabin and ignored the polar bear hunt on deck: an adult bear with two half-grown young bears became the vic-tims of a fusillade from twelve marksmen, who fired a hundred shots at a range of about a hundred yards (Ohlin 1895a: 127). It was on the West Green-land coast south of Avanersuaq that, in 1850, a British naval party from HMS *Pioneer* fired four pounds of small shot, "a waistcoat-button and the blade of a knife, which by great ingenuity, they had contrived to cram down one of their muskets" at a polar bear without seriously harming it (Osborn 1865: 39–40). It seems that neither the needs of the Inuhuit nor the sport of white men has made serious inroads on the polar bear population of northwest Greenland.

The wolf (*Canis lupus*) was probably never more than an occasional visitor to Avanersuaq in historic times (Dawes et al. 1986: 127–28), but two other land mammals played a significant role in Inuhuit subsistence, the fox and the hare. The skin of the Arctic fox (*Alopex lagopus*) became an object of trade at the close of the nineteenth century. Even before then, winter fox trapping, which was carried out exclusively by the women, was essential to meet the Eskimos' clothing requirements (Holtved 1967): the man's hooded outer coat required eight fox skins, the woman's coat required seven, the *amaat,* or woman's coat with special hood in which to carry a baby, required nine fox skins, and the woman's trousers (Fig. 5) were made from twenty-three sepa-rate pieces of skin from at least two different animals, one white and one blue. The Arctic fox holds its own in Avanersuaq in spite of commercial trapping by the Inuhuit. At Thule Air Base it has learned to live and breed in close association with people. In 1983 it was common to see one waiting for scraps outside the back door of Dundas Dining Hall (Fig. 10), and a litter of cubs was raised in a culvert. These animals were thought to constitute a threat to health and were subsequently shot. The Arctic hare (*Lepus arcticus*), abundant in Avanersuaq, was trapped by the Inuhuit both for its fur and its flesh. The fur, at least in former times, was used for stockings and inner mitts. Two skins were required for one stocking. Hares were formerly caught by means of snares fixed between low stone walls (Holtved 1967, Vibe 1981).

It is, of course, marine, not terrestrial mammals that have formed the mainstay of the Inuhuit subsistence economy (Vibe 1950). These mammals are the narwhal (*Monodon monoceros*), the beluga or white whale (*Delphinapterus leucas*), the walrus (*Odobenus rosmarus*), and the three species of seal, the ringed seal (*Phoca hispida*), the harp seal (*Pagophilus groenlandicus*), and the bearded seal (*Erignathus barbatus*). The impact of humans on some of these animals merits consideration.

The narwhal is a small whale around 15 feet (4½ m) long, the male of which has a single ivory tusk that grows in a spiral fashion to a length of 6 feet (2 m). It is a common summer visitor to Avanersuaq. Before the introduction of the kayak in 1862, the Inuhuit hunted it from the ice edge. Ross (1819: 131) described how they killed it with "a harpoon, the barbed part of which is about three inches long, having a line attached to it of about five fathoms [30 feet or 9 m] in length, the other end of which is fastened to a buoy of a seal's skin made into a bag and inflated. The blade is fixed on the end of the shaft in such a manner that it may be disengaged from the handle after it is fixed in the animal, and the shaft is then pulled back by a line which is tied to it for the purpose." The animal plunged but was quickly tired out by the drag of the buoy and was dispatched with spears. Nowadays the rifle does the work of the spear and the motorboat supplements the kayak.

The narwhal formed an essential element in the Inuhuit economy because its blubber was by far the best fuel for the lamps with which the winter houses were lit and warmed, food was cooked, and clothes were dried. It also provided extra strong sinews for lashing and for sewing boots, outer clothing, tents, and the like. The tusk, which was used from the early period of contacts with white men as a trading article, was also used in the construction of spears and sledges. The meat was eaten with relish by both dogs and people and the skin, called *mattak,* was regarded as a delicacy and was much prized for sustenance on a long sledge journey. The annual narwhal catch in Avanersuaq is concentrated in Inglefield Gulf (Silis 1984) and appears to have been fairly stable, at around 150 animals, since World War II (Malaurie 1982: 435, Born and Olesen 1986: 73). It was probably no higher than that before then (Vibe 1950: 79). Since on one occasion in August 1984 Erik Born and Lars Olesen (1986, and Born 1986) counted 4,043 narwhals swimming past their observation post on the island of Qeqertat, the largest of the Harvard Islands, at the head of Inglefield Gulf, it looks as though the Avanersuaq narwhal population, with its probable annual recruitment of 10 percent newborn animals, cannot have been seriously endangered by Inuhuit hunting in the past.

The narwhal, with its beautiful ivory tusk, was under pressure from explorers and whalers as well as from Eskimos. Captain John Gravill knew what he was doing when he harpooned some while the *Diana* was delayed by ice off Cape York in 1866: narwhal ivory was then worth up to thirty shillings a pound (0.5 kg), and he had had tusks weighing up to 22 pounds (10 kg). The Eskimos visiting his ship were glad to go off with "their sledges heavily loaded with narwhale skin, blubber, the long sinews of the animal" (Smith 1923: 34–35 and MS. in Town Docks Museum, Hull) while he kept the tusks. The United States National Academy of Sciences instructed Captain Hall's North Polar Expedition of 1871 to collect as many skeletons of seals and whales as possible and mentioned the narwhal as "particularly desired" (Davis 1876: 653). The big game hunters were after narwhals, too, but Harry Whitney (1910: 346–69) had to be content with a single tusk only 3 feet (1 m) long after several narwhal hunts in 1909.

One of the purposes of the American Museum's expedition led by George Putnam in 1926 (Putnam 1926, Raven 1927, Streeter 1929) was to obtain specimens of the narwhal for a new exhibition in the Hall of Ocean Life. After visiting the seabird colonies in Parker Snow Bay and narrowly escaping shipwreck on Northumberland Island, where their ship the *Effie M. Morrissey* went aground, the expedition called at Qaanaaq. During a midnight hymn-singing session with the pastor and missionary Jens Olsen, whom the American visitors dubbed the "Hunting Bishop from Holsteinborg," narwhals were spotted offshore swimming up the fjord. Author Daniel W. Streeter was with the expedition; he gives us a lively descripton of the narwhal hunt that followed (1929: 265–67):

> Suddenly there was an excited cry. The noise ceased abruptly. Narwhal! There they were, shoal after shoal, running down the Gulf! A babble of wild yells broke out. The Bishop acted like one possessed—and that's just what he was, possessed with the single idea of capturing one of those narwhal. The hymn was forgotten. In ten seconds he had transformed from Prelate to primitive hunter. With one bound he jumped through the narrow sod window and galloped for his kayak, running into the water up to his knees in shoving it off. Ten seconds after the narwhal were sighted the house was deserted.
>
> The gulf was alive with arched rolling bodies. Their moist skins gleamed and sparkled. As they rhythmically rose and fell, the air forced from their enormous lungs through a vent on top of their heads hissed audibly, and formed a plume of mist that hovered above them like an evanescent halo.

The long twisted ivory tusks projecting from their snouts were plainly visible. There were dozens of them. Here was meat for the long winter rolling right past the front door.

The chase commenced. Down from the head of the gulf the narwhal continued to come, shoal after shoal. . . .

It was a splendid exhibition of primitive hunting, staged as though for our especial entertainment directly in front of the Bishopric. Half a dozen kayakers were strung out in a long row, motionless as bronze images, waiting for their prey. The narwhal were obliged to run a gauntlet composed of primitive man after meat. . . .

Singly, and in groups, the narwhal were pursued by the kayakers. It looked like some kind of aquatic game. Harpoons were flicked, recovered, and flicked again, but none seemed to reach their marks. Soon fish and hunters had vanished into the labyrinth of bergs, and the surface of the gulf once more threw back, unbroken, the reflection of the serene Arctic sky.

The hunt eventually proved successful. Five adult narwhals were hauled on board the *Morrissey*. Plaster casts of heads, tails, and fins were made, photographs were taken from every angle, measurements were made, and strips of skin were removed, all with a view to the construction of a life-size model narwhal in the museum. Finally, the Eskimos helped strip the meat off the bones so that the skeletons could be taken back to New York; the meat, of course, was given to them. Having provided the museum with its narwhal, they now at once set out to obtain walrus specimens for it.

The mussel-feeding walrus, which is still an abundant animal year-round in Avanersuaq, has been a vital source of meat for Inuhuit and especially for their dogs. Without walrus meat they could not survive through the winter months. Moreover, the tusks were in great demand for toolmaking. The present-day annual catch of a little over two hundred animals provides around eighty tons of meat for the dogs on which winter transport and communications in Avanersuaq are still based. According to Malaurie (1982: 435), "One walrus provides a team of ten dogs with food for two months in the winter"; he adds that around 1950, the annual walrus catch was also about two hundred animals.

Before the introduction of the kayak in 1862, the Inuhuit hunted walruses either when they came ashore to rest or from the ice edge using a harpoon and line. The line was anchored to the ice with an iron-pointed ice hook or *tooq* and was made out of the entire skin of a bearded seal cut spirally off the carcass in a single long strip (Kane 1856a: 411–14, 1856b: 71). Buoys made of inflated sealskins were used to tire out the animal and prevent its carcass from sinking. The coming of the rifle has simplified the Inuhuit's walrus hunt, but the animals still have to be securely harpooned before they are killed with the

1. Looking over Inglefield Gulf from Qaanaaq in early July. The sea ice has not yet broken up, but shallow meltwater pools are scattered over its surface. The tracks are made by the trucks which collect ice during the winter from the still frozen-in icebergs. Eskimo sleds and dog teams can be seen parked on the edge of the sea ice beyond the wide shore lead, which is negotiable only by using the ice floes as stepping stones. Photograph by the author, 1984.

2. The North Water south of Cape Atholl, 17 July 1983. On the horizon, mist-enshrouded Conical Rock, onetime whalers' landmark, appears to the right of Cape Dudley Digges. Under flights of dovekies, the last remnants of the winter's land-fast ice or ice foot are drifting out to sea in the foreground. Photograph by author.

3. The mountain and former Inuhuit settlement of Uummannaq. The word means "the place which resembles a heart" (Vahl et al. 1929: 457) and originally referred to the mountain. The winter houses, abandoned in 1953 when their occupants were evacuated to Qaanaaq, were built of wood in place of the earlier stones and given outer walls of turf. Photograph by the author, 1985.

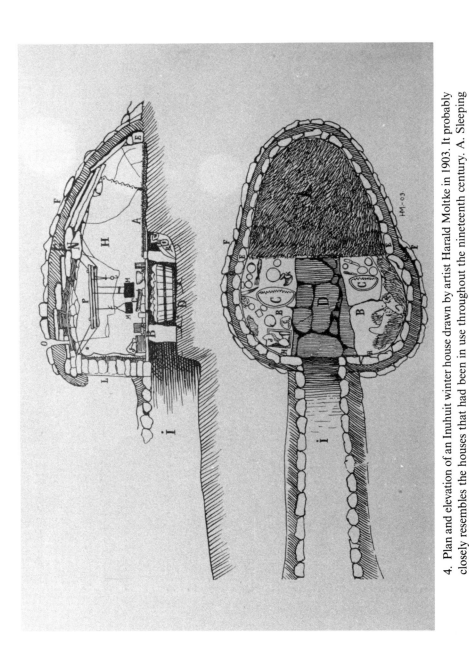

4. Plan and elevation of an Inuhuit winter house drawn by artist Harald Moltke in 1903. It probably closely resembles the houses that had been in use throughout the nineteenth century. A. Sleeping platform. B. Meat shelf. C. Soapstone blubber lamps. D. Floor stones. E. and F. Internal and external wall stones. G. Turves. H. Space above sleeping platform. I. Entrance. J. Meat box. K. Woman's knife. L. Gut skin window. M. Cooking pots. N. Roofing stones. O. Air hole. P. Clothes drying rack. R. Space under sleeping platform. From Mylius-Erichsen and Moltke 1906: 456.

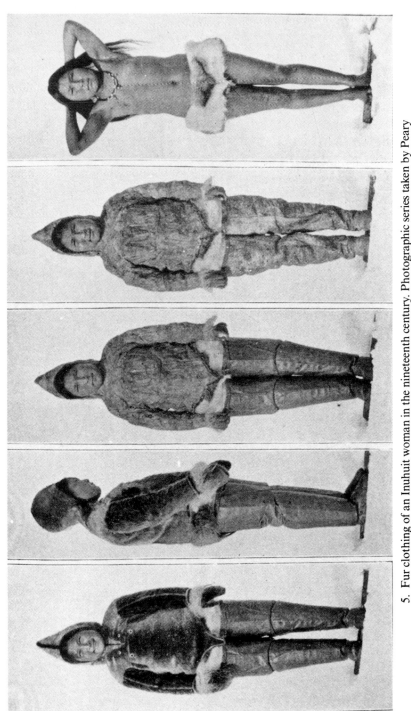

5. Fur clothing of an Inuhuit woman in the nineteenth century. Photographic series taken by Peary (1898a: 495 and 510) in the 1890s showing the complete costume in nine separate pieces worn by a young woman. In the two left-hand photographs she is shown wearing hooded sealskin coat, sealskin mitts, and sealskin boots. In the center, coat and mitts removed, the hooded bird skin shirt with feathers inward is revealed. In the left hand of the two photographs on the right she has removed her sealskin boots, revealing caribou skin stockings. Finally, on the extreme right, she retains only the short fox skin trousers that fill the gap between the upper and lower garments and are visible in all the photographs.

6. The meeting of Inuhuit and Europeans on 10 August 1818. Commander John Ross and Lieutenant William Parry are shown exchanging gifts with four Inuhuit. According to Ross, the plate, only part of which is shown here, is an exact copy of a drawing made by his West Greenlandic interpreter John Sacheuse and afterward presented to him by the artist, who may have depicted himself holding out a shirt in the background. From Ross 1819: facing p. 80.

7. Inuhuit men on board Amundsen's ship *Gjøa* on 14 or 15 August 1903. They offered their services as laborers and helped load heavy cases of provisions onto the *Gjøa* from the depot left on Dalrymple Rock by two Dundee whalers. Their fur clothing is that normally worn by Inuhuit men in the nineteenth century, fox skin coats, bearskin breeches, and sealskin boots, which are substantially shorter than the women's thigh-length ones. From Amundsen 1907: 30.

8. The Wanderers' Home. On 10 July 1984 my son and I found the ruins of the hut built and lived in by the withdrawal party from Kane's expedition led by Hayes (1860) in autumn 1854. Parts of a cast-iron stove, fragments of wood, copper nails, pieces of cloth and leather, and bits of broken glass were strewn about. Comparison of photographs shows that hardly a stone has tumbled from the walls since Peary halted briefly here and photographed the hut in August 1894. Photograph by author.

9. Josephine Peary gives away unwanted expedition utensils while packing up at Red Cliff House in August 1892 (Peary 1893: 204–5). The photograph, captioned in Fitzhugh Green's book on Peary (1926: 176) "Seamstresses rewarded. Mrs. Peary distributing prized pots and pans to faithful native needleworkers," shows her Inuhuit household staff wearing the traditional women's thigh-length seal-skin boots and short fox skin trousers shown in Figure 5.

10. Arctic fox at Thule Air Base, 1983. The animal is waiting for scraps outside Dundas Dining Hall. The Inuhuit economy has always been partly dependent on fox skins, which in the nineteenth century were used for their clothes and in the twentieth for trading. In spite of a probable annual cull of up to a thousand animals throughout both periods, the species remains abundant in the coastal regions of Avanersuaq. Photograph by the author.

11. Dovekies or little auks at Iterlak near Cape Atholl, 17 July 1984. Once a vital element in the Inuhuit diet, this starling-sized seabird is Avanersuaq's most abundant bird. It breeds in swarms in the steep coastal scree slopes, laying a single bluish-white egg deep among the rocks, hopefully out of reach of the Arctic fox. Photograph by the author.

12. The Tent, largest of the Cape York meteorites, being loaded aboard the *Hope* on 20 August 1897. This largest meteorite so far recovered is one of the highlights of the American Museum of Natural History in New York, where it is exhibited in the Arthur Ross Hall of Meteorites. It comes first on "a short list of some of the more unusual and famous objects on exhibition in the museum," according to an official brochure. From Peary 1898b: 581.

13. Comer's Midden at Uummannaq photographed in 1937 by Danish archaeologist Eric Holtved (1944a: 145). This Inuhuit rubbish tip, partly excavated in 1916, partly washed away by the sea, was on the south shore of Wolstenholme Fjord directly in front of one of the Eskimo houses evacuated in 1953 and now in ruins. Holtved removed nearly all of what is visible below the house, returning in 1946 to complete the job.

14. Thule Air Base, looking south across the broad valley called Pituffik from the North Mountain. The center of the lake on the left is still ice-covered. The 810-meter-high summit of P-mountain is hidden by clouds. In the part of the base visible, from front to rear, one can see oil storage tanks, barrack blocks and other buildings, three giant hangars, and a part of the main runway. Photographed on 5 July 1983 by the author.

15. Qaanaaq, capital of Avanersuaq, which on 1 January 1984 was reckoned to have had a population of 439 persons (Ministeriet for Grønland 1985: 144–45). The fifty or so Danes live in the larger, more spaced-out houses nearest the camera, which is pointing westward along the shore of Murchison Sound. Photographed by the author on 17 June 1985 from a helicopter.

16. An Inuhuit dog team at Qaanaaq enjoys a well-earned rest during the summer. Still the sole means of winter transport in Avanersuaq, dogs like these carried Peary and Cook, Rasmussen and Koch, and many other Arctic explorers to their destinations and back. For the Inuhuit they once also formed an essential meat reserve against times of famine, and their pelts were often used for clothing. Photograph by author, 9 July 1984.

rifle. Otherwise many wounded walruses, sinking below the surface, would be lost. According to Born and Kristensen, fewer than a quarter of those struck are subsequently lost.

The Inuhuit walrus hunt, which required a highly developed technology and a remarkable degree of skill and involved a relatively small number of animals, was very different from the wholesale slaughter of walruses with rifles which the nineteenth-century explorers considered excellent sport. On 3 July 1861 Hayes (1867: 404–10) and his companions attacked a herd off Foulke Fjord. Although they "killed at least a dozen, and mortally wounded as many more," they contrived to secure only two dead animals, one of which Hayes described as "a fine specimen to add to my Natural History collections." Peary organized walrus-shooting as a joint Eskimo-American enterprise. Edward J. House, who hunted big game all over the world, devoted part of his book *A Hunter's Camp-Fires* (1909) to a description of such a walrus hunt in Whale Sound in August 1899 on board the *Diana*. A single hunt yielded fifteen walruses, "a small portion" of the number killed and taken to Iita that autumn to provide dog food for Peary's coming overwintering. George Borup took part in the Peary walrus hunts of August 1909 and wrote about them as follows (Peary 1910: 80):

> Walrus-hunting is the best sport in the shooting line that I know. There is something doing when you tackle a herd of fifty-odd, weighing between one and two tons each, that go for you whether wounded or not; that can punch a hole through eight inches of young ice; that try to climb into the boat to get at or upset you,—we never could make out which, and didn't care, as the result to us would have been the same—or else try to ram your boat and stave holes in it.
>
> Get in a mix-up with a herd, when every man in the whale-boat is standing by to repel borders, hitting them over the head with oars, boat-hooks, axes, and yelling like a cheering section at a football game to try to scare them off; with the rifles going like young Gatling guns, and the walruses bellowing from pain and anger, coming to the surface with mad rushes, sending the water up in the air till you would think a flock of geysers was turned loose in your immediate vicinity—oh, it's great!

Seals (Vibe 1950, Holtved 1967) were formerly hunted by the Inuhuit on the ice, either by stationing a hunter armed with a spear at each breathing hole or by stalking them on the surface of the ice, in which case the hunter lay down, moved along on his elbows, and made grunting noises, indeed, pretended to be a seal (Fisher 1819: 60, Hendrik 1878: 34–35). Nowadays nets are used and a white canvas shooting screen is often employed to conceal the hunter approaching a seal on the ice. Every part of the animal was traditionally used by the Inuhuit. The meat was enjoyed boiled, frozen, or raw; the blubber was used for lamps or for food; the skin for tents, covering kayaks, making coats or boots, lashings, dog harnesses, buoys for kayak hunting, bags for storing dovekies (little auks), and a hundred and one other things. The intestines also had many uses, for example, for making egg sausages. Of the three species of seal mentioned above, the ringed seal was by far the most important for the Inuhuit, but the bearded seal provided for a few specialized needs: the skin made strong elastic lines and straps, parts of it being excellent for boot soles, which would last a whole winter, and the small intenstine, if not eaten, for it was regarded as a great delicacy frozen or broiled, could be inflated, dried, split, and then sewn together to make translucent window panes for winter houses. The harp seal was less often killed by the Inuhuit; in 1950 the catch was estimated at some fifty animals each summer.

Birds were also killed by both Eskimos (Ekblaw 1919) and whites. One species in particular, the dovekie or little auk (*Alle alle*) (Figs. 2 and 11), has been of great importance to the Inuhuit. Indeed, it seems possible that before the introduction of the kayak in 1862, they were entirely dependent on the dovekie for food in the months of July and August, when the fjords were unfrozen. Many of their most frequented settlements were situated near the scree slopes where these tiny seabirds nest in hundreds of thousands. Their colonies, which are tenanted between May and August, are to be found wherever suitable rocky slopes occur near areas of unfrozen sea, that is, where the North Water touches on the Avanersuaq coast. The Inuhuit settlements of Savissivik, Cape York, Siorapaluk, Neqi, and Iita were or are all close to such dovekie colonies. In 1875 the naturalist of the British Arctic Expedition, H. W. Feilden, reasoned that "from the large amount of bones and feathers lying around the huts of the Eskimo village of Etah, it is evident that these birds contribute largely to the support of the Arctic Highlanders during summer" (Nares 1878b: 215).

Dovekies were caught in flight at the breeding colonies with "a small net, made of light strings of seal-skin knitted together very ingeniously. The staff by which it was held was about ten feet long" (Hayes 1867: 391) and, according to Kane, was a narwhal tusk. Traditional hollows among the boulders were used as catching stations. As many as eight or ten birds could be caught with one sweep of the net; they were killed instantly either by finger pressure on the heart or by crushing the head between the teeth and then cached on the spot, under piles of stones. The caches were apparently indicated by marker stones: Fisher (1819: 62–63) describes how, in August 1818 on the scree slopes near Cape York, near each of these caches, "several stones were set up on end, or two or three laid over the other; these we supposed to be intended for marks to direct them to their respective collections, in the case of their being covered by a fall of snow before their return."

On Northumberland Island in December 1855 Hayes (1860: 305) and his companions were treated to a meal of dovekies by their Eskimo hosts:

> Northumberland Island is, during the breeding season, a favourite resort of the little auk; and with a providence which I had not seen among the Esquimaux in other places, the people here seem to have collected the birds in great numbers. Soon after our arrival one of the women brought into the hut a solid cube of them, a foot in diameter. This was the contents of one of their *caches,* made during the last summer. The birds had been thrown in as they were caught, and they were now all frozen together *en masse.* We were at liberty to break them off with a stone, one at a time, and, after removing the skin, to eat them in their actual condition,—or to wait until the women should have cooked them. We practised both alternatives. The pot would not hold more than half a dozen birds at one time, and it was replenished as fast as emptied.

But not all the dovekies were cached. Fisher's commander in 1818, John Ross (1819: 107), mentions that one of the Eskimos who came aboard "had a bag full of little awks, took out one in our presence, and devoured it raw." A favorite method of storing and eating these birds was to cram a hundred or more into a specially prepared sealskin with the blubber still adhering to it. The sackful of auks was then left under a pile of stones for several months, by which time the carcasses had blended with the blubber and fermented. The meat that resulted was known as *kiviaq* and was one of the greatest delicacies known to the Inuhuit.

Another important food bird for the Inuhuit was the thick-billed murre or Brünnich's guillemot (*Uria lomvia*), called *agpa* or *appa* by the Eskimos. The cliffs at the western end of Saunders Island seem to have been the main source of supply of these birds. Those that the Eskimos gave to the withdrawal party from Kane's expedition in autumn 1854 when it was living in the Wanderers' Home near Booth Sound came from this colony. More than one hundred of them were brought in a single month; on one occasion the Americans watched an Eskimo woman eat four of them at a sitting.

A third bird species that has been a significant element in the Inuhuit diet is the common eider (*Somateria mollissima*). In this case the bird's eggs have been more important than the bird itself. It nests in thousands on a handful of small offshore islets in Avanersuaq which, before the reintroduction of the kayak, could have been reached in the birds' breeding season only with difficulty across rotting sea ice, if at all. Kane implies that, in a late season, if the breeding islets were still surrounded by ice, the birds' egg-laying was delayed (1856b: 238–39), and Freuchen seems to have believed that, before the 1862 immigration, the Inuhuit had to go out to the eider breeding islets before the ice melted and then remain on them through the summer (Freuchen and Salomonsen 1958: 209–10). In the late nineteenth and twentieth centuries common eider eggs were certainly collected and cached by the Inuhuit and much prized when they were eaten frozen in the winter, after the shell had been removed. Whitney describes how, when he camped out on McGary Rock off Littleton Island in summer 1909, his Eskimo companion cached over a thousand eider eggs. At this same place, in 1975, Danish biologist Henning Thing (1976) noted that twelve Eskimo boat crews collected eggs on 23–26 June and that each crew took between three hundred and four hundred eggs. Early in the 1980s, Born (1987) reported that two thousand to twenty-five hundred eggs were taken annually.

In the past the Inuhuit ate any bird they could lay their hands on. Kane (1856b: 202) watched two youngsters at Iita squabbling over a snowy owl (*Nyctea scandiaca*) they were eating raw. Crocker Land Expedition member W. Elmer Ekblaw mentions twelve species in his study "The Food Birds of the Smith Sound Eskimos." During the present century Inuhuit pressure on bird life has declined, but large numbers of dovekies are still taken, especially at Siorapaluk.

The Inuhuit not only ate birds, they were also dependent on them for an essential article of clothing—the hooded birdskin shirt, worn by both men and women next to the skin with the feathers inside (Fig. 5). The species normally used for this purpose was the dovekie, and Gibson (1922), reckoning 50 skins apiece for each of the new shirts required by the 250 Inuhuit each autumn, concluded that 12,500 dovekies were required annually for clothing. Sometimes the thick-billed murre was used for this purpose, and Ross (1819: 125), who regarded this shirt as a lining of the sealskin coat, claims that eider skins were sometimes used. The Inuhuit seem not to have made any use of eiderdown.

During the nineteenth century the dovekies and common eiders breeding in the south of Avanersuaq fell victim almost annually to the whalers' need for fresh meat and eggs. The dovekies were shot down by the dozen as they flew near the ships in their habitual dense flocks. In 1849 the surgeon of the Dundee whaleship *Advice,* R. A. Goodsir (1850), noticed that "every ship in the fleet had their davits strung with hundreds." Captain William Barron of Hull claimed to have brought down 35 dovekies "with one charge of sparrow shot" (1895: 94–95), apparently in 1858, and the surgeon of the Hull whaleship *Diana* recorded that on 18 June 1866, offshore somewhere south of Cape Atholl, 172 dovekies were killed in less than two hours, 17 with a single shot (Unpublished MS., Town Docks Museum, Hull). In the last quarter of the

nineteenth century the whaleships also developed the tradition of stopping at
Dalrymple Rock to collect common eider eggs. Over a thousand eggs would
be taken at a time; the record take was the 7,200 said to have been collected
there on 27 June 1903 by the crew of the Dundee whaler *Diana.*

Naturally the explorers took a leaf out of the whalers' notebook. The Royal
Navy showed the way. Ross and his companions shot dovekies off Cape York
in 1818; so did Franklin and his men in July 1845. In 1852 Captain Sir
Edward Belcher (1855a: 69–70), dubious about the value of killing dovekies
for food, for the bird is only 8 inches (20 cm) long, went to the trouble of
appointing a committee of officers aboard HMS *Assistance* to inquire into the
matter. The naval gentlemen found that "twelve of these birds were not
deemed more than adequate to one pound of meat." On this basis, 1,080 birds
would be required to give the crews of the two ships one meal. Nor could so
large a number easily be obtained: Sir Edward's men, armed with four double-
barreled guns, killed only 150 birds in an hour. But the Royal Navy, at least
the officers, continued to eat dovekies. Captain M'Clintock (1859: 135, 139)
and his men brought down a thousand or so near Cape York on 26 June 1858;
and the naturalist on HMS *Discovery* at Iita in 1875, H. C. Hart (1880),
records that "the flesh of these birds was highly esteemed when made into a
pie for the ward-room mess."

Exploring expeditions visiting Avanersuaq made use of as much fresh food
as possible to ward off scurvy and to supplement the often inadequate supplies they brought with them, and common eider eggs and other birds besides
dovekies were likewise welcome to them. Thus Kane and his men, on their
way south in open boats in 1855, collected 1,200 eider eggs per day for three
days at Dalrymple Rock on 1–3 July, and on 10–17 July near Cape Dudley
Digges the famished travelers feasted on thick-billed murres and kittiwakes
and their eggs and took 250 dried murres with them when they left (1856b:
265, 270–74). When the British Arctic Expedition of 1875–76 touched at the
Cary Islands on 27 July, one member of the party admitted that "they misera-
bly slaughtered ten eider ducks, swimming about with their young broods.
There was no help for it; in the Arctic region 'the pot' is peremptory" (Moss
1878: 14). When Peary first arrived in Avanersuaq he sent a boat expedition
on 12 August 1891 to Hakluyt Island to raid the thick-billed murres breeding
there and "obtain as many of the birds as possible." They bagged 132 (1898a:
98). On 15 July 1892 near the head of McCormick Fjord, while awaiting her
husband's return from the Inland Ice, Josephine Peary shot an oldsquaw
(long-tailed duck) (1893: 171). "The breast gives us one meal," she wrote, "and
the rest of the bird stew for another."

In addition to the killing of birds and animals for food, the depredations of
naturalist-collectors in the name of science affected the fauna of Avanersuaq.
In 1818 the lords of the admiralty accepted the Royal Society's recommenda-

tion that Edward Sabine, "a gentleman well skilled in astronomy, natural history, and various branches of knowledge," accompany John Ross's expedition to assist him "to collect and preserve such specimens of the animal, mineral, and vegetable kingdoms, as you can conveniently stow on board the ships" (Ross 1819: 9–12, 245). Ross later issued special orders "relative to objects of natural history" (Fisher 1819: 95), which seem to reflect a personal interest in the matter:

> It is my direction that every specimen of the animal, vegetable, and mineral kingdoms, which may be found or procured by any person employed in the ships under my command and orders, shall immediately be brought to me, that I may give such directions respecting their disposal as I may think fit; and all officers going on any service to the shore, or ice, or having communication with the natives, are to use their utmost endeavour to collect and procure any thing which may contribute to the advancement of natural knowledge. And of the larger animals and other objects which cannot be removed, sketches and descriptions are to be taken; and all such reports, descriptions, &c. are to be signed by the officer, and sent to me for his Majesty's service.
>
> Given under my hand, on board the Isabella at sea this 17th day of August, 1818.
> (Signed)   JOHN ROSS, Captain.

The general public in 1818 seemed to regard the collection of museum specimens with a certain mocking hilarity. In the previously mentioned cartoon by George Cruikshank, entitled "Landing the treasures, or Results of the Polar Expedition," the procession led by Captain Ross is just arriving at the "MUSEUM" with a bizarre collection of curiosities, which, besides the specimens of *Larus sabini* and "Red Snow," include a large yellow container labeled "worms found in the intestines of a seal by a volunteer for Brit. Mu." carried by a black man; an absurdly long narwhal tusk with the inscription "Lance made of Horn of ye Sea Unicorn used in common as a walking stick"; and, of course, the inevitable polar bear. Nevertheless, the procurement of natural history specimens continued to be an important activity of nearly all the explorers in Avanersuaq for more than a century to come. Justified on the grounds of science, this collecting often failed to serve science: Kane's specimens had to be abandoned; information about Hayes's collections was never properly published; and the ornithological results of the 1936 Danish Natural History Expedition to Northwest Greenland (Salomonsen 1943) amounted to sixty-seven skins of birds shot in Avanersuaq and tucked away in the Zoological Museum in Copenhagen without any detailed publication of the expedition's ornithological observations. Even since World War II, egg collectors have been active in Avanersuaq. In 1967 the English egg collector William Hobson (1972) found three knots' nests (*Calidris canutus*) containing eggs on the stony plateau above Uummannaq by dragging a long rope over the ground. All the eggs were apparently taken. Honor is due to the Danish marine biologist Henning Thing, who was the first naturalist to visit Avanersuaq and publish observations in detail without collecting birds or their eggs. Thing visited the area between 13 May and 22 July 1975.

Local laws have restricted the killing of animals and birds, whether for subsistence or science, since 1929, when Rasmussen and the Hunters' Council he set up gave some protection to the walrus, the fox, and the common and king cider. The shooting of walruses without harpooning them first was prohibited (Sand 1935, Vibe 1950: 22–23). Members of the 1936 Danish Natural History Expedition were among the first to suffer a fine under these laws. They were busy skinning three king eiders (*Somateria spectabilis*) they had shot near the Thule Trading Station when the manager, Hans Nielsen, who was also chairman of the Hunters' Council, and two of its members, pointed out that they had broken the law. They had to pay a fine of fifteen Danish crowns; their Danish government permit, dispensing them from all the Greenlandic conservation laws then in force, was not valid in Avanersuaq, which was not annexed by Denmark until the following year (Vibe 1938: 143–44).

In 1939 the Inuhuit accepted some of the game laws then in force in West Greenland, including the close season for caribou in the spring (Gilberg 1977a). Since World War II the principle behind the conservation laws in Avanersuaq has been to protect any species of bird or animal thought to need protection but not to the extent of adversely affecting the Inuhuit's traditional subsistence hunting and gathering. Thus until 1978 they were allowed to shoot snow geese in the spring as well as later in the year, but since then in September only. They are still permitted to collect common eider eggs but only on 23–25 June (Born 1987) and to catch dovekies. They may still hunt the polar bear, the caribou in autumn only, and their traditional prey species among the sea mammals (Vibe 1981).

7

The Meteorite Rush

John Ross and the officers of his expedition were certainly curious about and may well have been astonished by the iron-bladed knives in the possession of the "Arctic Highlanders" who sledged out over the sea ice to their ships off Cape York on 10 August 1818. "Each of the natives was provided with a kind of knife," wrote the surgeon of HMS *Alexander* in his journal for that day (Fisher 1819: 57), "made of small pieces, or plates of iron, which were set close together in a groove made in a piece of narwhal's horn: the end piece was rivetted, but the others were kept in their places merely by being driven tightly into the groove." He added later that these knives averaged about 10 inches (25 cm) in length and that the flakes of iron forming the blade were not set exactly in line so that the edge "was serrated at the parts where the different pieces of iron were joined" and somewhat resembled a Malay kris. The ship's armorer on board HMS *Isabella* examined some of these knives and pronounced them to be made from "pieces of iron hoop, or from flattened nails" (Ross 1819: 95), which might accidentally have drifted ashore, but some of the officers remained doubtful of this explanation, believing the iron to be native, and Edward Sabine (1819: 81) thought that "the peculiar colour of these pieces of iron, their softness, and freedom from rust, strengthened the probability that they were of meteoric origin."

From the surviving accounts it is clear that a great deal of trouble was taken by the ships' officers to ascertain the truth about the origin of this iron, and their repeated inquiries seem to have severely tested interpreter John Sacheuse. Surgeon Alexander Fisher summarized the information thus obtained after a second group of Eskimos had visited the ships on 13 August (1819: 58–59):

> It appears from what Sacheuse could gather from them, that they procure the iron of which they [the knives] are made, from a mass of native iron, distant, agreeably to their information, about a day's journey to the eastward of this place. They likewise told him that their only object, in coming so far from

their own country, which lies to the northward, is to procure some of this iron, which they break off with great difficulty by the means of stones, and then beat out into the small plates of which the knives are made. Thus far their description agrees so well with what we find these rude instruments to be, that I think there cannot be any doubt of the truth of what they have related.

On being afterwards more closely questioned respecting this iron, they said that there were two insulated masses of it, the largest of which they described as being about the size of the skylight over Captain Ross's cabin, which is about four feet across. The other mass was reported by them to be considerably smaller. The place where these masses lie, is called by them Soowilik [Savissivik], from Soowik [*savik*], the name of iron in the Esquimaux language.

Ross's instructions from the admiralty did not permit him to linger unnecessarily at Cape York, and he left on 16 August without having visited the meteorites from which it appeared that the Inuhuit obtained their iron. The meteoritic origin of some of this iron was subsequently confirmed by Sir Joseph Banks, who had one of Sabine's specimens analyzed (Jones 1875), and by a Dr. Wollaston, to whom Ross submitted a piece for analysis. Wollaston sent the following carefully qualified report to Ross (1819: Appendix, p. lxxxix):

With respect to the iron, of which you obligingly gave me a specimen, it appears to differ in no respect from those masses of which so many have now been found on various parts of the surface of the earth; and which, in some few instances from tradition, and in all from the analysis, appear to be of meteoric origin. They all contain nickel, and this contains about the usual proportion of that metal, which I estimate between three and four per cent., as inferred from the quantity of crystallized sulphate of nickel which I obtained from it; but, though I can thus speak with decision as to the presence of a considerable quantity of nickel, I cannot undertake to pronounce with accuracy upon proportions deduced from so small a fragment as could be spared for this examination.

Ever since the publication of Ross's book in 1819 the armorer's opinion that some of the Eskimos' knives were made of wrought iron has been forgotten or rejected, along with the statement on the same page of Ross's book that John Sacheuse was told by the Eskimos that "a piece of wood with some nails had come on shore, and been picked up." A walrus harpoon point tipped with a single iron flake, which has been in the Museum of Natural History in Vienna since it was bought in England in 1838, and which certainly derived from Ross's expedition via a public auction in London, had always been assumed, therefore, to have been of meteoritic iron. But examination in an electron microprobe in 1979 indicated no nickel content, and Danish experts Vagn

Fabritius Buchwald and Gert Mosdal (1985) concluded that this harpoon blade is of "cold-worked" wrought iron. Thus as early as 1818 the Inuhuit had at least two sources of iron, one meteoritic, the other industrial. So far there is no evidence of their use of native iron from Disko, farther south in Greenland.

There was nothing unusual about the Inuhuit's use of meteoritic iron for the manufacture of knives or other objects. Such use has been recorded from all parts of the world and from all periods of human history. Parts of what was probably a dagger unearthed at Ur of the Chaldees in 1927 and ascribed to about 3100 B.C. contained around 10 percent nickel and were evidently of meteoritic iron, and predynastic iron beads from ancient Egypt found at Gerzah in 1911 are also meteoritic. A meteorite that fell at Toluca in 1776 was "forged by the Mexicans into agricultural implements." All this was discussed by T. A. Rickard (1941), who pointed out that though native iron of terrestrial origin was extremely rare, nature, through meteorites, provided a natural alloy of iron and nickel that was "much the best metal available" before the development of smelting: "Primitive man had thus the use of a natural alloy superior to any metal smelted for manufacture previous to 1890, when artificial nickel-steel was produced, and put on the market under the name of 'meteor steel.'"

Yet the identification of one of the Inuhuit's main sources of iron by Ross and his officers was a noteworthy achievement. After all, about fifty years before, a group of French scientists headed by the great Antoine-Laurent Lavoisier had declared the fall of objects of cosmic origin to earth to be physically impossible. Only in 1794 had the German scientist E. F. F. Chladni published the book that finally established the existence of meteorites. He drew attention to the lumps of iron brought to Leningrad from Siberia by the traveler-naturalist P. S. Pallas and bequeathed his own collection of meteorites to the University of Berlin. It was soon found that all apparently genuine meteorites contained a relatively high percentage of nickel. In 1808, Alois van Widmanstätten described the characteristic pattern found on the polished surface of meteorites after etching with acid (Garboe 1961). Early in the nineteenth century people began looking for and collecting meteorites. Every respectable museum had to have at least one, and the larger museums vied to obtain the biggest meteorite ever recovered.

John Ross's account of his 1818 voyage became one of the classics of the nineteenth-century literature of exploration and was widely read, not least in Denmark and Sweden. Around 1840 that keen amateur naturalist and scientist King Christian VIII of Denmark, who presided over the Royal Danish Scientific Society in Copenhagen, conceived the idea of sending a special expedition from the Upernavik district to recover the Cape York meteorites, or at least to bring back some of the meteoritic iron to Denmark. The expedition, led by Christian Lynge, was accompanied by the Danish pastor at Upernavik,

G. M. Q. Christophersen, one other Dane, and two West Greenlandic Eskimos, with five sledges. Pastor Christophersen seems to have volunteered for the trip in case his services as a missionary were required among the "Arctic Highlanders." The expedition was probably doomed from the start. Years later, in 1903, it took the Literary Greenland Expedition three weeks to sledge from Tasiusaq to Cape York; Lynge in 1843 had provisions for only two weeks, and he relied on his two Greenlanders to shoot seals to feed the expedition's dogs. Moreover, his starting date from Tasiusaq, 29 April, was almost certainly too late to enjoy good sea ice for sledging over the whole route; the Literary Expedition left Tasiusaq a good month earlier in the year. In any event, Lynge's expedition was dogged from the start by bad luck. After the first day, when they shot three or four seals, no more were seen. They were delayed by leads of open water, and on 2 May a southwest blizzard held them up. By 5 May the two Greenlanders were snowblind and in pain and could not shoot, and the starving dogs had eaten their leather traces and every one of the straps off Christophersen's traveling trunks. The expedition returned on 5 May to Tasiusaq (Garboe 1964 and see Freuchen 1936: 74).

Little was heard of the Cape York meteorites during the middle years of the nineteenth century, though Hayes was given some flakes of iron said to have been chipped from a large boulder near Savissivik by an Eskimo at his winter quarters near Iita early in 1861. The Eskimo told him he had kept them to make into a knife blade and that he and others often went to Savissivik to obtain iron (Buchwald 1964, Hayes 1862). In 1870 public attention was attracted to the Cape York meteorites by the discovery of large iron boulders on Disko island at a place called Uivfaq (formerly spelled Ovifaq) by the Finnish-Swedish explorer Adolf Nordenskiöld, as a result of an appeal to the local inhabitants. Convinced that the Uivfaq boulders were meteorites, Nordenskiöld persuaded the Swedish authorities to send a naval expedition the following summer to recover them. After some tricky negotiations with the Danish government, two Swedish warships, the gunboat *Ingegerd* and the brig *Gladan,* under the command of Frederik Wilhelm von Otter, were sent to Disko and returned in triumph to Stockholm with the three heaviest boulders, weighing around twenty-two tons, seven tons, and four tons, and several smaller ones. Some of the stones unfortunately disintegrated on the journey. One exuded sea-green droplets. Another crumbled to a reddish-brown powder. The largest of these alleged meteorites was set up in the hall of the Royal Academy in Stockholm; the second largest went to the Museum of Mineralogy of the University of Copenhagen; and the third was given by Nordenskiöld to the Finns and now graces the Botanical Garden in Helsinki. The sixth or so largest stone found its way to the British Museum (Jones 1875, Leslie 1879: 173–75, Thorén 1979). It scarcely mattered that learned scientific opinion soon rallied to Nordenskiöld's critics, who insisted that the Uivfaq ironstones were telluric, that is of terrestrial origin, and not meteorites at all. After all, they were and still remain the largest lumps of nonmeteoritic native iron ever found.

It was apparently Nordenskiöld's activities and the controversy surrounding them that induced the British admiralty to include the collecting of meteorites in the scientific program of the 1875–76 Arctic expedition (Jones 1875, Nares 1878). The expedition was warned that the meteorites might disintegrate in the air and perhaps should be stored in casks of water. The explorers visited Uivfaq briefly while they were at Godhavn but did not search for meteorites in Avanersuaq.

At Cape York, where Denmark and Britain had failed, might not Sweden, disappointed at Uivfaq, succeed? In 1883, Nordenskiöld (1885) organized another expedition to Greenland, in the *Sofia,* the main aim of which was the further exploration of the Inland Ice (Kjems 1981). He planned to lead a party along nearly the same route he had followed in 1870 more or less due east from a point south of Christianshåb (Qasigiannguit). Other aims of the expedition were to investigate the ocean currents and drift ice off the southeast coast of Greenland, collect living and fossil plants, and recover the Cape York meteorites. On 3 July 1883, before he set out over the Inland Ice, Nordenskiöld (1885: 290–92) placed Dr. A. G. Nathorst in charge of the rest of the expedition with instructions to sail north to Cape York. He was to remain there six days, during which time he was to investigate "Sivalik Hill," take on board the smaller meteorite, whole if possible, and try to obtain implements made from the Savissivik iron.

As so often happens on an Arctic expedition, local conditions prevented the commander from carrying out his instructions. It was a late season and a poor ice year in Melville Bay. Hans Hendrik, whom the Swedes had engaged as interpreter to communicate with the Inuhuit, declared that he had never seen so much ice there. A solid sheet of it barred Nathorst's way toward Cape York; instead of going there he had to be content with a brief visit to Parker Snow Bay, where he anchored off the tiny impermanent settlement of Issuvissooq. All he achieved there was a collection of botanical specimens and Eskimo artifacts. He could do no more than confirm the existence of meteoritic ironstone by conversation with the handful of Eskimos he met at Issuvissooq. Nordenskiöld must have returned home disappointed: no meteorites had been collected, and his Inland Ice reconnaissance had produced no trace of the ice-free lands he believed existed in the heart of Greenland.

More than anything else, it seems to have been the achievements and failures of Nordenskiöld that inspired the earliest Arctic explorations of the young United States Navy civil engineer Robert E. Peary. Not only did he follow in Nordenskiöld's footsteps on the Inland Ice in 1886, he must have owed his passionate interest in meteorites to the same source, though perhaps indirectly through Professor Angelo Heilprin. Heilprin was the leader of the West Greenland Expedition of 1891, mounted by the Academy of Natural Sciences of Philadelphia with the dual purpose of taking Peary to the north and conducting scientific research and collecting. He was a geologist and the executive curator of the academy. He made use of the expedition's delay at Cape York on its way home to lead a party up "what are known as the Iron Mountains" through a gale of sleet and snow in search of the Cape York meteorites. No trace of iron was found; indeed, it is doubtful if the professor was looking in the right place because he seems merely to have ascended one side of the Cape York promontory and returned down the other. Later on the same voyage, when the expedition ship *Kite* was delayed at Godhavn to take on ballast, Heilprin hired an umiaq with its crew of seven Greenlanders and set off on the tedious eight-hour sea voyage to Uivfaq, where Nordenskiöld's supposed meteorites had been found. He discovered one large and several smaller iron stones, which he proudly took back to the academy's museum, though he conceded that they were not meteorites (Keely and Davis 1893).

Since 1891 Peary had wanted to investigate the "Iron Mountain" near Cape York (see Peary 1894, 1898b: 128–55 and 553–618, Green 1926: 125, 140–54, Hobbs 1936: 167–74, Weems 1967: 142–46). In the winter of 1891–92 at Red Cliff House he obtained information about the supposed meteorites and learned that many living Inuhuit had seen one or more of them. But it was not until May 1894 that he was able to travel to Savissivik himself. He was accompanied by his colleague Hugh J. Lee and assisted and guided by Aleqatsiaq, whom he had employed as a postman two years previously. Aleqatsiaq assured Peary that he knew the precise whereabouts of three *saviksue* or "great irons," which he had often seen, and agreed to take Peary to them. The sledge trip from Anniversary Lodge, near the head of Bowdoin Fjord, which Peary and Lee left on 16 May, to Savissivik, where they arrived on 27 May, was accomplished mostly over the sea ice, but long and arduous detours inland had to be made to avoid the open water at Capes Parry and Atholl. Lee recorded that on the return journey, three separate marches on 2–6 June covered around 100 miles (160 km) each and were made with little sleep and virtually no food. Nevertheless, the object of the trip was achieved. On the lower slopes of the mountainous mainland peninsula called Ironstone Fjeld, some 9 miles (14 km) north-northeast of Savissivik, Aleqatsiaq was able to dig down through three feet of snow and reveal the "brown mass" of the meteorite called the Woman, encased in a "half-inch-thick coating of ice." Before leaving the spot, Peary "scratched a rough 'P' on the surface of the metal, as an indisputable proof" of his having found the meteorite and left the following record in a cairn "112 yards distant" (Peary 1898b: 147):

Sunday, May 27, 1894

This record is deposited to show that on the above date R. E. Peary, U.S. Navy, and Hugh J. Lee of the North-Greenland Expedition of 1893−94, with Tallakoteah, an Eskimo guide, discovered the famous 'Iron Mountain', first mentioned by Capt. Ross, and have carefully examined the same.

[Signed] R. E. Peary, U.S.N.,
Comd'g Expedition.

From this moment on Peary seems to have been determined to recover not only the Woman but also the two other meteorites the Eskimos had told him about, the Dog, which lay near the Woman, and the largest of the three, the Tent, which lay near the northeast coast of Meteorite Island, about 4 miles (6 km) northeast of Savissivik and 5 miles (8 km) due south of the Woman and the Dog. During the summer of 1894, in the weeks following his discovery of the Woman, he decided to try to ship one or two meteorites home at once, apparently with a view either to selling or exhibiting them to raise funds for future expeditions (Green 1926: 125). But although the *Falcon* arrived to take Mrs. Peary and some of the expedition members home, ice prevented Peary from getting the ship anywhere near the meteorites in August 1894. His opportunity came a year later, when he was able to force the *Kite,* after it had collected him and his colleagues Lee and Henson from Anniversary Lodge, through the Melville Bay pack and to make her fast to the ice only a mile offshore from the slope where he had seen the Woman exhumed from its winter snow covering fifteen months before. Now, in the absence of snow, it became clear that the Woman had been used in the past by the Inuhuit as a source of meteoritic iron. The original surface of the stone above ground level had been pounded and worked and eventually in this way entirely removed by the Eskimos, though below the original ground level its surface was undisturbed and typically meteoritic. All around the Woman were piled up, to a height of about 6 feet (2 m), the hard, rounded boulders that many generations of Inuhuit had brought to use as hammers to detach small flakes of iron from the meteorite. Nearby were three or four stone constructions that had been used as shelters by the Eskimos while they worked to obtain the iron (Hoppin 1897). With the help of the Eskimos, and under the able supervision of Mrs. Peary's brother, engineer Emil Diebitsch, the two meteorites were dragged down to the shore, ferried across the open water on massive ice floes, and then slid from the ice to the ship on a tramway of planks. The Woman was later found to weigh 897 pounds (407 kg). The smaller Dog had also been worked at by the Eskimos to remove flakes of iron, but much less so than the Woman.

While at work in August 1895 on the recovery of the two smaller meteorites, Peary visited and inspected the much larger Tent on Meteorite Island. The ground all around it was excavated to a depth of three feet without revealing its base, and an unsuccessful attempt was made to break off part of it by driving tapered bolts into a row of holes drilled into it. In the following summer, 1896, a larger ship, the *Hope* of 307 tons, was chartered. Only with great difficulty was Peary able to secure leave from the Navy Department for another Greenland voyage; financial support was provided both by the American Museum of Natural History and by its president, Morris K. Jesup. Peary took with him, presumably for a fee, scientific parties from the Boston School of Technology and Cornell University, which were put ashore in West Greenland near Uummannaq and Kullorsuaq respectively, as well as some fare-paying passengers or tourists and a party of mica prospectors from Newfoundland. One of the passengers, Benjamin Hoppin, of New Haven, Connecticut, wrote a diary of his trip which he later had privately printed (1897). One gets the impression that he was somewhat bored at Meteorite Island between 23 August and 3 September while the Tent was gradually raised with jacks and then slowly rolled over and over amid showers of sparks down a rough road of stones to the shore where the *Hope* was anchored. His entries read laconically, "Work on the meteorite" or "Iron is getting nearer the ship," but on 2 September he records the chorus sung by the Newfoundland seamen while at this work, which is a version of a well-known sea chanty, the usual form of the name being Johnny Boker (Doerflinger 1972: 9, 341–42):

> Oh my Johnny Voker
> We will turn this heavy Joker
> We will roll and rock it over
> We will turn the heavy Joker
> Oh my Johnny Voker, Haul!

Hoppin spent some time exploring Meteorite Island and even persuaded Peary to name the eastern of its two hills after him, though Mount Hoppin never made its way onto a map. He also tried his skill at skating on a glacier there but, not surprisingly, found it "rather rough and sloping." Eventually, having laboriously brought the giant meteorite down to the shore, Peary was forced to abandon his efforts for that year by the ice driving ashore from Melville Bay in a southeasterly gale, which threatened to crush the *Hope*.

Only in 1897, after a second summer voyage in the *Hope,* was Peary finally able to bring the largest meteorite ever recovered safely to New York. On this occasion he took with him even more professors, besides heavy lifting equipment in the form of powerful hydraulic jacks, massive steel chains, bolts, and tools. Also on board the *Hope* were two mighty beams of 14- by 16-inch white oak (35.6 x 40.6 cm), 60 feet (18 m) long, to form the backbone of a ship-to-shore bridge and a supply of 30-foot (9 m) "standard steel rails of the New York, New Haven and Hartford Railroad, weighing one hundred pounds to the yard." After five busy days and nights of almost continuous fog and driving snow starting on 15 August 1897, with the help of at least nine Inuhuit from Cape York the Tent was brought aboard, draped in the Stars and Stripes, and safely stowed in the hold (Fig. 12).

At Cape York the *Hope* halted briefly. Here, Peary writes (1898b: 591), "I sent my faithful Eskimos ashore, accompanied by several barrels of biscuit, and loaded with guns, knives, ammunition and numerous other articles which I had brought to reward them for their faithful service." He acknowledged (pp. 594–95) "the invaluable assistance" of the officers and crews of the *Kite* and the *Hope* and of "my faithful little band of Eskimos, who, handling heavy rails and timbers, working with pick and shovel and bar, and pumping on the jacks, did all they could to put into my possession the 'Iron Mountain' of their forefathers." He waxed almost poetic with pride in his own achievement (1898b: 594):

> Saturday, October 2, 1897, the hundred-ton floating crane at the New York Navy Yard, through the courtesy of the Navy Department, lifted the giant from the *Hope* and deposited it upon the quay wall, the largest known meteorite in the world, and a meteorite with human associations such as attach to no other.
>
> Three years of persevering efforts had won. The great Star Stone of the North, traced to its icy matrix and torn therefrom, had been brought safely out through the ice, the storms, and darkness of the Arctic seas.

Peary and his admirers consistently exaggerated his achievement in discovering and bringing back the Cape York meteorites. One would not dispute that they form perhaps the finest exhibit in the world's finest natural history museum, the American Museum of Natural History in New York. But it is scarcely fair to suggest, as often has been, that the Inuhuit revealed the secret of the location of the "Iron Mountain" to Peary after six earlier expeditions had failed to elicit it. This story derives from the admiring biographer of Peary, William Hobbs (1936: 166–67), who states that earlier expeditions "had made serious efforts to secure" the meteorites "but had not overcome the suspicion of the natives or their reluctance to disclose the site of the iron masses." In contrast to these earlier explorers, Hobbs continued, Peary had won the "complete confidence" of the Eskimos. Hobbs had taken the cue from Peary, who claimed that the meteorites had "for seventy-six years baffled all efforts to locate their hiding-place" (1898b: 617).

In reality, not one of the expeditions that supposedly failed to locate the Cape York meteorites actually looked for them, let alone tried to secure them. John Ross would surely have been shown the meteorites by the Eskimos had a favorable break in the weather not induced him to sail on northward. The officers of the *North Star,* overwintering in Wolstenholme Fjord in 1849–50 and described by Peary as having been "unsuccessful in locating the iron," were nowhere near Cape York and there is no evidence that they made any attempt to locate the meteorites (pace Bøggild 1927: 11). We have seen why the Danish expedition of 1843 failed to recover them, and the failures of the British Arctic Expedition and of Nordenskiöld's 1883 expedition occurred because the former did not have time or the latter opportunity to search for them. Peary was assuredly not the genius who succeeded where others before him had failed, though the recovery of the meteorites was a product of that same single-mindedness and resolve which had taken him over the Inland Ice from one side of Greenland to the other and was to take him to the North Pole or somewhere near it.

The American public was at first skeptical that Peary's meteorites were authentic. He complained that "paragraphs appeared repeatedly in the press, both in this country and abroad, asserting that the discovery of these irons was not new, that scientists had decided their telluric origin, and that I was taking a great deal of trouble to secure comparatively uninteresting specimens" (Peary 1898b: 602). Nor was this skepticism confined to the press. "Some eminent gentlemen, in advance of any personal acquaintance with the meteorites or the facts connected with them, did not hesitate to class them with the Nordenskiöld irons." But these critics were easily and decisively silenced. In December 1897 Peary's friend and supporter Morris K. Jesup sent specimens removed from the Tent to mineralogists Lazarus Fletcher of the British Museum (Natural History), E. A. Weinschenk of the Bavarian Institute of Minerals in Munich, and Professor A. Brezina of the Austrian Natural History Museum in Vienna, asking their opinion about the origin and nature of the iron. The verdict of these experts was unanimous. Fletcher wrote, "The character of the etched surface is decisive as regards the extra-terrestrial origin"; Weinschenk reported that "it is absolutely and without doubt a meteorite"; and Brezina stated laconically but confidently in a cable: "Cutting sent is a Montahedral [sic] Meteorite."

A more telling criticism of Peary claimed that, by removing or stealing the meteorites, he had deprived the Inuhuit of their traditional source of iron. This view was expressed most forcefully, in his usual exaggerated manner, by Frederick A. Cook (1911: 435n. and 512–14), who alleged that the Inuhuit complained bitterly that "Peary has stolen the iron stone," which, "owned by the Eskimos," "had been passed down from generation to generation as a tribal property" and was "put by Mr. Peary on his ship . . . without Eskimo consent." It was "the natives' last and one source of mineral wealth and ancestral treasure. That it was these people's great source of securing metal meant nothing to him." Peary replied that the Eskimos had not used the Cape York meteorites for obtaining iron for generations. He was probably right.

The Tent remained at the Brooklyn Naval Shipyard, New York, for ten years after it had been deposited on the wharf there in 1897. It caused a sensation when, in 1906, it was brought up the East River by barge and hauled to the 77th Street side of the American Museum by twenty-eight horses. It and the other meteorites had come into the museum's possession in a roundabout way. Peary gave them to his wife, Josephine; she sold them to Mrs. Jesup for $40,000; and Mrs. Jesup then donated them to the museum (Cook 1911: 514, Freeman 1961: 49, Weems 1967: 168, Harper 1986: 78–79, Preston 1986: 40–41).

Peary was convinced that there were no more meteorites to be found in Avanersuaq, but it was not long before he was proved wrong. Some time after the establishment of the Thule Trading Station at Uummannaq, Knud Rasmussen offered a reward for the finder of another meteorite, the existence of which had long been known among the Inuhuit but not its exact whereabouts. The reward—a brand new gun—was claimed by Qilluttooq, who later confessed to the murder of Ross Marvin. He discovered the stone in question near the top of a hill on the peninsula of Saveqaafik, somewhat over 6 miles (10 km) northeast of the spot where the Tent had been found. Naturally, it was Peter Freuchen who first told the story, which has been repeated in Danish sources (Buchwald 1964), that MacMillan planned to acquire this meteorite for the Crocker Land Expedition and thus also for the American Museum but that the ground was cleverly cut from under his feet by Knud Rasmussen, who forestalled him by pretending that he had already promised it to the Museum of Mineralogy in Copenhagen (Freuchen 1954: 144–45). The truth seems to be that the meteorite had already been promised to the Danish government or, rather, to Copenhagen University's Museum of Mineralogy, when Qilluttooq arrived at the Crocker Land Expedition's headquarters at Iita on 19 December 1913 to tell the Americans, among other things, about his find, and that MacMillan sent W. Elmer Ekblaw off to inspect it (MacMillan 1918a: 40–42, 388–96; Wissler 1918: 164–66) at Rasmussen's request. The expedition's surgeon, Harrison J. Hunt (Hunt and Thompson 1980: 45), recorded in his diary for 3 January 1914: "Ekblaw and Koodlookto have gone south. . . . Koodlookto will show Ek a meteorite he has found, and they hope to bring back a piece of it." The intense cold prevented them from obtaining more than a tiny fragment, which they broke off with a sledgehammer. They noticed that, as with the Woman, heaps of boulders that had clearly been specially brought and used as hammers to detach flakes of iron from the meteorite lay piled around it.

In 1915, at the request of the Museum of Mineralogy in Copenhagen, Peter Freuchen made a special trip south from the Thule Trading Station to investigate ways of transporting the Saveqaafik stone to Denmark. Traveling by sledge with three Inuhuit, Freuchen reached the meteorite on 12 October. His subsequent report to the museum was optimistic, though he wrongly assessed the weight of the meteorite at about ten tons; it was later found to be only three and a half tons. Ekblaw had proposed to let the meteorite down the mountainside with a steel cable, but Freuchen suggested rolling it to the crest of the slope and then pushing it over the edge. It would then descend a good 150 meters (164 yards)—"a small hop for a meteor. Naturally it would be somewhat damaged and scratched on the way, which the Museum people may not like." He offered to do the job himself with the help of some of the Eskimos; there was no need to send out an engineer from Denmark (Garboe 1961: 44–45).

Evidently Copenhagen University's Museum of Mineralogy thought Freuchen's attitude somewhat flippant. Instead of taking up his offer, it sent engineer Holger B. Hansen to Avanersuaq. He set to work on the stone in August 1923, but, though it weighed only a little more than the Woman and only a tenth as much as the Tent, the Savik meteorite, as it came to be called, caused the Danes nearly as much trouble as the Tent had the Americans. With the help of 48 dogs, Hansen shifted the stone onto a special sledge but could move it only five yards before it got stuck in the snow. Worsening weather and shortening hours of daylight forced him to leave, but not before he had returned the meteor to its place with tackle. He set to work again the following February, managed to get it down to the shore, but was forced to leave it there when his specially constructed sledge broke down. Finally, in February 1925, the manager of the Thule station, Hans Nielsen, with Eskimo assistance, transported it across the sea ice to Bushnan Island with sledges lashed together and a total of 175 dogs. The Danish government paid the transport costs so far incurred, and from Bushnan Island to Copenhagen the meteorite was shipped free of charge on the Thule station's *Søkongen,* where it played havoc with the ship's compass (Garboe 1961). It now graces the courtyard of the Museum of Mineralogy, next to the Uivfaq nonmeteoritic ironstone donated years before by Nordenskiöld, except for a small piece that was sliced off in the Royal Dockyard at Copenhagen and is exhibited inside the museum (Bøggild 1927). This meteorite had found its way into a museum in a more straightforward manner than had the Tent, but this time there was little financial benefit for the finder. It was described as having been "purchased" from the Inuhuit by Rasmussen and Freuchen (Commission for Scientific Research in Greenland, *Newsletter,* December 1984, p. 19); subsequently Rasmussen gave it to the museum, which expressed its great indebtedness to him "for his magnificent donation" (Bøggild 1927: 13).

The rush to secure Cape York meteorites for the world's museums had not ended. In 1936 Qaavigarsuaq told the Danish biologist Christian Vibe (1938:

161) that the recent retreat of the Inland Ice had uncovered another large meteorite somewhere near Savissivik. This stone has not been seen again unless it is the twenty-ton one found after a long search of the area by civil engineer V. F. Buchwald in July 1963. Named after the place where it was found, Appalilik, 3 miles (5 km) north-northwest of Meteorite Island, this meteorite was removed to Denmark in 1967 and also set up on display at the Museum of Mineralogy, next to the Savik meteorite. Meanwhile, in June 1961, Augo Suersaq, a young Eskimo hunter, had found a small meteorite weighing about 17 pounds (8 kg) on the shore near where the Savik meteorite was found. This too is exhibited in Copenhagen's Mineralogical Museum, so that that institution has four of the Cape York meteorites and the American Museum three; but New York holds thirty-four tons of these meteorites and Copenhagen twenty-three.

What of the future? In the summer of 1984 yet another meteorite, apparently weighing something under a ton, was found below the high-water mark on Meteorite Island. Named Tunorput, it was shipped to Copenhagen for examination but has now been returned to Greenland. Alone of the Cape York meteorites, it will be permanently exhibited in its country of origin, in the National Museum of Greenland at Nuuk (Godthåb) (Commission for Scientific Research in Greenland, *Newsletter,* December 1984. p. 19, and Buchwald 1988).

The total weight of the meteoritic fall at Cape York, now tipping the scales at around fifty-eight tons, makes it the largest single fall so far recovered unless the giant meteorite at Hoba in Namibia is ever dug out of the ground and weighed: it is provisionally estimated at sixty tons.

Long before the rush to discover, appropriate, and remove the Cape York meteorites so that they could be exhibited in America and Europe, the Eskimos had begun to search for and take away fragments and smaller stones associated with them and to chip flakes of metal off at least two of the larger ones. The best known of the unworked fragments or smaller meteorites that belonged to the Cape York fall is the fist-sized chunk of iron "showing signs of pounding" (Wissler 1918: 166), called Akpohon, which W. Elmer Ekblaw acquired from an Eskimo on Ellesmere Island in 1914. He was a member of the American Museum's Crocker Land Expedition, and the meteorite in question is now displayed in that museum alongside the other Cape York meteorites. It was found near an old Eskimo house ruin and was presumably taken to Ellesmere Island on a sledge by Eskimos, possibly around A.D. 1000 to 1300 or some time before then. It is likewise generally accepted that the meteoritic fragment which Knud Rasmussen acquired from an Eskimo on Northumberland Island in 1928 had been taken there from the Cape York area by Eskimos.

Other lumps of meteoritic iron deriving from the Cape York fall have been identified among the material excavated in Avanersuaq by Danish archaeologist Erik Holtved in 1937 and 1947 (Holtved 1944a,b and 1954a,b). Two such lumps, one small, the other quite large, came from Comer's Midden at Uummannaq. But at "New" Nuulliit, on the Steensby Land coast, Holtved found no less than twenty-three "unworked pieces of iron," all apparently of meteoritic origin. Subsequent examination has confirmed that eleven of these fragments derive from the Cape York meteoritic fall (Buchwald and Mosdal 1985). Associated with these unworked lumps of iron excavated from ruined Eskimo houses at Nuulliit were at least six iron knife blades, some of them certainly of meteoritic origin (Holtved 1954b: 73), and at least a dozen corroded iron flakes, all but one of meteoritic iron (Buchwald and Mosdal 1985). In contrast to this relative abundance of meteoritic iron in the abandoned Eskimo settlement at Nuulliit, dating probably from around A.D. 900–1200, there were only five iron or partly iron objects among the twelve thousand or so finds Holtved recovered from excavations in Inglefield Land and at Uummannaq in 1935–37 and 1947. Two of these are the already mentioned lumps from Comer's Midden, the other three are a knife, an adze, and an *ulu* or woman's knife, all with the blades made of meteoritic iron.

All the evidence points to the accuracy of Peary's claim that the Inuhuit abandoned meteoritic iron for artifact manufacture soon after 1818. They already possessed at least one harpoon point made from industrial iron when Ross discovered them in that year. Two of the knives obtained through barter by Ross, measuring 12 and 13.5 inches (30.48 and 34.29 cm) in length, and still in the British Museum, are undoubtedly made from meteoritic iron from the Cape York fall, but no one since Ross's time has obtained artifacts from the Inuhuit made of meteoritic iron which were actually in use. None of the nine metal samples from Inuhuit artifacts collected in 1891 and tested by James W. VanStone (1972b) were of meteoritic origin; nor could Wissler find anything of convincingly meteoritic origin in the rich collections made by the Crocker Land Expedition in Avanersuaq in 1913–17. Peary himself, the meteorite enthusiast, during all the time he was in Avanersuaq between 1891 and 1910, recovered only two artifacts made with meteoritic iron, a knife fragment and a small *ulu* or woman's knife, both of which were dug out of old house ruins in 1895 at Natsilivik and Kangerlussuaq (1898b: 612–13). In 1931 Junius Bird obtained "from the Eskimos at Cape York" the fragment of a knife with a bone handle, the *ulu,* and the harpoon point that are now displayed in the American Museum alongside the Cape York meteorites (Rickard 1941: Plate 1). These, too, must have been ancient relics.

A fair number of meteoritic iron flakes deriving probably or certainly from the Cape York fall have been recovered in recent years from outside Avanersuaq. None of those that can be dated is more recent than about A.D. 1400. Most have been found in Eskimo house ruins in Ellesmere Island and elsewhere in Canada, as far south as northern Hudson Bay. On Somerset Island, in 1976, of thirteen iron fragments excavated in "two large Thule age sites, 10 could be proven to come from the Cape York iron meteorite strewnfield" (Buchwald and Mosdal 1985: 42). Compared to the numerous finds in Canada on the western shores of Smith Sound, which are constantly being added to (McGhee 1987), finds of Cape York meteoritic artifacts from West Greenland south of Avanersuaq can be counted on the fingers of one hand. There seem to be only three. One, the farthest away from Avanersuaq, is the arrowhead almost certainly made from Cape York iron, mentioned in chapter 2, which was found in the Viking site at Nipaitsoq near Godthåb (Nuuk). The second was a knife found near Jakobshavn (Ilulissat) and described by Johannes Lorenzen in 1882. Although Buchwald and Mosdal were convinced from Lorenzen's account that the knife was indeed made from Cape York iron, they could not confirm it because Lorenzen had used half the knife for his analysis and the other half had been discarded or lost. Third and last of the Cape York iron artifacts found in Greenland south of Avanersuaq is a knife, the blade of which consists of a single flake of meteoritic iron, almost certainly from Cape York, which was excavated at Cape Seddon in Melville Bay in 1979 by the Danish Knud Rasmussen Memorial Expedition (Jacobsen et al. 1980). It was recovered from house ruin no. 11 at Illuminerssuit, which could be dated to A.D. 1000–1200. This settlement had evidently been occupied intermittently by the Inuhuit.

It seems reasonable to conclude that between about A.D. 1000 and 1300, artifacts made from the Cape York meteorites were in use in Avanersuaq itself, in the eastern Canadian Arctic, and to a lesser extent in West Greenland south of Melville Bay. Whether the iron was disseminated in the form of flakes or unworked fragments is uncertain, but the evidence so far available points to fragments. The Norse settlers in Greenland may well have played some role in the dissemination of this meteoritic iron. Curiously, according to Buchwald and Mosdal, most of the worked flakes so far recovered derive from separate, now lost, fragments and smaller meteorites belonging to the Cape York fall rather than from the large meteorites now in New York and Copenhagen.

No doubt future excavations will reveal further artifacts made with Cape York meteoritic iron, and more fragments of the original fall surely await discovery. We have certainly not yet heard the last word about the Cape York meteorites.

8

Archaeology and Anthropology
The Eskimo as Research Material

*J*ust as specimens of the natural history of Avanersuaq have been indiscriminately collected, taken home, exhibited in museums, and occasionally made the subject of scientific research and publication, so too have the
Inuhuit been irresistibly tempting subjects for collection and research—which
often amounted to the same thing. Favorite pursuits of most of the early and
many of the later European and American visitors to Avanersuaq have included removing skeletal remains from graves, collecting artifacts, digging in
ancient or supposedly ancient house ruins, and even counting and measuring
the Inuhuit themselves. These activities and other more colorful ones have
nearly always been carried out in the name of science. All have recently become much less indiscriminate, and most, such as the removal of artifacts, are
now prohibited by a protective Greenlandic government.

It would be no simple matter to classify and then discuss systematically the
multifarious, often overlapping studies of the Inuhuit and their material remains which have been undertaken since 1818, many of them wreathed in a
smoke screen of academic jargon. No attempt will be made here to distinguish
between or define demography, genealogy, ethnomusicology, anthropomet-
rics, human ethology, and the rest. What follows is merely a description of the
different ways in which the Inuhuit have been exploited, studied, or otherwise
treated or maltreated in the interests of what might vaguely be termed anthropology and archaeology.

John Ross, in August 1818, initiated the study and collection of the clothes
and implements of the Inuhuit. He bartered with them to obtain two sledges,
a dog, knives, a spear, and a dog whip. One sledge and two of the knives are
still in the British Museum (King 1982, Buchwald and Mosdal 1985). Ross
(1819: 108–109) was also interested in the intellectual culture of the Inuhuit,
and he persuaded two of them to demonstrate their drum song. This was pre-
ceded by a dance, which consisted of "a variety of extraordinary gestures and
attitudes, accompanied by the most hideous distortions of countenance." Ross
thought these gestures contained "indecent allusions." Though unable to go
ashore to inspect the Eskimos' settlements in person, he did his best to ascer-

tain their number but was confronted with the interpreter's inadequate time-worn phrase "plenty people" and a vague wave of the arm toward the north. He was able, however, to give a detailed description of the physical appearance of the men; he saw no women or children. Information about the health of the "Arctic Highlanders" was necessarily lacking, though Ross tried to ascertain if they had any diseases or cripples among them. These lines of inquiry, which he could not pursue any further, were taken up and continued by subsequent visitors to Avanersuaq.

Ross was followed or imitated by others in using barter to acquire what in the nineteenth century were called ethnographic collections. When A. E. Nordenskiöld sent Dr. A. G. Nathorst north toward Cape York for a few days in the *Sofia* during the Swedish expedition to Greenland in 1883, he instructed him to barter items purchased beforehand "on as large as possible a scale" to acquire objects of ethnographic interest. Nathorst did his best, obtaining a narwhal horn, a complete outfit of fur clothing, soapstone vessels, and animals carved out of walrus ivory. Indeed, the Swedes obtained nearly everything the small group of Inuhuit they met had with them, for the Eskimos were on a temporary summer visit to the spot.

Eight years after the Swedes' three-day visit to the Inuhuits' temporary summer outpost Issuvissooq in Parker Snow Bay, Peary began his series of sustained and repeated expeditions to every part of the area. The acquisition of ethnographical material was a crucial objective on his first expedition, the North Greenland Expedition of 1891–92, during which he and his wife overwintered in Red Cliff House and he and Eivind Astrup crossed the Inland Ice to northeast Greenland. Indeed, it was the collection of Eskimo artifacts that brought him much of the financial support that made the expedition possible.

In preparation for the celebration of the four hundredth anniversary of Christopher Columbus's discovery of America in 1492, materials were assembled for the World's Columbian Exhibition in Chicago in 1893. Frederick Ward Putnam, curator at the Peabody Museum of American Archaeology and Ethnology at Harvard University, was given the task of mounting a comprehensive anthropological exhibit from all over the world. Field parties were sent off in different directions, and Peary's expedition became one of them. Putnam agreed to pay him $2,000, about one-fifth of his total costs, for "ethnological and archaeological materials from the Polar Eskimo" (VanStone 1972a). At the same time Peary enjoyed the support of the Academy of Natural Sciences of Philadelphia, which also wished to acquire ethnographical material. Putnam, worried about obtaining his share of the spoils now that a rival had taken the field, drew up an agreement with Peary on 2 June 1891, a few days before the expedition's departure. In return for his $2,000, Peary promised to take photographs, measurements, and molds of men, women, and children and to obtain "all objects of past and present times he may be able to secure . . . their weapons, utensils, ornaments etc. and several sets of garments with which to dress a series of moulds of men, women and children. Also a stone house" to be carefully taken down so that it could be rebuilt in Chicago with the aid of drawings, photographs, and descriptions, and "with this house to be all its contents—beds, lamps, utensils, etc." Drawings and photographs of a snow house were required "so that a model of one can be made in Chicago; the contents of such a house also to be secured for furnishing the model" (VanStone 1972a: 32–33).

Putnam's doubts about Peary's interest in ethnography seem to have been well founded. He halted briefly at Natsilivik on 24 July on his way to establish winter quarters farther north, but hopes of obtaining "a native house, sledge, kayak and various native utensils and implements for the World's Columbian Exposition" (Peary 1893: 30) apparently were disappointed. Then in August, the expedition's ethnologist, Frederick Cook, obtained "many valuable ethnological specimens" (Peary 1898a: 111) by barter from the inhabitants of Northumberland Island, though the primary purposes of the boat trip there were to secure meat for the winter, in the form of seabirds, and to bring some Eskimos back to Red Cliff House. Putnam was afterwards so disappointed in the paltry results of the expedition that he balked at paying the last $500 installment he had promised Peary.

At the end of July 1891, after leaving Peary, the other members of the North Greenland Expedition, and the prefabricated wooden building that was soon christened Red Cliff House on the south shore of McCormick Fjord, the enthusiastic representatives of the Academy of Natural Sciences of Philadelphia lingered at several Eskimo settlements on their way home to collect materials for their academy (Keely and Davis 1893). At Cape York, in exchange for a gun and ammunition, they obtained a kayak, sledge, and some narwhal tusks. The following year, at Natsilivik, an hour or more's feverish trading with "Needles, knives, scissors, thimbles and other useful things" secured for the Academy of Natural Sciences "a rich collection of West Greenland ethnological material." As if to swamp the market, the academy representatives then distributed gifts. One wonders how the Inuhuit had any artifacts or possessions left, but the demand for them continued and one can imagine that in the years that followed, they fabricated bows and arrows and harpoons for the world's museums while actually using modern repeating rifles obtained in barter for their subsistence hunting. Even so, Gilberg's (1984a) innuendo that Peary made the Inuhuit dependent on imported merchandise by buying up all their weapons and equipment cannot be taken seriously.

By 1897 Peary was busy collecting for the American Museum of Natural History where Putnam had become curator of anthropology. New York needed Inuhuit exhibits just as much as Chicago and Philadelphia, and in 1899 A. L. Kroeber published a detailed account of this material titled "The Eskimo of

Smith Sound" in the famous museum's *Bulletin,* illustrated with many excellent line drawings. Less dynamic or less wealthy institutions were by no means so rapid in publishing or even successful in preserving their Inuhuit collections. Those formerly in the museum of the Philadelphia Academy could not be found when VanStone hoped to examine them. He had to be content with what was left of the 1893 World Fair's exhibit, which had been transferred to the Field Museum of Natural History in Chicago. There VanStone found that the bulk of the Peary collection still survived: he located 280 items out of a total of 366 with catalog numbers. Many of the specimens were in poor condition: two kayaks had disintegrated, and the fur clothing was in shreds, but VanStone was able in 1972 to publish an excellent account of the collection that had been acquired in 1891. Illustrated with photographs, it appeared in Volume 63 of *Fieldiana Anthropology.*

By the early years of the twentieth century, excavation was beginning to replace barter as the chief means of meeting the demand for artifacts. The last bout of bartering with the Inuhuit on behalf of a museum seems to have taken place in July–August 1909 at Uummannaq and perhaps Cape York. The museum was the National Museum of Denmark in Copenhagen and the anthropologists who "bought up a collection of clothing and implements" were H. P. Steensby and deputy curator Thomas Thomsen (Steensby 1910: 267 and Krabbe 1930: 117). Their activities yielded a collection for the National Museum described under some 160 catalog entries (Gilberg 1976b: 85).

Ross's interest in Inuhuit drum singing and dancing was also taken up by subsequent explorers, who attempted to transcribe and translate the songs and even to reproduce them in modern musical notation. Kane (1856a: 212, 383), Bessels (1879: 372, 1884: 881), and Astrup (1895: 278–80) all made a start at this, but the first real enthusiast to study Inuhuit songs was the Silesian-born American geologist Robert Stein (1902b; Barr 1982), who visited Avanersuaq with Peary in 1897 and returned there in 1899–1901, when he also lived for a time with some Inuhuit on Ellesmere Island. He recognized the words of one song as similar to those written down by Ross nearly a century before, but when he tried to sing the song Kane had transcribed and set to music, there was little positive response from the Eskimos. At first, Stein thought they had only one song, but at Cape York one day he heard Iggia singing the song of the snow bunting (*kopainu;* a Baffin Island name is *kopenuak,* the West Greenland name is *qupaluarssuk*). Encouraged to greater efforts by the gift of "enough wood to build the frame of a kayak" and the loan of Stein's gun to shoot seals for its covering, Iggia obliged and so did his companions, and Stein eventually went home with a collection of thirty-eight different songs, many of them in an archaic, poetic language the singers claimed they no longer entirely understood.

It was left to a compatriot of Eivind Astrup, the Norwegian musicologist Christian Leden (1910, 1952), to take a phonograph to Avanersuaq to record Eskimo songs properly. He traveled to Uummannaq in 1909 partly in company with Knud Rasmussen, T. N. Krabbe, H. P. Steensby, and the two West Greenlandic missionaries who were to set up a mission station on the shores of North Star Bay. A voyage to Avanersuaq was no simple matter. Leden traveled on the *Hans Egede* from Copenhagen as far as Egedesminde (Aasiaat), then transferred to a Norwegian freighter for the six-hour crossing of Disko Bay to Christianshåb (Qasigiannguit). For the next stage of his journey north to Claushavn (Ilimanaq) Leden hired an umiaq rowed by a crew of five Eskimo women and steered by an ancient Eskimo helmsman. A gale forced them to camp the night ashore en route and the 22-mile (35-km) trip took them the best part of two days. The next leg of the journey, along the 9-mile (15-km) stretch of coast to Jakobshavn (Ilulissat), involved crossing the mouth of the mighty Jakobshavn Glacier and running the gauntlet of the numerous icebergs that break off from it and float out to sea. The women were unwilling to row their frail craft through this hazard, but Leden managed to hire a wooden boat and a new crew. He was anxious to see the great glacier at close quarters but was disappointed to meet with fog, which persisted throughout the five-hour trip. In answer to Leden's question to his Eskimo helmsman, how he could find his way in the thick fog without a compass, the helmsman pointed to his forehead with the words "Here, compass." After a stay at Jakobshavn, Leden boarded the Danish steamer *Godthåb* for the rest of his trip to Uummannaq, where he soon got busy with his phonograph, recording the Inuhuit during late-night singsongs after they had completed a hard day's work helping to unload supplies and equipment and to erect the mission station. Only with difficulty and Knud Rasmussen's help were they persuaded that the phonograph was harmless. Apparently their apprehension of it derived from their conviction that the song was part of their soul and that if it went into the white man's machine, they might die.

Christian Leden's trials and misfortunes had only just begun in Greenland in 1909. Long delays dogged his efforts to publish his findings. His colleague at Uummannaq, Knud Rasmussen, who had taken down the words of the songs while Leden recorded them on the phonograph, became involved in his famous series of Thule expeditions. Shortly before Rasmussen's death in 1933, Leden had written asking him for his notes on the songs if he could no longer find time to help in person with the establishment of the words. Eventually, when Leden had everything ready for publication, his manuscript was destroyed in a German air attack on Oslo in April 1940. Undeterred, he produced a new version, but that was lost when his briefcase containing it was stolen. For a third time he had to go through and rework his phonograms. At last in April 1948, he wrote the foreword to his magnum opus on the music of the Smith Sound Eskimos and its relationship to the music of the American Indian, which was finally published in German in 1952 in the famous periodical published by the Commission for Scientific Research in Greenland, *Meddelelser om Grønland.* A renewed interest in Inuhuit drum songs has recently led to further studies by Danish musicologist Michael Hauser (1986) and his associates.

In spite of the publication in 1875 of the English version of Henrik Rink's classic *Tales and Traditions of the Eskimo,* little attention was paid to the myths and stories of the Inuhuit until the very end of the nineteenth century. Then, in the winter of 1897–98 anthropologist A. L. Kroeber (1899b and c), stimulated by the arrival of a group of Inuhuit brought to New York by Peary, published an English translation of some 35 stories or fragments of stories he had obtained from them. We are not told exactly how they were taken down or by whom they were translated. Not long afterward, in 1903, Knud Rasmussen began transcribing the tales and fables of the Inuhuit while he was a member of the Danish Literary Expedition, and these were published in Danish in 1905 titled *Nye mennesker* and in English in 1908 in *The People of the Polar North.* In 1925 Rasmussen's entire collection of Inuhuit stories appeared in the third volume of his *Myter og sagn fra Grønland.* Finally, in 1951 Erik Holtved's edition of 178 tales appeared, with a phonetic transcription, a phrase-by-phrase literal translation in English, and an English translation of each story. Most of these were taken down and disk-recorded from two narrators, Amaannalik (a woman) and Pualorsuaq (a man), born in 1907 and 1891 respectively, in 1935–37 and 1946–47. These stories have been printed virtually without comment, comparison, or discussion by their successive editors, not one of whom has troubled to inform the reader where each has previously appeared in print. It is high time somebody made them the subject of study. According to Malaurie (1982: 240), the Inuhuit possessed a stock of around 200 stories, half of which might be known at any one time to a good raconteur.

Ross's curiosity concerning the size of the Inuhuit population was shared by many of his successors. From 1854 on, when Kane compiled a list of 140 names (not published) of Inuhuit from three independent informants and believed he could have missed only a few, counting the Inuhuit became the rage (Gilberg 1976b: 12–16). The first three counters, Kane, Hayes, and Bessels, only visited the extreme north of the district and, even accepting the nomadic nature of Inuhuit society in the nineteenth century, their figures of about 140, 100, and 112 respectively may have been low because of inadequate coverage of the Cape York area in the far south. Frederick Cook undertook the first census made by the Peary expeditions in 1891–92. Angelo Heilprin (1893) stated soon after the event, "The exceedingly accurate work of Dr. Cook, the ethnologist of the Peary expedition, whose census comprises not only the number, but the names, relationships and points of location of most of the members of this exceedingly interesting people, increases the number to 233, all between Cape York and the north shore of Robertson Bay." There is no reason to suppose that Cook's successors Hugh J. Lee and Ross G. Marvin, who compiled lists of names, were any less thorough; their totals were 253 and 207 respectively, for 1895 and 1906 (Peary 1898a: 511–14 and 1907: 391–93). According to Peary (1898a: 511), the Inuhuit at first somewhat resented Lee's persistent cross-examination about their "children, relatives and ancestors," but "finally they came to look upon it as a harmless indication of mild insanity." The reason for Marvin's lower figure seems to have been an epidemic in the winter of 1901–02, which apparently caused the death of 36 people. Except for this marked dip to around 200 to 220 in 1903–11, the Inuhuit population probably remained fairly stable at around 250 between 1895 and at least 1938. From 1910 on, the census work initiated by Peary was continued with substantially increased accuracy by the mission authorities at Uummannaq, beginning with Gustav Olsen's count in 1910 of 99 women and 118 men, distributed in nine settlements. The Danish official national censuses, which began to include Avanersuaq in 1921, distinguished between persons born in and out of Greenland but not between Inuhuit and West Greenlanders. In 1926 the American Museum Greenland Expedition counted 133 male Inuhuit and 138 females, giving a total population of 271 (Heinbecker and Pauli 1927), and in 1950–51 Jean Malaurie arrived at a total of 302. Rolf Gilberg (1976b) has been able to establish the exact annual increment of the population at least since about 1920.

Along with attempts to ascertain the total population of the Inuhuit went an abiding interest in the structure of that population and in their genealogy. The work of Cook and Lee in 1891–92 and 1894–95 was taken up by Mylius-Erichsen in 1903. He describes how on 25 April on Saunders Island he began to compile a list of all the island's inhabitants, even attempting an inventory of the belongings of each: weapons, sledges, kayaks, dogs. They were neither used to talking about their own property nor to counting. Their names, which were often shared by several individuals, were difficult to write down. "Agpalarsuarsuk" pronounced his name "Abalasuahw." The latest spelling fashion makes it Aapilarsuaq (Ulloriaq 1985). Family relationships were complicated by the practice of polygamy and wife exchange, and their investigation was hindered by the Eskimos' unwillingness to talk about the dead. Poor Mylius! He struggled on, like Lee before him, with a minimal knowledge of the Inuhuit language (Mylius-Erichsen and Moltke 1906: 229–30, 274). These early efforts were continued and taken a good deal further by Jean Malaurie in 1950–51. They have been refined in recent years by the meticulous research of Rolf Gilberg of Denmark's National Museum in Copenhagen

(1976b, 1985) and his collaborators, a veritable family concern. When Avanersuaq's first doctor, Mogens Holm, was appointed by Knud Rasmussen in 1928, his duties included the collection of genealogical information, a task he found perplexing because, at that time, the Inuhuit had no surnames. His work was continued in 1938–39 by Åge Gilberg, aided by his wife, Lisbet. Their son Rolf took over the research project in 1963 and brought it to a triumphant conclusion in 1978 with the publication of 630 numbered family diagrams containing genealogical data for each Inuhuit nuclear family (Å. Gilberg et al. 1978).

A fourth line of inquiry inaugurated by Ross in 1818 was the health of the Inuhuit. He could learn of no serious diseases among them, and subsequent explorers in the nineteenth century confirmed this. Cook, who was not only an ethnologist but a medical doctor as well, when questioned after a lecture he delivered on 16 January 1894 to the New York Obstetrical Society, reported that the Inuhuit suffered from very little illness except rheumatism, occasional tonsillitis, and mild forms of influenza; that they had no "no system of medical treatment for their diseases"; and that their teeth, "though short and worn," were in good condition. This last finding was corroborated by later examination of live Inuhuit and skeletal remains: in 1910 Ales Hrdlička was able to report the complete absence of dental caries among them. According to Peary (1907: 384), the main causes of death were "lung and bronchial troubles" and accidents while out hunting. When, in the 1930s, the Inuhuit were provided with European-style medical services, this assessment was confirmed. Åge Gilberg, Avanersuaq's second resident doctor, reckoned in 1940 that half the deaths were caused by tuberculosis or pneumonia and 13.8 percent resulted from accidents. On the credit side he was able to report the complete absence among the Inuhuit of appendicitis, scurvy, venereal disease, and cancer. Curiously, in 1908–9, Dr. Goodsell (1983: 36, 139) had noticed several cases of what he believed was gonorrhea.

That most notorious though almost never fatal Inuhuit ailment, which has acquired the name *piblokto* or *pibloktoq* in the literature and has also been called "Arctic hysteria," is not mentioned, so far as I can ascertain, by any of the nineteenth-century travelers to Avanersuaq before Josephine Peary. This is the more remarkable because Kane and Hayes were both medical doctors, both give very full accounts of the Inuhuit, and both describe in detail the symptoms of a very similar disease that killed many of their dogs. Cook made no mention of *piblocto* in his 1894 lecture, and it seems that several years elapsed before this disease came to the notice of Peary, who does not mention it in his appendix "The Smith Sound Eskimos" at the end of the first volume of his classic work *Northward over the "Great Ice"* published in 1898. But when he republished this appendix under the title "My Eskimos" in 1907 in *Nearest the Pole,* he added two paragraphs about *piblocto* introduced with the words, "There exists among these people a form of hysteria known as *pib-locto*" as if this was his first announcement of it, and he mentions a case that occurred in 1898. Mrs. Peary (1893: 125), however, was told in April 1892 by the Inuhuit woman Mannik that another woman, who was struggling and screaming, "was pi-blocto."

The word *piblocto* was a corruption of the Greenlandic word *perlerorpoq*, used alike for a person who is out of his mind or a dog suffering from frenzy. For whatever reason, there seems to have been a sudden increase in the number of persons going *piblocto* in the first decades of the twentieth century. During its lengthy stay among the Inuhuit in 1903, the Danish Literary Expedition recorded only one case, but Whitney witnessed at least four attacks involving two individuals during his stay in Inglefield Land in 1908–9, and MacMillan described it as "common among the women" on board Peary's ship the *Roosevelt* in 1908–9. These attacks, which were accepted by the Eskimos as perfectly normal and natural, caused some hilarity among the explorers. MacMillan (1934: 101) writes as follows:

> The show was always well attended. Everybody was up to see what would happen next, and something always did happen with startling rapidity. We found fat old In-a-loo flat on her back far out on the packed drift ice, blowing like a porpoise and cramming pieces of ice under her sealskin coat on her bare breast. We handled her with gloves. Although she was well along in years, she could certainly scratch and kick. With a sling around her waist the boys "heave ho'ed" her over the rail. Her husband promptly sat down on her feet, a son on each arm and a lady friend on her head, and there they remained until the tumult subsided. Weak, dazed, and with eyes bloodshot, she was finally put to bed. When in the unladylike condition of "piblockto" her special forte was an insane desire, followed by the attempt, to walk across the ceilings of our cabins. She never quite reached the top.

It was in the same summer of 1909 that the Danish anthropologist Steensby (1910: 337–38) described an attack he witnessed at Uummannaq suffered by the woman Inaalliaq, which was also described by the newly arrived missionary Sechmann Rosbach (1910a). Later, on the Crocker Land Expedition of 1913–17, MacMillan took a series of seventeen photographs of an Inuhuit woman suffering *piblocto* which, along with other expedition material, are in the possession of the American Museum of Natural History in New York. In more recent years *piblocto* has apparently become rarer. Neither of the Danish doctors in Avanersuaq in 1938–41 mentions it (Gilberg 1948, Beck 1946). Malaurie, who discusses the subject (1982: 77–80), never saw a case in 1950–51.

Recent medical opinion has not departed significantly from Dr. A. A. Brill's diagnosis of hysteria, which that distinguished neurologist announced in 1913 in a lecture before the New York Neurological Society. In 1960 two learned scientific papers on *piblocto* among the Inuhuit were published. Zachary Gussow reprinted some of the published accounts of attacks of it and added some unpublished ones, accepting that it was a form of hysteria. That same year, A. F. C. Wallace and R. E. Ackerman proposed that modern science take note of what they considered a still unsolved problem. They suggested that an interdisciplinary research program be established to study the syndrome known as *piblocto,* whose possible causes they listed, with a fine display of scientific terminology, as follows:

1. Hypocalcemia induced by a low-calcium high-protein and potassium diet, possibly aggravated by a low vitamin D3 intake in winter.
2. Psychomotor epilepsy due to inbreeding.
3. Spontaneous functional hypoglycemia brought about by severe depletion of the liver glycogen, caused in its turn by a low carbohydrate diet and insufficient gluconeogenesis from protein.
4. Psychogenic hysterical fit, a result of emotional conflict brought about by situational stresses etc.
5. Food poisoning due to the consumption of shark or other flesh containing nerve poisons eaten during periods of hunger.
6. An endemic virus infection like encephalitis.

Perhaps it is just as well for the Inuhuit that this formidable research program never got under way.

In addition to collecting artifacts by barter, musicology, and demographic and medical studies, Ross was the inspiration for subsequent ethnic studies of the Inuhuit. Had he not claimed that these people had for some time been cut off from the rest of mankind? Here again the Inuhuit were the innocent victims of Western scientific curiosity: they must be examined, measured, and photographed. Shortly before his first expedition set out in 1891, Peary was asked by Franz Boas, professor of archaeology and ethnology at Harvard, for measurements and descriptions of the local Eskimos. Boas sent him a pair of calipers and asked for an exact description of the Eskimos' ears (Fogelson 1985). In 1892 Peary was able to report, not without pride, to the Philadelphia Academy of Sciences that he had photographed many of the same seventy-five individuals from whom Cook had taken "anthropometrical measurements." He was planning to make complete sets of photographs "consisting of front, side, and rear elevations of between 50 and 60 individuals of both sexes and all ages" and thought that "this material will answer the interesting question, 'Whence came these strange people?'" (Peary 1892: 347). In the appendix to the first volume of *Northward over the "Great Ice"* (1898a) Peary published some of these photographs. Two plates each have four full-length photographs of an

Eskimo. In one photograph the subject is shown facing the camera, fully dressed; in another, nude except for a loincloth, facing the camera; in the third in profile, totally nude; and in the fourth, from behind, again completely nude. The plates are captioned "Male ethnological series" and "Female ethnological series." The author takes pains to warn the reader "in connection with the numerous partially nude figures in this appendix, that it is not the usual custom of the Eskimos to omit portions of their clothing. It was done at my request to show physique and muscular development."

The demands Peary made on the Inuhuit went much further than measuring them and photographing them in the nude. In 1896 and 1897 he took artist Albert Operti with him on the *Hope* to make plaster casts of some of them while work proceeded on the recovery of the third and largest of the Cape York meteorites. The purpose was exhibition rather than research. Peary (1898b: 614), who hoped all along that his meteorites could be sold to the American Museum, dreamed of "making them the central feature in a life-size group representing the ancient method of utilising them." To this end Operti made "a complete series of casts, measurements, and sketches, as well as studies of the surroundings. I assisted, with my camera," continues Peary, and "the costumes and all accessories of the group were then purchased, and packed away with the casts."

The taking of these first plaster casts of Inuhuit in 1896 was described by Operti (1902) in an article entitled "An Artist in the Frozen Zone." The artist's materials, "5 barrels of plaster of Paris, 3 gallons of vaseline, 200 lbs of modelling clay," together with some salt and a few iron pails, were specially shipped from New York to Sydney, Nova Scotia, and there put on board the *Hope*. At Cape York, about twenty of the Eskimos who visited the ship and were plied with coffee and ship's biscuits were selected as models. These victims were "allowed to remain on board to make fur clothing, be measured, painted, photographed and cast." Operti got to work with half-frozen fingers while the *Hope* pushed her way through the ice to Whale Sound. He was hampered by the up-and-down movements of the ship as she thumped into the ice, rose up, then slid back. Every now and then came the deafening noise of masses of ice crunching and grinding against the ship or violent shudders when a snow squall descended on them from the Inland Ice. His subjects were by no means enthusiastic. The heat from two oil stoves was insufficient to encourage them to undress, and Operti had to get Peary to speak to "one of my subjects about disrobing." He found that "the promise of presents very soon conquered their objections." The unfortunate subject was first cleaned with a piece of canvas tied over the end of a stick and then scrubbed with soft soap and warm water from the engine room, which became cold in less than ten minutes. Some castings were done in the hold by candlelight, the model lying on his or her back, a quill in each nostril and tissue paper over eyes and mouth. "The skin was well oiled, clay built around the head, and plaster poured over all." Later, in a tent pitched ashore on Meteorite Island, full-figure casts of a man and woman were made, though not without difficulty. The fires in the stoves were extinguished by the rain, snow, and wind. The wretched man (or woman) stood half frozen while a wall of clay was built around him and he was painted all over with vaseline. Then pail after pail of plaster was mixed and poured over his shivering body. "I believe the chattering Eskimo was promised a gun to stand this dose," wrote Operti. When Captain John Bartlett and five sailors responded to a call for help, they burst out laughing on entering the tent and seeing Operti and a colleague standing there with their arms around a mass of man, clay, and plaster trying to hold it all together. After the plaster had set, they had to "cut the 'husky' out of his crust," a process that took one and a half hours of hard work with hammer and chisel. The luckless Eskimo was then rushed to the galley fire and resuscitated with brandy and coffee while two of his friends rubbed him all over with canvas to restore his circulation.

In 1897 Peary became responsible through an error of judgment for a tragic event that brought him opprobrium because it smacked of kidnapping and murder. His erstwhile colleague, later rival and enemy, Frederick Cook, made the most of this disastrous episode in his *My Attainment of the Pole* (1911: 514–15).

> At about the same time a group of seven or eight Eskimos were put aboard a ship against their will and brought to New York for museum purposes. They were locked up in a cellar in New York, awaiting a market place. Before the profit-time arrived, because of unhygienic surroundings and improper food, all but one died. When in the grip of death, through a Mrs. Smith, who ministered to their last wants, they appealed with tears in their eyes for some word from Mr. Peary. They begged that he extend them the attention of visiting them before their eyes closed to a world of misery and trouble. There came no word and no responsive call from the man who was responsible for their suffering. Of seven or eight innocent wild people, but one little child survived. That one—Mene—was later even denied a passage back to his fathers' land by Mr. Peary.

What is the truth behind this bizarre story? Understandably, Peary makes no mention of it in his own books, and his biographers either omitted it altogether (Hobbs 1936, Weems 1967) or glossed it away by neglecting the all-important details. From Fitzhugh Green's brief mention (1926: 157–58) it appears that in the autumn of 1897 Peary was desperately short of funds and heavily in debt. Besides the hope and expectation that the triumphant recovery and sale of the meteorites, which were brought back in autumn 1897, might help to improve matters, he had also thought of bringing back some Inuhuit to the United States in the hope that, besides providing "an interesting ethno-logical and anthropological study," they would generate publicity that would help promote fund-raising. The story of these unfortunate Eskimos has been put together by the Canadian writer Kenn Harper (1986; see Lauritzen 1987) from many scattered sources, and the main facts are now established.

In 1894, Mrs. Peary, at the end of her second overwintering in Avanersuaq, had taken back with her to America a twelve-year-old Eskimo girl, Eqariusaq, whom the Pearys dubbed "Miss Bill" and whose photograph adorns one of Peary's books in two places. According to Peary (1898a: 487), the "first and only thing [in America] that elicited expressions of vivid surprise and aston-ishment" from her "was the sight of a Chinaman upon the street," whom she evidently mistook for a fellow countryman. In 1903 Eqariusaq was discovered by the Danish Literary Expedition alive and happy on Saunders Island (Mylius-Erichsen and Moltke 1906: 99, 211–12). She had been well treated in the United States, but her longing for Eskimo food, they were told, was the main reason she was safely restored to her friends and kinsmen in the summer of 1895, when she was taken north on the *Kite.* Peary describes how, when her father, Nuktaq, reached the *Kite,* anchored in McCormick Fjord, and boarded the ship, she was awakened and told of his arrival. Even though she had not seen him for a year, she promptly went off to sleep again and had to be reawak-ened. Father and daughter, as is customary with Eskimos, showed no sign of emotion when they met, but Peary was told that, once they were alone, Eqa-riusaq "had talked to him an unceasing stream through nearly two entire watches (eight hours)" (Peary 1898b: 537–38).

In 1897, when Peary's ship the *Hope* steamed homeward from Cape York late in August, she had on board a party of six Inuhuit: Qisuk, Nuktaq, Atan-gana, Aviaq, Uisaakassak, and Minik. Peary is said to have taken the Eski-mos back with him to the United States because they requested him to, but the idea may have originated with Franz Boas, who had just become an assistant curator in the American Museum. Boas wrote to Peary that "it would be of the greatest value if you should be able to bring a middle-aged Eskimo to stay here over winter" (Harper 1986: 33). Boas and his colleagues may have been startled by the arrival of six Eskimos in place of the one hoped for, but they were all housed and taken care of in New York at the American Museum of Natural History, where, however, they soon began to cough. By November they were in hospital with pneumonia, and within nine months four of them had died, probably of tuberculosis. Qisuk, said to be "a chief of the tribe," who was the son of Qulutana, who has figured largely in these pages in connection with the expeditions of Kane and Hayes, succumbed first, in Bellevue Hospital, New York, on 17 February 1898, aged about forty-five. Nuktaq's wife Atangana died on 15 or 16 March 1898, aged about fifty-five. Nuktaq himself died on 14 May in the same year and at about the same age, and their twelve-year-old daughter Aviaq died on 19 May (Spitzka 1902, Hrdlička 1910, Harper 1986). Qisuk's son, eight-year-old Minik, survived an attack of tuberculosis and was adopted by William Wallace, an employee of the museum. He took the name of Mene Wallace, was privately educated in New York, and after returning to Avanersuaq, where he stayed from 1909 to 1916, went back to New York and subsequently died of influenza in "a lumber camp in the woods of New Hampshire" (MacMillan 1934: 270) in 1918 or 1919 (Harper 1986, Lauritzen 1987).

Almost a year after the six Inuhuit had left home on the *Hope,* Peary brought the other survivor, Uisaakassak, back to Avanersuaq on board the *Windward.* Uisaakassak told so many tall stories about America, which he called "the great scramble," to his friends that he was soon nicknamed "the big liar." According to Freuchen (1954: 103), he told them he had seen houses "rushing along on iron rails," people living "on top of each other" like birds on the ledges of a cliff, and, most absurd of all, he had spoken to Peary through a thin thread when he was far away in another town. It has been claimed that either because of these strange stories of trains, skyscrapers, and telephones, or because his visit to America had made him arrogant and autocratic, or for both reasons, Uisaakassak was never thereafter fully accepted into Inuhuit society. At any rate, he withdrew in 1905 to found an isolated colony of his own far to the south of Avanersuaq at Tuttulissuaq on the Melville Bay coast. After his return from there to the Inglefield Gulf area he was murdered by Silluk and Oodaaq, probably in 1910. The killing could be justified theoretically. For one thing, in a society in which, according to Peary's figures, there were only eighty-one women for every hundred men, Uisaakassak insisted on having two wives; he also had a reputation as a womanizer (Mylius-Erichsen and Moltke 1906: 406). For another thing, he kept a team of nine dogs while others went short. But there were pressing practical reasons for the crime. Silluk claimed that one of Uisaakassak's two wives, Aleqasina, was his, though she had been married to Uisaakassak until she deserted him for Silluk in 1904, and she had returned to Uisaakassak in 1908–9, after Silluk deserted her when he signed on with Peary for the North Pole trip. The other murderer, Oodaaq, had recently lost his wife and badly needed another. Thus by shooting and killing Uisaakassak both Silluk and Oodaaq solved their marital problems: Silluk remarried Aleqasina and Oodaaq married Uisaakassak's other wife, Meqo (Rasmussen 1935: 178–88, Freuchen 1936: 41–44, 1954: 102–3, Gilberg 1969–70 and 1970, Harper 1986: 166–69). Both Rasmussen and Gilberg have done their best to rehabilitate Uisaakassak, whom Freuchen regarded as a scoundrel. Gilberg excused his stealing of other men's wives on the grounds that he had remained childless in a society that regarded children as a status symbol.

The unfortunate Inuhuit who were taken to New York in 1897 were exploited in the interests both of fund-raising for Peary and for science. Uisaakassak, complete with his Arctic fur clothing and hunting equipment, accompanied Peary on a lecture tour as an exhibit (Mylius-Erichsen and Moltke 1906: 274). Kroeber used their presence in New York to record and publish some of their legends. Before they died, Uisaakassak's companions were examined, measured, and described, and they were mentioned in a paper published in 1910 entitled "Contribution to the Anthropology of the Central and Smith Sound Eskimo," written by the anthropologist Ales Hrdlička and published in the *Anthropology Papers* of the American Museum. As soon as he died, Qisuk's remains became the object of a dispute between the Bellevue Hospital and the American Museum. According to the *New York Daily Tribune,* it was settled by allowing the medical students to make as much use as they could of the body in the hospital dissecting room; thereafter the skeleton would be mounted and preserved in the museum (Harper 1986: 91). Hrdlička—known to his friends as Hard Liquor—was able to secure and describe the brain of Qisuk immediately after his death, and the *American Anthropologist* published his paper on this macabre subject in 1901. It was only the fourth Eskimo brain to be scientifically described; the owners of the other three had died of smallpox in Paris in 1881, and their brains had been the subject of a monograph by a certain Chudzinski. In 1902, volume 2 of the *American Journal of Anatomy* carried a paper by E. A. Spitzka called "Contribution to the Encephalic Anatomy of the Races," the first part of which dealt with "three Eskimo brains from Smith's Sound." In the second and third parts, "A Japanese brain" and "two brains of natives of New Guinea" were inventoried. Needless to say, the "three Eskimo individuals whose brains are here presented" (p. 29) were those of the luckless Nuktaq, Atangana, and their daughter Aviaq. Their brains were weighed, drawn, and preserved in "a mixture of formal and alcohol" and then deposited in the Anatomical Laboratory of Columbia University, New York. Although they belonged to the "lower races," then thought to be dying out, these Eskimo brains were found to weigh more than the average European brain.

Fortunately for the Inuhuit, Peary's immediate successors in the exploration of Avanersuaq and in the study of its inhabitants, the Danish members of the Literary Greenland Expedition of 1903, lacked the means to take plaster casts or abduct people en masse to Copenhagen. They were supposed not to be scientific but literary. Nonetheless, their leader, Ludvig Mylius-Erichsen, did not rest content with a census. He was an anthropologist at heart. He soon acquired a reputation among the Eskimos for incipient lunacy after he had insisted on measuring Kale and his wife Asivaq "anthropologically" and pulling out some of their hair by the roots. Mylius measured head shape, arm span, and chest width, described skin color, and also measured kayaks, sledges, and tents, while his colleague Knud Rasmussen was busy recording legends, and the third Danish member of the expedition, Harald Moltke, painted the Eskimos' portraits (Andreassen 1984 reproduces fourteen, eleven in color) (Mylius-Erichsen and Moltke 1906: 223, 328–29, 370–73). The expedition did take one man, Uusaqqaq, back to Copenhagen. He returned to West Greenland in the summer of 1905 with Knud Rasmussen, settled in the Uummannaq district of West Greenland, and, on being baptized, took the name Knud Mylius Moltke Rasmussen.

Anthropological and medical studies of the Inuhuit have continued to the present day. In 1926 the American Museum Greenland Expedition took blood samples from them to ascertain their blood group (Heinbecker and Pauli 1927). From 1963 on the Danish Gilberg family research team has carried out an intensive research program that included taking fingerprints, recording the color of the pupil and the shape of the eye and eyebrow, and collecting blood samples (L. and Å. Gilberg 1986).

Ethnologists have thus seized on and somewhat indiscriminately exploited the research potential offered by the very small and relatively isolated population of Inuhuit. The studies so far described have centered on living Eskimos, forced or bribed to allow themselves to be measured, photographed, and so on, but at the same time archaeologists and other less professional enthusiasts excavated the relics of dead Eskimos. The nineteenth-century craze for rifling graves was accompanied by a passionate craving for artifacts or souvenirs, which found expression in the wholesale excavation and plundering of the ruins of ancient Eskimo houses and of the middens that were sometimes found near them.

Elisha K. Kane began the fashion of grave robbing in Avanersuaq. At the start of his explorations, on the shores of Lifeboat Cove on 7 August 1853, when removing boulders to heap over the boat and supplies he cached there, he and his men uncovered some graves. Some "Esquimaux instruments" taken from these graves are the subject of one of the illustrations in his book. Kane was far surpassed as a grave robber by Hayes, who, during his expedition of 1860–61, when he overwintered near Iita, managed to collect, load on board his ship, and take back to the United States of America no fewer than 101 Inuhuit crania complete enough to measure accurately. No mention of this is made in his published works. The measuring was undertaken by Emil Bessels in about 1874, at which time some of the skulls were still in Hayes's possession and the others were in the Museum of the Academy of Natural Sciences of Philadelphia (Bessels 1875, 1879: 350–73, 1884). That academy's appetite for Eskimo skulls had apparently still not been satisfied. In its *Proceedings* for the year 1891 the leader of the West Greenland Expedition, Angelo Heilprin, reported that they had brought back a complete Eskimo skeleton and 22 Eskimo crania, not all of them from Avanersuaq (Heilprin 1891). The American Museum was also interested in Eskimo skulls: in 1896 Peary opened the very recent graves of three Inuhuit he knew by name and sold it their skeletons (Harper 1986: 30, 244). By the end of the nineteenth century there were tourists on the lookout for Eskimo skulls as well; a passenger on the whaleship *Esquimaux* out of Dundee in 1899 wanted to land on Bushnan Island to see if he could find one (Walker 1909: 31–32). In 1905, Nicholas Senn, professor of surgery at the University of Chicago, who should perhaps have known better, came across a recent grave at Uummannaq. The bones were mostly exposed, and he took the opportunity "to secure a real Eskimo skull, which I brought with me among other equally interesting souvenirs to Chicago."

Kane had rightly pointed out in his *Arctic Explorations* of 1856 that "the Esquimaux never disturb a grave." Nevertheless, he and many a white man after him chose to ignore this taboo, though grave-robbing anthropologists of the present century like Therkel Mathiassen did it furtively and perhaps with guilty consciences (de Laguna 1977: 91–92, 98, 122, 141). The journalist leader of the Literary Expedition, Ludvig Mylius-Erichsen, was such a clandestine grave robber. After midnight, on 9 June 1903, at the settlement of Itilleq on the south shore of Inglefield Gulf, he stole out of his tent so as not to disturb his sleeping Eskimo companions and made his way to a burial place where on a former visit he had noticed two Eskimo crania in reasonably good condition (Mylius-Erichsen and Moltke 1906: 343, author's translation):

> Under cover of the snowfall and mist, in the course of an hour or so I worked both skulls loose from the frozen ground and carried them to my tent, where I hid them in a kitbag. I did not want to go to the graves openly, partly to avoid offending against the piety of the Eskimos, and partly so as not to risk the effects of any possible resentment. But the importance of bringing home these skulls from this area, where the Eskimo race can be taken to be as good as pure, is so self-evident that I feel justified in procuring a reasonable number of them even at considerable risk.

Could Mylius have been unaware of the existence in America of more than one hundred Inuhuit skulls and of the publication of an exhaustive series of measurements of them by Bessels in volume 8 of the journal *Archiv für Anthropologie?* In any event, he persisted with his nefarious practices. On 4 July, when he removed the skull from a grave he had found on Saunders Island, he made sure he was not seen. But an Eskimo boy put his head through the entrance to their tent while Mylius was showing his find to his colleagues Rasmussen and Moltke. Later two Eskimos entered the tent to look at the skull and expressed their disapproval. Worried by this incident, Mylius took the trouble to entertain these two in the tent by plying them with biscuits, explaining that skulls had to be measured just like living people's heads, thus implying that that was all he wanted it for. Finally he made them a present of some pieces of wood they badly needed for their kayaks.

The ruined and often long-abandoned winter houses of the Inuhuit or their predecessors in Avanersuaq must have been excavated or dug into by many a nineteenth-century expedition without any record being made of what was done or found, still less publication. The Inuhuit habitually rebuilt and reused these old ruins. The last two great American intrusions into Avanersuaq before recent times, those of Peary and the Crocker Land Expedition, procured comprehensive collections of artifacts, many of which were recovered by digging in abandoned houses, but did little systematic excavation of house ruins. Neither Peary or MacMillan took an archaeologist on their expeditions. By chance, the whaling captain and enthusiastic amateur archaeologist George Comer was stranded with the Crocker Land Expedition between 1915 and 1917. He surveyed and excavated fifty-three house ruins between Parker Snow Bay and Rensselaer Bay (Wissler 1918: 111). Nor was the Danish Literary Expedition of 1903 equipped for or inclined toward the archaeology of house ruins, though its artist, Harald Moltke, drew with care and skill the plan and elevation of an occupied house (Mylius-Erichsen and Moltke 1906: 456) (Fig. 4).

The treasure-hunting variant of archaeology practiced by the nineteenth-century explorers meant that their successors in the twentieth century, the allegedly scientific archaeologists of the years between the two world wars (1918–39), were often hard put to find house ruins that had remained undisturbed since their inhabitants abandoned them. Nonetheless, if by traveling to some far-off place, never before visited by whites, members of this new school of archaeologists did find abandoned houses that had not been dug into and plundered, they immediately set about digging and plundering. A classic example is the English expedition led by J. M. Wordie in 1938, which explored the Cary Islands and visited Ellesmere Island. On Isbjörn Island they found five ruined "long houses" that had "never been disturbed." They noticed whale bones "visibly jutting through" the turf covering of the longest house. "The turf was therefore stripped," revealing "a complete framework of rafters of whale bone." They also dug in one of the smaller houses. At least this expedition, which was from the University of Cambridge, had an archaeologist, the subsequently renowned T. C. Lethbridge. In 1934, Oxford University had sent an expedition to Ellesmere Island (Shackleton 1937), which overwintered at Iita. It had no archaeologist, but the members dug into any house ruins they could find "on the chance of finding some relics" (p. 229), and elsewhere we are told that they "were anxious if possible to obtain some relics which might be of archaeological value" (p. 209). Fortunately, they did not try very hard and seem to have done little damage.

Infinitely more methodical and painstaking than either of these English expeditions was the Danish archaeologist Erik Holtved, pupil of Mathiassen, whose first systematic excavations of Eskimo house ruins in Avanersuaq, at Uummannaq and in Inglefield Land, were carried out in 1935–37, the years between the two English expeditions. Holtved was more interested in quantity than quality: he brought more than twelve thousand objects back from his first expedition after excavating more than forty ruins in Inglefield Land, representing nearly all those he found. His archaeological campaign in the Uummannaq ruins was equally all-embracing, for he seems to have excavated every single one of the twenty-six ruins he found outside the area of the still inhabited settlement. He returned in summer 1947 to dig in the deserted village of Nuulliit, somewhat north of the mouth of Wolstenholme Fjord, where he undertook what might be called a rushed job (Holtved 1954a and b). He managed to "identify with certainty 62 major or minor ruins—in other words, the largest hitherto known ruin site in Greenland." Between 24 June and 24 July, working with one or two Eskimo assistants, he excavated no less than forty of these ancient houses. More recent Danish archaeological practice has fortunately discarded such a breathtakingly speedy tempo, which Holtved himself sometimes found "rather strenuous." Instead of excavating at high speed as many house ruins as possible during the brief summer season of six weeks or so, the Danish archaeologists of the Knud Rasmussen Memorial Expedition of 1979 excavated only three of the ten house ruins they found at Illuminerssuit on the peninsula of Tuttulissuaq near Cape Seddon in Melville Bay (Jacobsen et al. 1980). Even here, however, the old story was repeated of the joyful discovery in an inaccessible spot of unspoiled remains, in this case graves, which the archaeologists immediately proceeded to disturb—and, we may assume, despoil (p. 44).

It would be wrong, while deploring the irresponsible or unnecessary destruction of house ruins and graves by explorers and archaeologists, to assume that the destruction of middens, or rubbish tips, was a relatively harmless occupation. In fact, the hasty excavation of age-old Eskimo rubbish tips in a search for artifacts can destroy just as much valuable historical evidence as the opening up and pilfering of graves. This chapter may fittingly close with a brief account of the joint Danish-American attack on one of the most famous rubbish tips in the history of Eskimo archaeology: Comer's Midden at Uummannaq (Fig. 13).

On the low-lying and gently shelving shingle peninsula bordering the remarkable flat-topped hill Uummannaq is the Eskimo settlement of the same name

(Fig. 3). The two groups of ruined houses belonging to it, one abandoned long ago and excavated by Holtved fifty years ago, the other, next to it to the south, abandoned more than thirty years ago when its Eskimo inhabitants moved to Qaanaaq, are scattered over the slight hollows in a peaty area of long, coarse, tufty grass and one or two small pools. Both groups lie on very gently sloping or undulating ground behind a range of low basalt cliffs forming part of the south shore of Wolstenholme Fjord. At a point along this ice-bound shore, the inhabitants of ancient Uummannaq were wont to dump their refuse, which the accretion of years formed into a low mound. This mound was discovered in 1916 by Captain George Comer, who, on whaling voyages to Hudson Bay, had made the first American collection of Eskimo artifacts (Wissler 1918, Ross 1983). He set about excavating it with the help of the Crocker Land Expedition's doctor, Harrison J. Hunt (Hunt and Thompson 1980: 77), and eventually several hundred artifacts and other objects were recovered. These were sent to the American Museum with the rest of the Crocker Land Expedition's collection and were described and illustrated by Clark Wissler in his paper on the archaeology of the Inuhuit published in 1918.

The Americans, however, were not to have Comer's Midden to themselves. On 17 June 1916 a young Danish student arrived from Copenhagen at the Thule Trading Station with Knud Rasmussen. This subsequently famous explorer and cartographer was Lauge Koch. Freuchen (1954: 155–156), then manager of the station, describes how the youthful Koch was eager "to go to work at once" but had no idea what to do. He spent a great deal of time taking temperatures several times a day at the surface and 5 inches (12 cm) below it in snow, gravel, sand, and swampy earth. "Fortunately," continues Freuchen, "his energy was soon diverted into the study of archaeology" by Captain Comer. While Comer, aided by Hunt, worked at one side of the midden, Koch, aided by Freuchen, worked at the other. The Danes obtained 259 objects but did not publish anything about them until Therkel Mathiassen's classic account of the archaeology of the Central Eskimos appeared in 1927. He named the culture, remains of which Knud Rasmussen's Fifth Thule Expedition of 1921–24 had unearthed across Arctic North America, the Thule culture because it was, first and foremost, represented in the Danish share of the contents of Comer's Midden, which was only a few hundred yards from the Thule station. That share was later vastly increased by the indefatigable Erik Holtved, who recovered 3,299 finds from what was left of the midden in 1937 and hundreds more in 1946.

The quality of Inuhuit life has not been improved by the archaeological and anthropological research described in this chapter. They may have suffered inconvenience as a result of it but little harm. The products of their material culture have been removed, sold, and donated to museums. The ethics of present-day scientific inquiry suggest a different, more understanding, and more conservationist approach than in the past. Yet it cannot be denied that this approach is a product of the earlier activities. Indeed, the entire field of Eskimo anthropological archaeology that has been opened up in the last fifty years by such men as Eigil Knuth and James L. Giddings is ultimately based on the earlier, if now amateurish-looking, researches of men like Peary and Comer. And what of the future? Who knows what further archaeological and anthropological researches will be undertaken in Avanersuaq, where no excavation has been done in the last thirty years? Perhaps the Inuhuit themselves will one day investigate their own past. In 1990 the Danish National Museum returned to Greenland "339 ethnographic and about 6,600 archaeological objects" obtained in Avanersuaq by Danish expeditions. However, these went, not to a museum at Qaanaaq, but to Greenland's National Museum in Nuuk (Schultz-Lorentzen 1990).

9

America in Greenland

*K*ane's expedition of 1853–55, during which he overwintered for two successive years in Rensselaer Bay, Inglefield Land, marked the start of a series of private exploring expeditions to northwest Greenland launched by Americans and supported by the American Museum of Natural History and other American institutions. These expeditions included those of Robert Peary in 1891–1909 and of Donald MacMillan in 1913–17 and 1923–24. The last was the MacGregor Arctic Expedition of 1937–38, which overwintered in Foulke Fjord in the schooner *General A. W. Greely* (MacGregor 1939) and was primarily meteorological. The government of the United States had intervened only once, to send the expedition under Charles F. Hall in the U. S. ship *Polaris* "toward the North Pole." It was only a chance succession of disasters, beginning with Hall's death, that brought members of this expedition to Avanersuaq in October 1872.

Indeed, before the start of the present century no government had shown any interest in any of the lands on either side of Smith Sound. But patriotic private individuals arrived on the scene, willing to take action on behalf of their countries even if their governments were reticent. In 1903 Ludvig Mylius-Erichsen solemnly proclaimed at the start of the Literary Expedition that, in the name of King Christian IX, he had "taken possession for the Danish state" of the entire Melville Bay coast of Greenland from Kraulshavn (Nuussuaq) to Cape York (Mylius-Erichsen and Moltke 1906: 169). Thereafter, he raised the Dannebrog on a ski stick all along the coast of Avanersuaq, at Cape York, at Saunders Island, and, finally, at his farthest north on the Clements Markham Glacier on 25 May 1903, and declared that Danish interests in Greenland also extended to this most northerly inhabited stretch of coast (p. 315). But the Danish government ignored the subsequent requests of Mylius-Erichsen and Rasmussen that it take possession of Avanersuaq. Nor did the government of the United States show any more enthusiasm for Peary's activities at the North Pole on its behalf. On 6 April 1909 he hoisted the Stars and Stripes there and formally took "possession of the entire region and adjacent, for and in the name of the President of the United States of America" (Peary 1910: 297).

The first government to take possession of land in the Smith Sound area was that of the dominion of Canada: on 11 August 1904 A. P. Low (1906: 48), officer in charge of an official Canadian government expedition in the steamship *Neptune,* officially and formally took "possession of the island of Ellesmere Land and all the smaller islands adjoining it" in the name of King Edward VII. He deposited a sonorous proclamation to this effect in a metal box and built a cairn over it "on the conspicuous headland of Cape Isabella." A few years later the cairn was dismantled by the Inuhuaq Torngi. When his companion Rudolph Franke (1914: 120–22) explained the meaning of the proclamation to him he laughed uproariously and refused to rebuild the cairn. This sardonic incomprehension and the disrespectful deed that accompanied it have not deterred Canada from retaining possession of Ellesmere Island or the rest of the world from accepting its doing so.

When, in 1909 and 1910, the Inuhuit were taken over spiritually and economically by Danish explorers, missionaries, and businessmen, attempts were made to implicate the Danish government. The Dannebrog fluttered over the mission house and store erected on the shore of North Star Bay at the end of July 1909, and on 19 August 1910 it was unfurled by Rasmussen on the top of the mountain Uummannaq (Holtved 1960). Still there was no response from Copenhagen. But in 1916, the year Peary suggested that the United States should purchase Greenland from Denmark (Carlson 1962: 53), the United States government formally declared, in connection with the purchase of the Danish West Indies, now the Virgin Islands, from the Danish government for $25 million dollars, that it would not oppose the extension of Danish "political and economic interests to the whole of Greenland" (Skeie 1931: 45, Ancker 1977: 453). On 11 January 1917, when MacMillan (1918a: 276) received news of this at Iita, he thought it "of the highest interest to our Eskimos, hitherto free and independent, henceforth subject to the control of a foreign nation." That control was not put into effect until 1937, but the declaration showed how the strategic and security requirements of World War I had induced the United States to switch her attention from Greenland to the Caribbean. World War II and its aftermath brought Greenland and then the Arctic once again into her sphere of interest. Avanersuaq became subject to American intervention on an unprecedented scale and of an entirely new kind.

When the Germans occupied Denmark on 9 April 1940, that country's far-flung and extensive island possessions in the North Atlantic immediately became a focus of attention for belligerents and nonbelligerents alike. The Faroese and the Icelanders had to accept occupation by the British, but Greenland was a very different proposition. In 1939, the purchase of Greenland by the United States had again been proposed, this time in the Senate (Carlson 1962: 53). When asked by a reporter if Greenland was included in the Monroe Doctrine, President Franklin D. Roosevelt is said to have replied that Greenland's flora and fauna were American. Canada and Britain were warned off and, before the end of 1940, the U.S. Coast Guard had installed itself at Ivittuut, under Commander "Iceberg" Smith, to defend the vitally important cryolite mine. Furthermore, Greenlandic waters were being patrolled by the U.S. Coast Guard, an American consulate had been opened in Nuuk (Godthåb), and a representative of the American Red Cross had arrived there. Exactly a year after the German occupation of Denmark, on 9 April 1941, the representative of free Denmark in Washington, Henrik Kauffmann, signed the Agreement Relating to the Defense of Greenland with United States Secretary of State for Foreign Affairs Cordell Hull, which was subsequently approved by the Danish governor of north Greenland, Eske Brun, and his colleague in the south (text in Vibe 1946: 72–76 and see Sørensen 1983: 93–95). This treaty, which permitted the United States to build and operate air bases and weather and radio stations in Greenland for the defense of that country, was renewed in a modified form ten years later and continues in force to this day (Ancker 1977, Sørensen 1983, Brun 1950 and 1985).

American military activity in Greenland under the terms of the 1941 treaty was, according to the plan for the defense of Greenland approved in summer 1941, to be concentrated in eight defense areas, the two most important of which were at Narsarsuaq and Søndre Strømfjord, code-named Bluie West One and Bluie West Eight respectively, both busy airports to this day. Bluie West Eight, at the head of Søndre Strømfjord, was the site of the airstrip established in 1927–29 by the University of Michigan expeditions led by W. H. Hobbs (1930) and called Camp Lloyd. Also among the eight defense areas was Thule–Bluie West Six. On 24 August 1942 the Norwegian-American flyer Bernt Balchen, remembering that Knud Rasmussen had years before recommended it to him as a possible airfield, flew low over the Pituffik Valley near the Thule Trading Station and passed on the recommendation to the United States authorities (Balchen 1958: 192–93). A year later the U.S. Army erected a weather station in the valley consisting of several buildings on rising ground not far south of the Pituffik River. During the rest of the war this was manned by Danes based at the Thule station, only a few miles away across North Star Bay (Ancker 1977, Lufkin 1977, Ross and Ancker 1977).

Soon after the end of the war the United States Navy embarked on a research program in northern seas, including the Northwest Passage and the straits between Greenland and Canada. At the same time a joint Canadian-American project to establish a network of radio and weather stations in the Canadian Arctic archipelago was begun (Orvig 1981), in which Denmark also participated. These schemes occasioned a fresh wave of activity in the Pituffik Valley, which, together with neighboring North Star Bay, now became an important sea and air transport base. In the summer of 1946 a small U.S. naval armada of surface ships and submarines escorted by an icebreaker arrived in North Star Bay to the amazement of the local Danes, who had not been informed and are said to have feared an imminent United States invasion and occupation of Greenland (Pommier 1953: 98). A 4,000-foot long (1,200 m) gravel runway, with various buildings, was constructed a few hundred yards from the shore of the bay, and the first aircraft landed on 9 September 1946. This airstrip became the springboard for the reconnaissance and air photography flights over Ellesmere Island and north Greenland which the Strategic Air Command of the U.S. Air Force carried out in the summer of 1947 with a squadron of reconnaissance aircraft from Alaska, temporarily based at Pituffik. They provided the necessary photographic coverage in northern Canada and Greenland for the *World Aeronautical Chart*. Pituffik was also the base of operations for the establishment of the Canadian weather stations at Eureka and Resolute, in Ellesmere and Cornwallis islands, in 1947 (Ancker 1977, Clæsson 1983), and of Alert at the northern tip of Ellesmere in 1950.

Each year from 1947 on the United States Weather Bureau's Arctic Operations Office sent an icebreaker with a supply convoy to North Star Bay as soon as the ice there broke up in July. Equipment and supplies were unloaded with the help of lighters and taken across a mile of barren, gravely tundra to the airstrip, whence they could be sent by air to Eureka and Resolute. At this time Pituffik was still a deserted expanse of marshy tundra dotted with lakes, except for the Danish weather station with its six-to-eight-man staff and its few buildings, situated on rising ground just over a mile east of the shore of the bay and on the northern side of the valley, and the gravel runway with attendant buildings not much more than a mile away on the other side of the valley, almost tucked under the slopes of the surrounding hills. This remote and beautiful valley was no doubt still the breeding ground of Arctic birds, the snow goose and the king eider especially. It probably remained just as it was when lyrically described in 1905 by the University of Chicago professor of surgery Nicholas Senn (1907: 110).

> This wide valley is coursed by two streams which drain the ice-cap and a number of small glaciers. One of these streams is large enough to entitle it to the name of river. Owing to the gradual, steady incline of this river from the coast to the ice-cap, a distance of about twenty miles, the current is very swift, and is broken at short intervals by roaring, foaming rapids. On each side of the valley rise mountains from 1,000 to 2,000 feet high, surmounted by a rock-strewn plateau. From these plateaus, the valley beneath, with its

turbulent streams and numerous little fresh-water lakes, presents a magnificent sight. Much of its surface, especially on the west side, is covered by tundra with moss, grass, and an abundance of flowers. The great ice-cap, with its numerous nunataks along its edge, rising like black monuments above the surface of the sea of ice, although twenty miles away, yet appearing in the deceptive, clear atmosphere as though it could be reached in an hour's easy walk, can be seen stretching inland by a gradual incline for eighty to one hundred miles.

During the summer vacation of 1950, Daniel Lufkin (1977), an enterprising student at the Massachusetts Institute of Technology, signed on for a dollar a day with other students recruited to help load and unload supplies for the weather stations. But Lufkin was a photographer and was attached to the surveying team assessing the feasibility of establishing a major air base in the valley. His description and photographs give a last impression of the weather station and the airstrip while they were still only diminutive enclaves in the wild tundra landscape, before the giant new air base was constructed. He visited the radio station, school, church, hospital, and Royal Greenland Trade Department shop at Thule, and he visited and photographed the cluster of stone, wood, and turf houses of the Inuhuit at neighboring Uummannaq. Some of the Eskimos, including Oodaaq, who had accompanied Peary to the North Pole, were helping with the transfer of supplies from the shore of the airstrip, and Lufkin was impressed by their knowledge and intelligence: they could draw a map of the area as well as the surveyors could. These Eskimos told him the name of the place where the radio station and airstrip was situated. It was Pituffik, meaning *the place where dogs are tied up*, a name dating from a long time before when, during an epidemic among the dogs, the sick animals had been tied up there, some way from the settlement. The gigantic military installation, the site of which Lufkin and his colleagues surveyed in the summer of 1950, became, and still is, known to the world as Thule Air Base in spite of a recommendation by the local council at Qaanaaq in 1983 that its name be changed to Pituffik Air Base (*Hainang. Nordgrønlands Avis* [North Greenland's Newspaper], 27 May 1983; Lauritzen 1983).

The United States transformed the modest communications and meteorological facilities at Pituffik into Thule Air Base in 1950–53 because of developments in great power politics and weapons technology; the start of the Korean War in June 1950 greatly hastened its completion. The increasingly hostile confrontation between the United States and the Soviet Union had been reflected in the announcement of the Truman Doctrine and the Marshall Plan in 1947, the Russian blockade of Berlin in 1948, and the creation of the North Atlantic Treaty Organization in 1949. The Americans naturally drew up elaborate plans for attacking the Russians and for defending themselves against Russian attack. The atom bomb, of which the Americans enjoyed a monopoly in the immediate postwar years, and the strategic bombers were of crucial importance in the decision to build a military base at Thule, which was equidistant from Moscow and New York and astride air routes between the United States and the Soviet Union. Behind this thinking were two probably mistaken beliefs of American military strategists, namely that the war against Germany had been won largely by means of American daylight raids by heavy bombers on communications and industrial targets within Germany in May– September 1944 and that the Japanese had surrendered because of the atom bombs dropped on Hiroshima and Nagasaki in the summer of 1945 (Bjøl 1977). The American military presence in Greenland had been called into being against the Germans by the 1941 defense treaty with Denmark. It was confirmed ten years later in the 1951 defense treaty. But the enemy had changed in the meantime: Thule Air Base was unmistakably aimed against the Russians. Indeed, the activities at Pituffik from 1946 on including the construction of weather stations and the aerial photography of northern Ellesmere Island and Greenland, had all been undertaken with the possible dispatch of strategic bombers over the North Pole and northern Greenland to targets in the Soviet Union in mind.

The construction of Thule Air Base, code-named Operation Blue Jay, was virtually completed between February 1951 and October 1952. It was one of the greatest engineering feats of all time; its logistics have been compared to the Normandy landings of June 1944 and repeatedly described by journalists and popular writers in colorful and sometimes hyperbolic language. The Austrian Hans Thür (1958) even wrote a novel about them, with the conquest of the brutal and hostile Arctic by organization and technology as one of the main themes. Bernt Balchen appears in this book thinly disguised as the United States Arctic expert Ben Balten; the Eskimos, though forced to leave their homes, rescue some Americans from a drifting ice floe; and the engineering problems are compounded by every conceivable natural phenomenon— dreadful gales (which do occur at Thule), plagues of mosquitoes, and violent thunderstorms (which do not). At the same time Thule Air Base was constructed, the United States air bases at Søndre Strømfjord and Narsarsuaq were reactivated.

The principal partners in the building of the base were a consortium of four of the largest engineering and construction companies in the United States, which called themselves North Atlantic Contractors, and the U.S. Army Corps of Engineers. The entire operation was based in Norfolk, Virginia, and the airlift was from Westover Air Force Base, Massachusetts. A first contingent of six hundred men was flown in during the Arctic twilight days of March 1951. The main convoy of 120 ships, led by the icebreaker *Adak* and carrying cranes, bulldozers, tractors and other vehicles, prefabricated buildings, oil, stores and supplies of every kind, as well as some twelve thousand men, left Norfolk on 6 June 1951 and, after delays and damage occasioned by ice in Melville Bay, arrived to drop anchor in North Star Bay on 9 July 1951. While the landing of men and material from lighters got under way, a three-hundred-yard-long jetty was completed in record time on 14 August by sinking eight discarded landing craft salvaged from a ship graveyard in Florida. All super-structure had been cleared off them so that, secured end to end and sunk, they could be used at once for the jetty. That summer, oil tanks had to be con-structed ashore and filled, the largest seawater distillery ever made had to be constructed to provide drinking water, a steam central heating and drainage system for the entire base installed, streets laid out, extensive runways laid down, the enormous heated steel hangars erected, and hundreds of buildings constructed on concrete stilts or wooden blocks to ensure their stability on the permafrost. When autumn came, the entire area was bathed in electric light. In 104 days an airport had been built that could be used by any known aircraft. The last construction party was flown out on 23 October 1951 (Ancker 1977; Pommier 1953: 49–52; Ross and Ancker 1977; see too, Malaurie 1956, 1982).

Work on the new base continued in 1952 and was successfully brought to completion before the onset of the long winter night. On 9 September 1952 four F 94-B all-weather fighters from Fifty-ninth Fighter Interceptor Squad-ron were flown in. Two of these aircraft were supposed to be able to take off within five minutes of an alert to identify, intercept, and if necessary destroy any hostile aircraft within striking distance. Finally, on 1 November, the base was officially handed over by the Corps of Engineers to the U.S. Air Force. It lies in the center of a total defense area of 339,004 acres (137,193 hectares), which was soon intersected by 56 miles (90 km) of gravel roads.

Thule Air Base (Fig. 14) was constructed solidly and well. It remains much the same now as it was in 1952: hangars, runways, barrack blocks, the net-work of gravel streets and central heating and drainage pipes, and thirty-nine large cylindrical fuel tanks, which can store more than 100 million gallons of petroleum products, though many of them have been dented by fierce Arctic winds. But its purpose has changed more than once: Thule Air Base has a history. It was initially designed as an operational backup base for strategic bombers flying from airfields in the United States to targets in the Soviet Union, including the heavy industry concentrated during and after World War II behind the Urals. For this operation Thule would provide technical and logistic support and make it possible, by means of the tanker aircraft stationed and supplied with fuel there, to refuel the bombers in the air. Thule's second role in the 1950s was as a fighter base from which, it was hoped, long-range all-weather fighters could intercept and destroy Russian heavy bombers en route to targets in America. Thus a succession of Starfires, Scorpions, and Delta Daggers were stationed at Thule, which was protected by radar stations set up on the Inland Ice 93 miles (150 km) north and 186 miles (300 km) east of Thule but soon abandoned because of the cost of manning them, and by four batteries of surface-to-air missiles and a circle of anti-aircraft guns. The main radar warning and control center for the base was at first in the base itself, then on North Mountain just outside its northern perimeter, and finally on the mountain called Pingorssuit or P-mountain 21 miles (34 km) south of the base via a winding gravel road and 2,660 feet (810 m) above sea level.

Toward the close of the 1950s Thule's role in support of America's strategic air arm was made less significant by the development of a much longer-range strategic bomber (the B-52 Stratofortress), which did not have to be refueled in midair, and its role in air defense was diminished by the development of intercontinental ballistic missiles on both sides, which made fighters based at Thule seem irrelevant. But a new role for the base came into being in 1958–60, when it was decided to build the first of three Ballistic Missile Early Warning System (BMEWS) installations on a high ridge about 12 miles (20 km) to the northeast of the base. Said to be capable of giving fifteen minutes warning of the approach of a hostile missile and of detecting an orange thrown into the air from a distance of 3,000 miles (5,000 km) (Furnas et al. 1966: 103–7), this radar station is now manned and maintained by the Twelfth Missile Warning Squadron of the U.S. Air Force based at Thule. Completed in January 1961, BMEWS Site 1 is locally known as J-site and is now being updated and replaced by a new phased-array radar station using computers and electronics to track missiles and monitor objects in space. It is dominated by four gigantic sky scanners, each longer than a football field and as high as a fifteen-story building, which are the radar antennae. They are perched on a clifftop facing due north 885 feet (270 m) above the head of iceberg-strewn Wolstenholme Fjord, where three great glaciers flow into it. Under the station is a labyrinth of tunnels and underground rooms to house the personnel as well as computers and other equipment. The planned modernization of this early-warning radar station was the cause of a political crisis in Greenland in 1987 (the London *Times,* 12 March 1987).

Space surveillance was added to Thule's role as a missile-warning station after the construction of a tracking radar in 1961, and in 1983 Thule Air Base was officially transferred from the U.S. Air Force's Strategic Air Command to the newly set up Space Command. In the *Thule Times* of 25 May 1984 the editors featured an article in "an effort to help Thule's assigned servicemembers better understand the mission and operations of the Air Force's new Space Command" of which they now formed part. Some of it ran as follows:

The command's motto, "Guardians of the High Frontier", reflects the spirit and determination that our pioneer forefathers had as they met the

unknowns of a new continent. That same spirit and determination are hall-
marks of Space Command as the Air Force meets the challenges of the new
frontier—space.

Space Command's mission is to manage and operate assigned space
assets, centralize planning, consolidate requirements, provide operational ad-
vocacy, and ensure a close interface between research and development activities and operational users of Air Force space programs. Space Command is
also the major command responsible for the strategic defense mission area.

Whether or not Thule's air force personnel found this passage enlightening,
their primary mission now is the tracking of objects orbiting the earth, as well
as the support of at least two "major contingency plans" that might be put
into operation in the event of hostilities.

Thule Air Base, combining airport, harbor, oil storage depot, warehouses,
barracks, gymnasium, hospital, churches, a post office, a shop, dining hall,
clubs, a hotel, and much more, is a small town. While under construction it
housed a labor force of up to 12,000 men. The peak permanent population
since then was reached in about 1959, when J-site was under construction: at
that time there were some 10,000 people at the base, 4,000 of them American
military personnel. Subsequently, numbers declined: in 1977 there were about
1,440, only 240 of whom where U.S. servicemen: of the remaining 1,200,
about 800 were Danes and 400 American civilians. In 1984, according to an
official handout, there were 1,400 "residents" at Thule Air Base, about 960
Danish and 220 American "contractor personnel" and about 220 U.S. Air
Force personnel. For the last twenty years, the great city in the Arctic, the
billion-dollar base, has been a sleeping giant. Many of its barracks and other
buildings have been and are empty, most of its enormous oil storage capacity
is used only to hold a significant proportion of the United States national reserve, its huge hangars are deserted. The space surveillance tasks of J-site use
only a tiny fraction of the base's vast resources.

Life at Thule Air Base differs in important respects from that at military
bases elsewhere. Thule is isolated. Its personnel are virtually sealed off from
the other inhabitants of Avanersuaq, the Inuhuit, and contacts in recent years
have been limited to annual sporting and social festivities on Armed Forces
Day (5 May). The field events are held on the ice of North Star Bay and include dogsled racing, games for Eskimo children, mukluk hockey (seven-a-
side using brooms and a slightly softened volleyball), and speed skating.
Afterward, buses transport the participants to one of the base's enormous
hangars, where food and music are provided. Eskimos gather for this gala
from the entire region—in 1983 thirty-nine dog teams participated in the four-
mile sledge race. In 1984 the winner was Miteq Qisuk of Qaanaaq, who

completed the course in ten minutes at a speed of twenty-four miles per hour (39 km). The winners were presented with Winchester repeating rifles, and hunting knives were distributed as consolation prizes for the losers. Very strict rules are enforced by the United States authorities on these occasions: participants are reminded that no bartering is allowed with the Eskimos ("the Royal Greenlandic Trade Department is the only organization allowed to trade with Greenlandics") and no alcoholic drinks are allowed on the ice, in the hangar, "or anywhere our Greenlandic guests are allowed. It is illegal to give Greenlandics any alcoholic beverages" (*Thule Times,* 29 April, 13 May 1983; 30 April, 15 May 1984). On these annual occasions the Inuhuit visitors camp near their former settlement of Uummannaq on the far shore of North Star Bay from Thule Air Base.

Because Greenlandair maintains regular helicopter flights, weather permitting, between Thule Air Base and the administrative center of Avanersuaq, Qaanaaq, 65 miles (104 km) due north of the base, as well as other Inuhuit settlements, Eskimos as well as Danes traveling between these places and Denmark are frequent visitors at the base as transit passengers. When bad weather detains them at the base they are allowed to eat in the refectory, Dundas Dining Hall, make purchases in the shop, the Base Exchange, visit the Knud Rasmussen Recreation Center, the theater, and the gymnasium, and, if necessary, they are put up for the night at the base's hotel, the North Star Inn. They may make free use of the base's buses and taxis but may not purchase wines and spirits at the Top of the World Club's duty-free shop, nor may they purchase any other goods that if imported into Avanersuaq would be subject to duty payable to the government of Greenland, namely beer, tobacco and cigarettes, chocolate, and sugar. Naturally they are forbidden to barter with base personnel.

The only other contact with the Inuhuit has been indirect. Recently, at Christmas, Operation Julemand or Father Christmas has been organized at Thule Air Base and has resulted in up to $10,000 being raised to buy presents for Eskimo children and for other purposes such as funding playground equipment for the children at Savissivik, providing "Siorapaluk with kayaks for use in the school curriculum," buying camping equipment for the Boy Scouts at Qaanaaq, and installing a generator for the Community House at Moriusaq (*Thule Times,* 14 January 1983, 15 May 1984).

Besides these occasional contacts with their neighbors, Thule Air Base personnel look forward with enthusiasm to the annual resupply by sea, which takes place in July and August. The first ship to tie up each year at the world's most northerly deepwater harbor is a U.S. Coast Guard icebreaker. In 1983 it was the cutter *Northwind,* famous for her 1965 cruise into the Polar Sea north of Siberia (Petrow 1967), which arrived on 4 July with a crew of 170 and two helicopters. She had struggled through three-foot-thick ice for the previous hundred miles. The only regular and frequent contacts between Thule Air Base and the rest of the world are by air. In 1984 aircraft were flying four times weekly between McGuire Air Force Base, New Jersey, and Thule Air Base, a distance of approximately 2,500 miles (4,022 km) each way (*Thule Times,* 29 June 1984). These aircraft fly fresh fruit and vegetables and eggs in to the base for consumption in the Dundas Dining Hall, as well as taking American personnel to and from the United States. In 1984 there was also a weekly flight from Thule to Søndre Strømfjord Air Base farther south in Greenland. Contacts with Copenhagen are fewer; Scandinavian Airlines System flies to Thule once every two weeks in the summer.

Besides its relative isolation from the outside world, Thule Air Base is unique in its situation at 76° 30′ north latitude—700 miles (1,100 km) north of the Arctic Circle and 800 (1,300 km) miles south of the North Pole, according to an official handout at the base. Life there tends to be dominated by the long winter darkness, officially reckoned from 22 November to 22 February, and the long summer day between April and August, when the sun never sets. The sun's first appearance is always good for a photograph in the *Thule Times* (naturally the world's most northerly newspaper), and since 1975 the Danish community at least has made use of the midnight sun on the eve of St. John the Baptist's day (Sankt Hans) or Midsummer Day, to celebrate with a bonfire in true Nordic fashion (*Thule Times,* 1 July 1983, 29 June 1984).

The low winter temperatures do not interfere with life at Thule as much as the recurrent Arctic winter storms, when very high winds can be expected, usually accompanied by blizzards. A warning system has been set up classifying these adverse weather conditions into three categories or phases. A Phase Alert is announced when bad weather is impending, and in these conditions no one is permitted to leave the base on foot. Three separate phases follow. Phase 1 is announced when winds reach a speed of twenty to thirty knots per hour; at this time the buddy system applies, and one is allowed to walk about the base only with a companion. Phase 2 implies winds of up to forty knots; nonessential work ceases, all base facilities are closed, including Dundas Dining Hall, and personnel are expected to return to and remain in their quarters. If winds increase to over fifty knots Phase 3 is announced; no movement is allowed, and one has to remain in the building one is in until the storm is over.

Danish civilian personnel outnumber United States Air Force and civilian personnel and this adds another dimension to life at Thule Air Base. The Danes all speak some English, and Danish lessons are available for Americans. Denmark is responsible for running all base facilities and services, including the fleet of buses that carry personnel around the base and to and from outlying places like the BMEWS site 1 or J-site, all other transport, the Thule

Port Authority, the Dundas Dining Hall, road repair, runway maintenance, weather services, loading and unloading of aircraft, and virtually everything else. All this is the responsibility of a consortium of six major Danish engineering firms, called Danish Arctic Contractors, which was set up in 1952 at the time the base was constructed.

Naturally such a large and well-equipped base as Thule offers many sporting activities. Perhaps the most remarkable of these is the annual golf tournament held since 1975 on the flat top of Mount Dundas (Uummannaq) at a height of 728 feet (222m) above sea level. The last, nearly perpendicular, section of the ascent is usually scaled with the aid of a fixed rope. So far the match has only once been "Phased Out" by bad weather. According to the rules of the Dundas Open, players may not use their clubs as walking sticks during the ascent of Mount Dundas; they carry a piece of carpet on which they are allowed to place their ball; snowdrifts "will be treated as casual Arctic water and played as such"; players going over the cliff after a ball, therefore out of bounds, "will be considered lost and severely penalized"; and "cheating will not be tolerated and will be punished by an invitation to next year's tournament" (official brochure of the Thule Country Club).

The humdrum life of Thule Air Base has twice been disturbed by exceptional incidents. On 21 January 1968 a B-52 bomber carrying four atom bombs, which had been flying high over international waters off Greenland, caught fire and crashed onto the sea ice in or outside Wolstenholme Fjord. Six of the seven crew members parachuted from the burning aircraft and all, miraculously, made their way safely to Thule Air Base, the last arriving twenty-two hours after the crash. The scene of the crash was not easy to investigate in the dark and in a temperature of −22° F (−30° C), and work continued through the following summer. An independent investigation was undertaken by the Danish Atomic Energy Commission, which found no plutonium concentrations dangerous to humans. Fragments of the bombs, which had not exploded when the chemical weapons the plane was carrying had exploded, were collected and removed, and seventy-one tanks of contaminated snow and ice, each holding twenty-five thousand gallons, were removed to a special area in or near Thule Air Base (Vigh 1970).

On 8 March 1972 Thule was hit by the worst storm in its history. Originating off the southeast coast of the United States, this storm increased in intensity as it moved north, passing Cape Hatteras on 5 March. When it reached Thule in the evening of 8 March the barometer dropped to 970 millibars. The base was placed on a Phase 3 alert and remained so for sixteen hours, experiencing winds of up to 100 knots per hour. On P-mountain the wind exceeded 120 knots during a period of three hours, and at the BMEWS Site 1 a wind of 180 knots per hour (205 mph or 330 km ph) was recorded on the evening of 8 March. This was the second strongest wind ever recorded, the strongest being during a storm at Mount Washington in New Hampshire on 12 April 1934 (Taagholt 1977).

Thule Air Base has served the needs of science as well as those of strategy, though much of the scientific research it has made possible has important military applications. This association of military and scientific aims was present in the first and largest-scale research program at Thule, initiated by several different units of the U.S. Army Corps of Engineers which were reorganized in 1958 to become the United States Army Polar Research and Development Center, with the motto *Scientiae servimus*. According to Danish glaciologist and Inland Ice expert Børge Fristrup (1966: 146) "the Americans were starting the most intensive geophysical and glaciological research programme that had ever been envisaged in any area of glacier or Arctic snow." The nub of this costly and protracted research effort was the study of the Inland Ice (Wager 1962, Daugherty 1963, Fristrup 1960a, 1966, 1977, Laursen 1972, Taagholt 1977).

American interest in the Inland Ice had a long history. With five companions, Hayes (1867) reached its margin above the head of Foulke Fjord on 23 October 1860 and marched inland the next two days, covering 55 miles (88 km) according to his account of this. The pioneer American aviator Parker Cramer had in 1931 been the first to fly across the Inland Ice a few days before his death in a storm over the North Sea. Then, in World War II, aircraft being ferried to Europe crash-landed on it and had to be rescued by other aircraft landing and taking off on the ice (Carlson 1962, Balchen et al. 1945). On 17 July 1942 a squadron of two Flying Fortresses and six Lightnings was forced to crash-land on the Inland Ice about 160 miles (257 km) from Ammassalik, apparently after being lured off course by false information radioed by the enemy. The crew of a Flying Fortress that crashed on 9 November 1942 on the edge of the Inland Ice in south Greenland was forced to winter by the crashed plane but was rescued nearly six months later. After the war, in 1947 and 1953, the United States, prompted by the Cold War with the Soviet Union, mounted two special expeditions, named Project Snowman and Project Mint Julep, which discovered suitable landing places for aircraft on the Inland Ice one hundred miles east of Søndre Strømfjord, in an area of frozen lakes (Carlson 1962). But it was the decision to build Thule Air Base, Operation Blue Jay, that made possible a systematic five-year plan of Inland Ice investigations by the United States.

Even before the completion of Thule Air Base, in the summer of 1952, preliminary explorations of the Inland Ice were made. French experts led by Paul-Emile Victor of Expéditions Polaires Françaises fame were called in with the snow tractors or Weasels they had tried out since 1948 in a series of Inland Ice expeditions farther south. Two places were found not far from Thule Air Base where, instead of the usual ice cliff or moraine of jumbled boulders, the margin of the Inland Ice sloped gently down to more or less flat ice-free land. One of these ramps, as they were called, on the Nunatarsuaq Peninsula across Wolstenholme Fjord from the base, was called Nuna Take Off or Nuto for short. The other, which was much more accessible from the base, being only 16 miles (25 km) to the southeast, was called Thule Take Off or Tuto. In July and August 1952 a joint Franco-American expedition, under the direction of Victor but led in the field by Robert Guillard, consisting of eleven men in five Weasels, drove up the Tuto ramp, across the Inland Ice to the head of Danmark Fjord on the northeast coast of Greenland, and then returned safely to Thule (Pommier 1953).

Camp Tuto, a small town with an airstrip and more than fifty buildings, which was designed as a headquarters for glaciological studies and for further motorized transport ventures over the Inland Ice, was constructed as a satellite of the main base. Completed in 1954, it was provided with a 3-mile (5 km) gravel road that enabled vehicles to drive up the ramp and onto the Inland Ice even when the summer snowmelt, which reduces the margins of the Inland Ice to a quagmire, was in full spate. Via Tuto, in 1954 and 1955, much heavier convoys of up to fifteen vehicles, among them ten-ton sledges and special caravans on runners for living in, crossed to northeast Greenland and back, and other convoys of heavy-tracked vehicles, called swings, took the material for a radar station called Site 2 being built on the Inland Ice about two hundred miles east of Thule Air Base. These expeditions were made much less dangerous by the invention of an electronic crevasse detector that was mounted in the front of the leading vehicle. Even so, a winter swing that drove south from Tuto in the last months of 1955 nearly ended in disaster. Temperatures of −58° F (−50° C) and fierce blizzards were experienced, and several vehicles had to be abandoned.

Meanwhile, at Camp Tuto, U.S. Army Engineers had begun excavating tunnels into the edge of the Inland Ice. Starting with picks and shovels in 1955, they soon had an electric chain saw and then a coal mining machine on the job, and by 1957 the tunnel was several hundred yards long. It was illuminated by electric light and is said to have offered opportunities for research on the storage of food and ammunition, on new types of Arctic housing, on how human beings react to a low-temperature environment, and on the movements of the ice. Near it another tunnel was excavated to study the permafrost, which was shown to be stronger than concrete. Above the entrance to this tunnel a board displayed the words "Camp Tuto Salt Mine. Little Siberia. Greenland."

This motoring over and tunneling into the Inland Ice was inspired by Bernt Balchen's vision of Greenland as a gigantic aircraft carrier and spurred on by fears of an imminent military confrontation with the Soviet Union. Might not radar stations, weather stations, and even air bases be set up on the Inland Ice in northeast Greenland, up to 600 miles (1,000 km) nearer the enemy than

Thule Air Base? Inaccessible by sea because of the pack ice, such establishments would have to be supplied from Thule, with its deepwater harbor, over the Inland Ice and by motorized transport. The climax of this Inland Ice exploration came in 1959–60 with the excavation and construction 7,218 feet (2,200 m) above sea level on the Inland Ice of Camp Century, the so-called "City under the Ice" (Wager 1962, Daugherty 1963). It owed its name to its planned position 100 miles (161 km) from Camp Tuto; in fact, the distance was 138 miles (222 km) over the ice, or 115 (185 km) by air.

Camp Century was not really a city; it could house only about two hundred persons. Nor was it at first "under the ice"; it was subsurface. It was based on a grid of enormous trenches cut out of the surface of the Inland Ice with a Swiss snow-clearing machine called a Peter Snow Miller. The main street was formed by a 437-yard (400 m)-long trench; other trenches at right angles to it contained prefabricated buildings for living quarters, storage rooms, lavatories, a mess, kitchen, library, gymnasium, and so on. These trenches, which were 20 to 30 feet (6 to 9 m) deep, were quickly turned into tunnels by roofing them with arched sections of corrugated iron covered by a thick layer of snow thrown onto them by the Peter Snow Miller. Nature does the rest: every winter up to three feet of compacted snow is deposited over the entire surface of the Inland Ice. Except for the ventilation funnels and escape hatches, little at Camp Century was visible above the surface, and as the years went by, the entire station was being slowly buried under the snow. Eventually, it would indeed be under the ice.

The most remarkable feature of Camp Century was its 1,500-kilowatt nuclear reactor, which provided all the energy required for heating and lighting the entire complex. Instead of an annual requirement of half a million gallons of diesel oil for conventional diesel generators, all that was needed was an annual supply of 110 pounds (50 kg) of uranium. The ten thousand gallons of water consumed daily at Camp Century were produced by melting the ice below the station with steam, forming an underground reservoir that could be drawn on as required. The American writer who visited Camp Century in 1960, C. M. Daugherty (1963), reckoned that the drinking water reservoir descended 400 feet (122 m) and that the personnel of the station were at that time drinking water that had been laid down in snow at about the time the Pilgrim Fathers landed at Plymouth, Massachusetts, in 1620. Camp Century was completed and occupied on 25 September 1960 and evacuated and closed down as a year-round station in August 1965. By that time the two radar early-warning stations, DYE 2 and DYE 3 (named from Cape Dyer in Baffin Island), on the Inland Ice had been constructed far to the south on stilts to ensure that they would not, like Camp Century, slowly be engulfed. By that time, Camp Tuto had also been closed down.

American Inland Ice studies based at Thule culminated in drilling down into the ice and removing a core in which the successive annual layers of snow could be traced and, ultimately, a long-term climatic record could be established. The French, at their Station Centrale, far to the south, had drilled down to 435 feet (151 m), but at Camp Century, where seismic measurements had shown that the ice was not more than 5,250 feet (1,600 m) thick, the power and facilities were thought sufficient to drill through it to the bedrock below. In spite of technical problems caused by the properties of ice, work proceeded throughout the period of occupation of Camp Century and beyond. The first boring, begun in 1961, had to be abandoned in 1962 when the drill head froze solid in the hole and then the drill shoe snapped off. A new boring was more successful and was continued year by year. New techniques were introduced in 1965 so that at the end of that season's drilling, cores had been extracted down to a depth of 3,199 feet (975 m). At last, in 1966, the boring was completed down to the rock, 4,564 feet (1,391 m) below the ice surface (Fristrup 1966, 1977). This Camp Century ice core has since become famous in climatological circles and is still the subject of active research. According to Willy Dansgård and his colleagues (1970), the upper 928 feet (283 m) of core span the last eight centuries. The lowest sections, which are thought to be between 125,000 and 425,000 years old, have been found to contain well-preserved microfossils in the shape of marine and freshwater diatoms whose presence may indicate a substantial enough shrinkage of the Greenland Inland Ice in a Pleistocene interglacial period to have exposed the entire northwest corner of Greenland (Harwood 1986).

From its inception Thule Air Base has played a vital role in the construction, maintenance, and supply of radio and weather stations in the north of Canada and Greenland. These stations serve the purposes both of strategy and of science; they also support scientific expeditions in the field and act as communication centers. Besides the Canadian stations already mentioned, Thule Air Base was the headquarters for the construction of Denmark's Station Nord on the extreme northeastern tip of Greenland, 700 miles (1,100 km) northeast of Thule. This somewhat hazardous undertaking was initiated in 1952, before Thule Air Base was completed, and carried out by air mainly by Americans. Only one Dane participated, meteorologist Edmund Nielsen (1960, Pommier 1953), who subsequently wrote an account of his experiences. The area selected was inaccessible by sea because of pack ice, on which the aircraft carrying equipment, including Weasels and supplies, had to land. Leader of the expedition was an American officer known as "Blowtorch" Morgan, who, according to French Arctic explorer Robert Pommier (1953: 57), "had become celebrated in the Arctic because of the blowlamp which he carried permanently attached to his belt like a revolver; it enabled him to start an engine even in the coldest conditions." It was −40° F (−40° C) on 4 April 1952 when the reconnaissance party arrived to mark out a landing strip on the ice. In spite of accidents and mechanical problems, Station Nord was in operation that year, was manned by four men in the winter of 1952–53, and was completed in 1953 following eighty-seven flights from Thule Air Base that brought in, among other things, eighteen prefabricated buildings. This remote station, runway, and fuel store, which, like Alert, also has a role in antisubmarine warfare, is still dependent on flights from Thule Air Base. In April 1984 a year's supply of more than eighty-five thousand gallons of fuel was airlifted there (*Thule Times*, 30 April 1984).

Thule Air Base has been the site of a great deal of meteorological and other scientific research (Taagholt and Andersen 1981, and see reports in the *Newsletter* of the Commission for Scientific Research in Greenland since then). Radiosondes have been sent aloft by rocket to obtain information about the upper atmosphere. In 1964 Danish scientist Jørgen Taagholt watched the firing of a 6.5-foot (2 m) Arcas rocket weighing 77 pounds (35 kg) from a ramp near the road to J-site; this operation was carried out by four men in white boiler suits and red helmets. The words "Rocket Son" were inscribed across their backs. Meteorological rockets are still fired at this site.

At Camp Tuto and, after 1966, at Qaanaaq, the U.S. Army Signal Corps ran a program of research into the ionosphere that was begun in 1957 as part of the activities of the International Geophysical Year (Lundbak 1956). At Tuto this was housed "in a shack full of instruments that goes by the name of the Signal Radio Propagation Station" (Daugherty 1963: 54). Here sensitive instruments recorded magnetic variations and electron density in the ionosphere as well as the constantly fluctuating height of the ionosphere layer, and radio signals originating in Antarctica were recorded to try to solve the puzzle of why radiocommunication between the Poles is relatively so good. This ionosphere research, vital for long-distance communication, continues at Qaanaaq and is still housed in the original "shack full of instruments," now staffed by Danish scientists of Copenhagen's meteorological institute, which was moved to Qaanaaq and reassembled there in 1966 (Taagholt 1977, Lauritzen 1983).

Another research program was carried out at the so-called Geopole Station on North Mountain immediately north of the air base by the U.S. Air Force Cambridge Research Laboratory. This outpost of Thule, which was built in 1958 and closed down in 1976, was manned by four scientists. Here an All Sky Camera using 16mm film took a photograph of the sky once every minute through the winter, a spectrometer tracked the aurora borealis or Northern Lights, and a cosmic ray counter recorded protons, mesons, and other particles. Studies of the earth's magnetism were continued after 1976, partly in a new installation at Thule Air Base run by Danish Arctic Contractors and partly at Qaanaaq, where a special geophysical station was built in 1953 (Taagholt 1977).

Yet another ancillary outpost of Thule Air Base was the so-called Loran (Long Range Navigation) Station, which was in operation between 1953 and 1975 near Cape Atholl, about 31 miles (50 km) southwest of the base. This radio transmitter was run by the U.S. Coast Guard, and its function in naval navigation was subsequently taken over by satellites (Clæsson 1983). The abandoned ruins of American installations like Camp Tuto, the North Mountain Geopole Station, and the Cape Atholl Loran Station, which disfigure the Arctic landscape around Thule Air Base, give an impression of decline and decay. Yet though American activities at Thule have been on the wane, the Danes look forward to making even more use of the base facilities in the future for at least two of their government research institutes, the Geodætisk Institut, which is responsible for mapping and surveying, and the Grønlands Geologiske Undersøgelse or Geological Survey of Greenland, which has carried on and developed the glaciological and Inland Ice studies originally started in the area by the Americans.

Thule Air Base has been used as a starting point and backup base for many expeditions and activities. In 1952, when it was only half completed, it became the headquarters of Project Icicle: the establishment of a United States Air Force scientific station on the floating ice "island" called T-3, at that time 103 miles (166 km) south of the North Pole. Four aircraft took off from Thule on 19 March 1952. They found that the surface of T-3 or Fletcher's Ice Island, as it came to be called after Colonel Joseph Fletcher, who first described the ice islands, was from 5 to 10 feet (1.5 to 3 m) above the surface of the surrounding pack ice and that the "island" measured approximately 9 miles in length and 5 in width (14.5 km × 8 km). It was later discovered to be 170 feet (52 m) thick in the center (Rodahl 1953, Carlson 1962). Ever since 1937 the Russians had been manning drifting stations on the Arctic pack ice; now the Americans could go one further, for T-3 was no ordinary ice floe like those used by the Russians. Like its fellows T-1 and T-2, it was an enormous chunk of ice that had probably broken off from the Ellesmere Island ice shelf years or even centuries before. When T-1, with a surface area of more than 200 square miles (320 km^2), was first sighted in 1946 less than 300 miles (500 km) north of Point Barrow, Alaska, the radar recorded it as land and it was first believed to be land, hence it was called an ice island. The U.S. Air Force station on T-3 has been abandoned and reoccupied several times and been renamed Bravo. In 1971, when the United States authorities allowed Italian alpinist Guido Monzino to use Thule Air Base as the starting point for his North Pole expedition, he and his colleagues with their dogs, sledges, and Eskimo guides visited the Americans then camped on T-3 on their way from Alert to the North Pole (Monzino 1971). More recently another drifting station, the so-called Polar Research Laboratory Ice Station Crystal, was maintained by aircraft from Thule (*Thule Times,* 29 April 1983).

Thule's role as starting point for polar exploring expeditions has involved the United States Air Force in some dramatic rescues. In 1952, when the base was still under construction and was serving as springboard for the Danish weather station Nord, the American station on T-3, and the Franco-American trans-icecap expedition in Weasels, it was also used by Royal Air Force Hastings transport planes to supply Northice, the Inland Ice station that was manned between 1952 and 1954 by the British North Greenland Expedition. When one of these aircraft crashed onto the Inland Ice while air-dropping supplies for the British station, the twelve British crew members, three of them injured, were rescued by the U.S. Air Force in two separate flights and taken safely back to Thule. Each rescue involved a flight of 480 miles (772 km) east from Thule over the Inland Ice. After taking aboard the stranded airmen, the rescue plane had to take off with the aid of rockets from the snow surface at an altitude of about 8,500 feet (2,600 m), higher than any previous Inland Ice takeoff, and then fly the 480 miles back to Thule (Mackersey 1954, Simpson 1957). A less dramatic rescue operation was directed in the spring of 1983 by the air base's search and rescue officers when two Cessna aircraft became lost near the North Pole and had to land on the pack ice after using up much of their fuel. The radio transmissions from their emergency transmitter were picked up by search and rescue satellite, and once their position was known, a rescue plane from Thule was able to land and refuel one of the Cessnas, which then returned to Thule. The other was recovered later in the same way, after repair (*Thule Times,* 29 April 1983).

Such, in brief, is the history to date of post–World War II American strategic and scientific activities in Avanersuaq and of Thule Air Base, the greatest Arctic military installation in the Western Hemisphere. Its effectiveness as a deterrent cannot easily be assessed, and it has never been used in anger. Yet it has been, and remains, the scene of varied scientific activity, especially as part of the United States collaboration in the 1957–58 International Geophysical Year, and its hospitality has been extended to numerous expeditions. The early promise that it might become an international airport for trans-Arctic flights was never realized, but this piece of America in Greenland will surely remain to fulfill new roles in the future. Then, the significance—never, perhaps, very clear—of the last part of the inscription that is posted on the giant hangar visitors walk toward after leaving their aircraft may escape them altogether. Under the large letters "THULE AIR BASE" one reads: "The Top of the World." Below, it says, "WELCOME. You have just arrived at FREEDOM frontier."

10

The Inuhuit in the Twentieth Century

*F*rom 1818 on, Avanersuaq was penetrated by a succession of whaling and exploring expeditions from Britain and America and successfully invaded and colonized by a small group of Inuit from Baffin Island. These incursions all impinged in important ways on the Inuhuit inhabitants of the region, but it is arguable that the arrival of their fellow Inuit from Canada in about 1862 had greater import than the visits of Europeans and Americans, at least before about 1880. In the twentieth century, the Inuhuit were confronted with the more or less sudden arrival not only of Danes in 1903–10 but also of the West Greenlanders they brought with them, and of these two it begins now to look as though the Danish impact on the Inuhuit is rapidly being overtaken in significance by the influence of their fellow Inuit from West Greenland.

During the course of the nineteenth century the Inuhuit managed to stave off the disaster of extinction which both Kane and Hayes had predicted for them. They likewise escaped the implementation of suggestions to evacuate them south to West Greenland made first by Kane (1856b: 253) and later by the Royal Greenland Trade Department (KGH). M'Clintock (1869: 114–15) describes how, at Godhavn (Qeqertarsuaq) in June 1858, he "received a request from the Royal Danish Greenland Company, through the Inspector of North Greenland, to convey from their isolated locality these arctic highlanders (numbering in all 120 souls), to the Danish settlements in Greenland." He adds that to carry out "so humane a project" would have given him "very sincere satisfaction."

No sooner had these perils been averted when, in the early years of the new century, a new force inspired by a new ideology made its appearance on the stage of Inuhuit history: Danish colonial patriotism. This was more intense and persistent than the impulses that had so far inspired whites to visit Avanersuaq, such as commercial gain, scientific curiosity, the spirit of adventure, the quest for the lost Sir John Franklin, and the search for the North Pole. Now a determined group of idealists who believed that their activities were based on moral rights and duties intervened in Avanersuaq. These people were convinced that Denmark, as colonizer of the Greenlandic peoples, had a natural and moral right to bring them all under a single Danish administration (Rasmussen 1921a: 517). As Mylius-Erichsen (Mylius-Erichsen and Moltke 1906: 279) explained in a lyrical passage in his journal of the Literary Greenland Expedition in 1903, Denmark is not just wooded peninsulas and islands between belts and sounds, it is also this barren district with its bleak coasts, where they were then encamped and where their country's language was being spoken and its flag had been hoisted. "Denmark has become extensive and mighty. Our fatherland is the nations' furthest cultural outpost towards the north."

In 1929, the humorous American writer Daniel W. Streeter (pp. 148–49), who visited Avanersuaq in 1926, drew up a list of things the local Eskimos had managed without up to the time of Peary in the last decade of the nineteenth century. Though meant in fun, the list is worthy of serious consideration. According to Streeter, the Inuhuit lacked

Government
Religion
Salt, pepper or other condiments
Written language
Stimulants, narcotics, drugs
Money or standard of value

Food, except { blood / blubber / meat

Any edible substance of vegetable origin (they didn't have any vegetables)

and Property except { clothing / hunting equipment / traveling equipment / skin tents

In spite of the enthusiasm of Mylius-Erichsen and Rasmussen to provide the Eskimos of northwest Greenland with government as soon as possible in the shape of Danish colonial rule, this first and foremost item on Streeter's list was not immediately forthcoming from Copenhagen. Instead, it was left to Knud Rasmussen and the so-called Cape York Station Thule Committee to provide the Inuhuit with orderly government institutions and laws that, for good or ill, were thought to be essential. After all, Rasmussen could not permanently rule "his" Eskimos as though he were the uncrowned king of Avanersuaq. Yet this was the image he projected. "At Thule Rasmussen, and the Danish committee which works with him in running the thing, have a regular kingdom," wrote schoolboy David Binney Putnam in 1926 (p. 105). "Dad calls it a benevolent dictatorship, which means that Rasmussen is just about a king, but runs everything for the good of the people." In 1927–29 Rasmussen set up for the Inuhuit what Malaurie (1973) described as a *société politique* in the form of the Hunters' Council, which then approved his Thule Law.

The fiction was and is still studiously maintained that both council and law were established according to the wishes of the Inuhuit and that the purpose of the council was to enable them to participate in the management of their own affairs. The alleged desire of the Inuhuit for a council (*efter befolkingens ønske,* Goldschmidt 1950) is about as meaningful as their alleged desire for a Danish mission and trading station or their alleged desire to be moved from Uummannaq in 1953. The composition of the council reveals the limited nature of their participation in self-government. Of the six members, three were permanent and ex-officio, namely the manager of the Thule Trading Station, the pastor, and the doctor, all of whom were appointees of Rasmussen or of the Cape York Committee. The other three, who were to serve only for a year at a time, were local hunters, one from the area north of Uummannaq, one from Uummannaq itself, and one from the south of Avanersuaq. All three were to be appointed by Rasmussen as owner of the Thule station; subsequently they were to be chosen by the Hunters' Council. Not until 1952, when their term of office was extended to four years, were these three members elected by universal suffrage (Gilberg 1977a). Even then, this so-called self-government was neither democratic nor representative.

Like every good statute, the new law was provided with a preamble in which its philosophy was expounded (Sand 1936: 57, author's translation):

> As owner of the Thule Station, Dr. Knud Rasmussen wishes the Station to help the Cape York Eskimos not only to obtain quality goods at low prices and sell their products on the best possible terms, but also to take part, like every other people throughout the world, in the management of their common concerns to their common advantage.
>
> Since it is impossible for every member of the tribe to be present at every deliberation, he wishes some good men to be chosen who will be in a position to make proposals or pass resolutions and take decisions of every kind in such a way that whatever these men are agreed about shall be valid for all members of the tribe.
>
> He has therefore established a Hunters' Council, in the same way as other peoples have a council of good and competent men, to cooperate in conducting their common concerns in the best possible way, partly by making stipulations called law, to be valid for all members of the tribe, and partly to see that this law is observed.
>
> All the tribe's members are named with the one word community and the community speaks through the Hunters' Council.

The Cape York Station's Thule Law of 7 June 1929 was drawn up by Knud Rasmussen with the help of his business manager Rudolf Sand and the approval of the Hunters' Council. In eight sections divided into thirty-five articles it laid down the organization and competence of the Hunters' Council (1–8), crimes and punishments (9–17), regulations for litigation (18–24), health measures (25–27), close seasons and other conservation measures for game (28–29), provisions for social security (30–33), rules for the payment of fines (34), and details about the entry into force and publication of the law (35) (Sand 1935). This law was confirmed by the Danish state in 1931. Under its terms, murder was punishable with a prison sentence of indefinite length; bodily harm, including rape and sexual intercourse with women under fifteen years of age, with a maximum prison sentence of one year. In the period 1935–45 no homicide or sexual crime was known to have been committed and no one was sentenced to imprisonment. The majority of the few crimes recorded were petty thefts and infringements of the game laws (Goldschmidt 1950).

The Danish government's declaration in 1921, in the face of vigorous Norwegian protests, that the whole of Greenland came under its sovereignty, had no immediate repercussions on northwest Greenland and its Inuhuit inhabitants. Nor were Avanersuaq's continued existence as a political no-man's-land and the Inuhuits' in a sort of independence affected by the 1933 judgment of the International Court of Justice in The Hague confirming Denmark's "possession" of Greenland or even by Rasmussen's death in that same year. On 10 August 1935 the Copenhagen office of the Cape York Station Thule issued a set of stamps to commemorate the jubilee or twenty-fifth anniversary of the foundation of the station. Designed by Harald Moltke, they portrayed Knud Rasmussen, walruses, Cape York, and the "Thule Mountain" (Uummannaq) together with the Danish flag (Lindskog 1959). The inevitable absorption of Avanersuaq and the Inuhuit into a national state came at last in 1937 (Brøsted 1988) when the political and economic destiny of these Eskimos was decided without even a pretense of consultation with the people in question. Inuutersuaq, who was a member of the Hunters' Council in 1937, was asked in a newspaper interview in 1983 if the council was consulted before Avanersuaq was incorporated into the rest of the Danish colony of Greenland and the Thule Trading Station taken over by the Royal Greenland Trade Department (KGH). His reply was negative; it merely received the information that this had happened (Lauritzen 1983). If Inuutersuaq (Ulloriaq 1985: 126) regarded this as an impairment of his people's independence, more was to come. In 1950, a Greenland Provincial Council was set up at Godthåb (Nuuk), and the Inuhuit thenceforth elected a representative to its sessions. In 1953, when Greenland was technically declared to be an integral part of the kingdom of Denmark and no longer a colony, the Inuhuit, like all other Greenlanders, found themselves Danish citizens. Still, the Hunters' Council and the Thule

Law remained in force until 1 January 1963, when the municipal system established in West Greenland in 1950 was extended to include the area hitherto loosely known as the Thule district, which later, together with the rest of North Greenland, officially became Avanersuaq commune or Avanersuup Kommunia. The new local council consisted of two members elected from Qaanaaq and one each from three other districts (Weidick et al. 1970). The process of political assimilation of the Inuhuit into a West Greenlandic–dominated Greenland went a step further with the introduction of Home Rule in 1979. Since then Avanersuaq has sent one elected representative to the new National Assembly of Greenland and has become increasingly involved in Greenlandic party politics. Such was the roundabout and arbitrary manner in which the Inuhuit were provided with the government they originally lacked and had never requested.

After government, religion was next on Streeter's list of things the Inuhuit had been doing without. By religion he meant Christianity: the Eskimos in northwest Greenland were heathens. Here, too, it was the private initiative of devout Danes that brought Christianity to them; the actual bringers were West Greenlanders or, as MacMillan (1934: 271) put it, "Half-breed Eskimos from South Greenland, brought up in the faith of the Lutheran Church, and educated at the 'University' of Godthaab." The Americans in Avanersuaq had shown little or no interest in converting the Inuhuit to Christianity, leaving that task to Hans Hendrik (1878: 34), who abandoned Kane's expedition in 1855 to live with them for a few years and did his best to tell them about God and Jesus Christ. Peary, indeed, strongly opposed any attempt to civilize, by which he meant Christianize, the Eskimos. In 1910, just as the missionaries were beginning their work, he wrote: "I hope no efforts will ever be made to civilize them." A Methodist minister replied: "I hope that the Eskimos will be brought to the light and that the darkness and fear of evil spirits that now engulf them will soon be lifted" (*Fram: The Journal of Polar Studies* 1, 1984: 692).

The Inuhuit, who had quickly learned to appreciate and use the white man's weapons, had few problems in adopting his religion, especially when it was introduced among them by fellow Eskimos from West Greenland. But there were some initial difficulties immediately after the arrival of the mission at North Star Bay complete with three years' supply of food and fuel on 23 July 1909 (Rosbach 1910a. For the following account, see especially Gilberg in Ulloriaq 1985, Gilberg 1984c, and Sandgreen 1989). At first, the Inuhuit and the West Greenlanders could not understand one another. Some of the Inuhuit thought that Pastor Gustav Olsen (1910) and his assistant Sechmann Rosbach were speaking Danish, so unintelligible to them was the dialect of West Greenland. The newly ordained priest and catechist, fearful above all of immorality among their future proselytes, were convinced, when Peary's ships arrived at the end of August and all the Inuhuit, both men and women, went aboard them and remained aboard as long as they were anchored in North Star Bay, that the women were being put to immoral purposes while their husbands were busy fetching water and transferring coal. Not surprisingly, the two missionaries found that the Inuhuit lacked any concept of sin, but they may have been somewhat premature in deciding that they did not indulge in some of the "most shameful customs" of their own forefathers in West Greenland and of the East Greenlanders, namely wife exchange, murder, the vendetta, and certain games played by men and women together after the lamps were extinguished.

In his first dispatch to the Danish Mission Society and the Committee for the Greenland Church Cause in Copenhagen on 27 August 1910, after the first year's work of the North Star Mission, Gustav Olsen (1911) reported that he had met all 217 inhabitants of the district except 4 who had been absent hunting musk-oxen in Ellesmere Island. He had had problems with Oodaaq's and others' views about marriage and remarriage, which did not square with his interpretation of the Christian view. He was upset by a case of female infanticide following the father's death. He and his colleague, unlike Mylius-Erichsen in 1903, when his comrade Moltke lay sick, had firmly refused to allow the *angakkoq* or shaman Soqqaq to hold a seance over him to cure him. Olsen confessed that he was curious to see what Soqqaq would do but stopped him because he was not prepared to risk Soqqaq claiming the credit for his recovery. He went on to describe how Sechmann had inadvertently held a service on 2 July, thinking it was Sunday when it was still only Saturday. But the error turned out to be fortunate because divine worship that Sunday was prevented by the arrival of the Dundee whaler *Morning*. The missionaries were disappointed that Captain Adams brought them no letter from the mission societies who had sent them but were pleased to receive "many nice things" from him, including a box of fifty cigars. Their first year's work closed with a tragedy. Uusaqqaq, who was the only living Inuhuit already baptized when the mission arrived, was killed by a shot through the heart from his own rifle as he sat in his kayak on 11 August 1910. A few days later Knud Rasmussen arrived in North Star Bay with Peter Freuchen to set up the Thule Trading Station.

Although they were accepted in a friendly manner by the Inuhuit and the work of the mission was never seriously hindered, the two missionaries had to face the hardships and tragedies that often accompany work in the Arctic. The annual sledge trip early in the year across Melville Bay with the post was fraught with difficulties. Sechmann started off with seven sledges on 18 January but was forced to return a week later because of bad weather. Another effort was made on 28 January and was successful, though the postmen did not arrive back at the mission until 11 March. They had made good progress southward, shooting four bears en route, which provided ample food for men and dogs. But on the return trip they were forced to feed the dogs the skins of the bears so that many died of constipation: only two dogs of the mission's two teams survived. That winter each of the missionaries, who had brought wives and children with them, lost a child through illness (Rosbach 1910b). In winter 1912 Olsen with his sledge and dogs had a narrow escape when he went through thin ice while on a trip to Cape York but was hauled out of the water by his Eskimo companions. This accident made it necessary for them to abandon the trip and return home, Olsen in discomfort. "The trouble was," he wrote, "that I had to wear the wet bearskin trousers for a whole day, because I had nothing to change into" (Olsen 1913b).

The mission's communication with the world outside and its supply of European food and coal were placed in serious jeopardy in its first years. No supplies were delivered in 1910 by Rasmussen's trading company ship because it was already fully loaded and in any case the mission had started in 1909 with three years' supplies. Moreover, though ships could reach North Star Bay for only a few weeks annually in the late summer, the Inuhuit could and sometimes did sledge south in the winter along the Melville Bay coast to Tasiusaq for urgent necessities. In summer 1911 a ship got through to North Star Bay with no luxuries and only two years' supply of bare necessities, but no ship was sent in 1912, and in 1913 the trading company's ship *Kap York* broke down en route and was unable to reach the mission. In autumn 1913 a letter from the mission reached Copenhagen via the last Scottish whaler to visit Avanersuaq, in which Olsen described their longing for a ship and their lack of virtually all European foods. Fortunately, game was plentiful and the pastor was an expert kayaker and hunter (Schultz-Lorentzen 1913).

In spite of these hardships, the mission's work progressed satisfactorily. The first baptism took place on 4 February 1912, of Ulloriaq and five others, and more followed. Those who wished were allowed to keep their own names; others exchanged their Eskimo names for biblical or at least Christian ones such as Maria, Helene, Thomas, and Moses (Olsen 1913a). Education went ahead alongside conversion and may have made a greater impact in the long run on the Inuhuit way of life: twelve children were soon being taught to read and write West Greenlandic (Olsen 1913b). In 1914, when Olsen visited Denmark, he was able to tell the annual meeting of the Greenland Church Cause that fifteen adults and three children of baptized adults had been baptized. Moreover, the morals of the Inuhuit had been improved. Christmas, which coincided with the traditional midwinter season of mutual conviviality, when the Eskimos tended to congregate at Uummannaq, was still the occasion for merriment and revelry, but its non-Christian elements were optimistically referred to in the past tense (Olsen 1914: 1–2, author's translation):

> But there is no doubt that at the same time there was scope for all kinds of heathen practices. I have not seen this myself, but have heard about it.

This time of hospitality offered the best opportunity for the *angakkut* to practise their art. Their aim was to make people obedient and willing to be guided by them, and their method was to frighten people with apprehension for all the misfortunes that might happen. They readily threatened the unwilling and neutral natives that they would cause some mischief to befall them. This was the way the *angakkoq* worked; he was concerned not with consolation, but with fear.

Nor is there any doubt that, at this season of visiting all sorts of heathen indecency took place. The Cape York Eskimos [Inuhuit] were ignorant of the crudest of these, which was practised by the heathen Eskimos in West and East Greenland, the so-called "putting out the lights". But there was much immorality. Women, whose husbands were away on a visit, felt themselves very free towards visiting male guests, and I have been told a good deal about what went on at this time.

On his next visit to Denmark in 1922, at which time another West Greenlandic missionary of the same surname, Jens Olsen, was preparing to take over from him, Gustav Olsen could report that 120 Inuhuit had been baptized, half the population (Olsen 1922; Petersen 1922). Jens Olsen established himself intermittently at Qaanaaq in 1922–29 but moved the mission's headquarters back to North Star Bay when a church was built there in 1930. The last Inuhuit adult to be baptized was Nukappiannguaq (Harington 1989). After several years' residence, the last two with his wife, in Ellesmere Island in the service of the Royal Canadian Mounted Police, he returned in 1933 to northwest Greenland and was baptized on 13 May (Ross 1934; Ulloriaq 1985: 125). Three years later, when the Danish state took over Avanersuaq, the Danish State Church formally took over the mission from the Greenland Church Cause, which had been founded in 1905 to initiate it (Larsen 1972: 85–91).

Few people seem to have offered any resistance to the Christianization of the Inuhuit, which was from the first enthusiastically supported by Knud Rasmussen, except for Thule station manager Peter Freuchen. He raised a lonely voice of protest that was not entirely muffled by the clause in the 1913 contract between himself and the Cape York Committee prohibiting him from criticizing the North Star Mission. Relations between the two were already strained. With manifest disapproval the mission had reported in 1912 that "Mr. Freuchen has married a heathen woman in a heathen manner and follows heathen cult in his home" (Christensen 1986). Freuchen saw the mission as a threat to the culture and way of life of the Inuhuit. His attitude is exemplified in the caption to the photograph in his book *Arctic Adventure* of Ittukusunguaq and his wife standing outside their summer tent with no clothes on the upper part of their bodies: "This was before a missionary had informed them it was a sin to go about undressed in their home."

The North Star Mission undoubtedly achieved its aim of transforming the Inuhuit way of life, though its task was greatly eased by the contemporaneous improvement in their material welfare brought about by the Thule Trading Station. Taboos have disappeared, burial practices have been changed, polygyny, infanticide, the drum song rituals, and the *angakkoq* have all gone (Gilberg 1984a). Some say that wife exchange has disappeared under missionary influence (Gilberg 1984a), but others claim it survives, at least in an attenuated form (Adler 1979: 126–28). Eskimo names and naming practices survived until the Inuhuit were compelled after World War II by the Danish Ministry of Ecclesiastical Affairs to adopt surnames (Gilberg 1984a; Ulloriaq 1985: 136). They threatened, however, in 1986 to take the ecclesiastical authorities to court for insisting that they spell their Eskimo names the West Greenlandic way, a practice I have, perhaps mistakenly, followed in this book. Thus Amaunalik must be written Amaannalik, Patdloq should be Palloq, and Osarqak had to write his name as Uusaqqaq (Fægteborg 1986). This insistence by the Christian authorities that the Inuhuit adopt West Greenlandic as their written language supplied another of the wants noted by Streeter. Since 1909 church services have been held in West Greenlandic, children have been taught to read and write West Greenlandic, the administration has used West Greenlandic, and even the local newspaper *Hainang* is printed in West Greenlandic as well as Danish (Søby 1979).

The Thule Trading Station, which was opened by Rasmussen and Freuchen next door to the North Star Mission in 1910, was also a shop. It ensured regular supplies of some of the dietary items noted by Streeter as unknown to the Inuhuit before Peary's time. Indeed, it soon made the Inuhuit partly dependent on European food, as well as on stimulants like tea and, later, alcoholic drinks. Malaurie (1982: 453) opposed the use of spirits in the Arctic and stated that "in 1950–51, alcohol was fortunately forbidden and unknown to the Polar Eskimo"; Dr. F. Jensen (1960), *locum tenens* or temporary doctor in summer 1959 in Qaanaaq, reported the same. British polar explorer Wally Herbert (1969: 73–74) found a very different situation when he wintered in Avanersuaq in 1966–67. At Siorapaluk on 1 March 1967, "by lunch-time half the village was tipsy." He continues:

> I had seen drunken Eskimos three times before—on the 1st December, 1st January and 1st February. On a points rationing system the inhabitants of the Thule District (Danish administrators and British Expeditions included) are allowed per person one bottle of spirits, two bottles of wine or twenty small bottles of beer a month. The Eskimos invariably buy a bottle of whisky and finish it off in one lurching tour of the village. At Qanaq our hut had been bypassed by most of the Eskimos, consequently we had not

become involved in the orgies on the first of each month; but at Siorapaluk, Allan and I were right in the thick of it and the focal point of interest.

With the exception of Inutasuak [Inuutersuaq], an old hunter of great dignity who had travelled in his youth with Edward Shackleton, every Eskimo in the village was rotten by nine o'clock. Men were squaring up to each other and then falling over, old crones were screaming like stuck pigs or sobbing, and wide-eyed children were cowering in the corners or hiding beneath thin blankets on sleeping-platforms on which their elders were wrestling in a stupor of fornication. From each hut in the village came the roars of lunatics and the thud of falling bodies. Doors were wrenched open and, framed for a moment in the light of a lantern, bow-legged drunks lurched out into the night.

Through the village at midnight I followed the old man. He was in a hurry, and the thin shaft of light from his torch did not for one moment change its angle, nor did he once look up. He was disgusted with his fellow villagers and ashamed that I had witnessed the "Inouit" (the man *par excellence*) in their weakness. "Drink and the Eskimos no good—no good, NO GOOD", he kept saying.

These monthly potations continued through the 1970s and shocked the German anthropologist Christian Adler, who noted how they brutalized Inuhuit life and brought everything constructive to a halt for two days each month (1979: 479–82). In the early 1980s, the local authorities were administering a more successful rationing scheme based on the allocation of points through an elected committee that was empowered to make exceptions in the form of extra points for weddings, confirmations, and other special occasions (Lauritzen 1983). Everyone was entitled to a personal allowance, not transferable to others, of ten points per week, and each point was worth a small bottle of beer. The system of extra points gave rise to abuses to which the vigilant editor of the local newspaper *Hainang* (6 February 1984) drew his readers' attention. In spite of the local council's decision that no more extra points were to be awarded for Christmas dinners, the alcohol committee had invited the councillors in writing to submit applications for such extra points. He also complained that though a married couple could obtain no extra points for a child's birthday, the election committee had obtained forty at its last meeting, presumably to promote discussion.

The switch from a diet of "blood, blubber and meat" mentioned by Streeter to one largely based on European food had disastrous effects on Inuhuit dental health. Around 1900 their teeth were entirely without caries. By the early 1950s, after forty years of "shop" food, visiting dentist O. Larsen (1955) found the Inuhuits' teeth to be as bad as those of residents of Denmark or West Greenland and laid the blame squarely on the shop. In the seventeen families then at Qaanaaq, eighteen people had false teeth. When Malaurie (1982: 405) revisited Avanersuaq in 1967 he found that two forty-five-year-old men, who had had excellent teeth when he knew them in 1951, were now entirely toothless.

Apart from the inexorable shift toward a money economy after 1910, the establishment of a shop cum trading station and mission had the effect of concentrating the Eskimo population in one place. Though the mission moved at times to Kangerlussuaq or Qaanaaq and shops were opened at Siorapaluk and Savissivik, Rasmussen found it necessary to forbid people to remain at Uummannaq for more than two years at a time, and in 1948 it was ruled that the flow of immigrants at Uummannaq was not to exceed the flow of emigrants (Fristrup 1960b). Even so, twenty-seven families representing more than one hundred people, or nearly one-third of the total Inuhuit population, were living at Uummannaq in 1953 (Gilberg 1976b: 12 and 1977b: 310). Concentration in one place has become more pronounced since then. According to the 1977 census, there were 702 persons living in Avanersuaq who were born in Greenland (no distinction was made between Inuhuit and West Greenlanders), 316, or 45 percent, of whom lived at Qaanaaq. The remainder were distributed among five settlements: 129 in Savissivik, 106 in Moriusaq, 63 in Siorapaluk, 45 in Qeqertarsuaq (Herbert Island), and 43 in Qeqertat (Petersen and Staffeldt 1978: 315).

This concentration and stabilization of the Inuhuit population was accompanied by changes in housing. From 1910 onward the old stone and turf houses were increasingly roofed and lined with wood bought from the shop, and because they were stocked with private effects, some of which were elaborate fixtures like coal-fired kitchen ranges (Ulloriaq 1985: 131, 185), these houses soon acquired the character of private property. This was in contrast to the older stone and turf houses that had been "private" only when actually occupied. The privatization of housing evolved further when, in the early 1970s, prefabricated do-it-yourself houses were introduced: the prospective owner paid 10 percent of the cost of the materials and an interest-free thirty-three-year mortgage covered the remaining 90 percent (Knudsen 1974). Nowadays in Avanersuaq the Eskimo owns his own wooden house in one or more of the settlements and, if he is a hunter, leaves it or them for extended hunting trips by motorboat in summer or by dogsled in winter (Gilberg 1985).

Along with these changes in their life-style, the Inuhuit have adopted new clothing and new hunting equipment since the beginning of this century, under the influence of both the Thule Trading Station and the North Star Mission. The West Greenlandic kayak was introduced to them after about 1920 by, among others, Thule Trading Station manager Hans Nielsen and Pastor Jens Olsen, and it has now replaced the heavier Baffin Island type in use before then. The motorboat, a further manifestation of private means and property, has also come into use: the Inuhuit owned eighteen in 1966 (Gilberg 1984a: 591). It is generally agreed that the opportunity offered to the Inuhuit after 1909–10 by the Thule Trading Station and its successor to sell the products of the hunt for money to purchase shop goods resulted in much substitution of cloth for skin in their material culture. Thus canvas or other materials replaced sealskin in the construction of kayaks and tents so that the sealskins could be traded. By 1936 the man's fox skin coat had disappeared for the same reason: in that year Holtved (1967) could learn of only one man who still had one. The trading station had bought up the Eskimos' fox skins and supplied them in return with caribou skins imported from Lapland for their coats, presumably making a profit on both transactions. Other transformations, including the widespread adoption of European clothing, came about more for reasons of convenience. Bird skin shirts had virtually been replaced by cotton in the 1930s (Holtved 1967: 39); iron sledge runner shoes were replaced by plastic ones in the 1970s (Holtved 1950: 275–77 and 1967; Gilberg 1984a).

These more or less gradual changes were in sharp contrast to the sudden jolt which the construction of Thule Air Base in the midst of their traditional hunting territories in 1951–52 gave to the Inuhuit in Avanersuaq. The event intruded most dramatically and immediately on the twenty-seven Inuhuit families then living at Uummannaq, which was less than two miles northwest of the base across the waters of North Star Bay, though the sprawling base was hidden from it behind a hill. The official Danish version of what happened claims that the inhabitants of Uummannaq, fearing that their walrus hunting activities around the islands in the mouth of Wolstenholme Fjord, their winter fox trapping in and near Pituffik Valley, and their sledge routes to the south would all be ruined by the base, decided to move elsewhere. The story was overplayed in a report issued by the American Associated Press on 23 July 1953, which claimed that the Eskimos were glad to be moving to new hunting grounds (van Kampen 1953). It was idealized or romanticized by Rolf Gilberg (1977b: 310–11) and Jean Malaurie, who saw in it a small but proud people bravely insisting on continuing their traditional way of life. "The kings of Thule had refused to raise their glasses in salute to the new era," commented Malaurie (1982: 395). The truth of the matter may perhaps never become entirely clear and is certainly complex, but it seems that the move was indeed forced on the Eskimos (see Skov 1966a and b *pace* Brun 1966a and b, and Brøsted and Fægteborg 1985) as a result of American pressure. The Americans had found it essential for the defense of the base to site a battery of anti-aircraft guns on the shingly peninsula in the immediate vicinity of the stone and turf wood-lined houses at Uummannaq (Gilberg 1977b and Brøsted and Fægteborg 1985 are the main sources for this and the following).

On 4 June 1953 the native inhabitants of Uummannaq loaded their sledges, harnessed their dogs, and set out on the long journey over the ice to the shores of Inglefield Gulf nearly one hundred miles to the north. Thirteen of the twenty-seven families involved, numbering in all 116 persons, settled at Qaanaaq in new wooden houses; the rest split between three other settlements. Current controversy (Brøsted and Fægteborg 1985) has exaggerated the significance of the 1953 evacuation. The presence of so many people at Uummannaq was more a consequence of the Danish mission, shop, and trading station that had been there since 1910 than of the settlement's intrinsic importance to the Inuhuit. From data given by the missionary Gustav Olsen (1910) it seems that about 35 Inuhuit overwintered at Uummannaq in 1909–10 out of a total population of 217 divided among nine settlements, giving an average of about 24 persons per settlement. Qaanaaq, too, where 61 people were planning to winter in 1894 (Peary 1898b: 267), had in the recent past been an important center: in the 1920s the missionary Jens Olsen established himself there for at least part of the year and up to about ten families consisting of 50 or more persons lived there (Holtved 1944a: 12). His motive, apparently, was the decline in the number of walrus in Wolstenholme Fjord (Ulloriaq 1985: 131); according to one report all the inhabitants of Uummannaq asked in 1925 to be moved north to better hunting grounds in the Qaanaaq area (Ahlman 1957: 129). The evacuation of the population of Uummannaq northward in 1953 should be viewed against this background and in the perspective of Danish policy in Greenland at that time. That year, in the Upernavik district, the removal of twenty-one families south from the remote Kullorsuaq area to larger centers was planned; it was carried out in 1954 (Lundsteen 1954; Knudsen 1964). Such removals, either to better hunting grounds or to more populous centers, had long been a normal feature of Greenlandic life.

There is no question that the impact of Thule Air Base on the Inuhuit local inhabitants was in some ways decisively negative. Apart from the forced evacuation from their homes, Wolstenholme Fjord was and still is seriously affected as a hunting area for sea mammals, especially walrus, and fox trapping in the area of the base has declined markedly or even disappeared. Moreover, the ancient Inuhuit sledge routes between the Savissivik area in the south and their Inglefield Gulf heartland have been seriously interrupted. On the other hand, the presence of the great base has enabled the Danish authorities to provide helicopter communications between the Avanersuaq settlements and to arrange regular flights to Søndre Strømfjord and Copenhagen. Another consequence of the construction of the base was that a substantial proportion of the Inuhuit population were provided with new wooden houses paid for by the Danish and American governments. In spite of Danish attempts to persuade them to build turf outer walls around these houses, the Eskimos preferred to do without them, and the move to Qaanaaq in 1953 marks the final demise of their traditional dwelling (Adler 1979: 475). It had been modified in the years after 1910 by the increasing abandonment of stone as a lining for the turf walls and roof and its replacement by wood; from 1953 on, the outside turf wall fell into disuse.

Both the establishment of the shop, trading station, and mission next door to Ummannaq in 1910 and the uprooting and dismantling of the Inuhuit settlement at Uummannaq in 1953 were accompanied by a persisting differential in housing standards between the Inuhuit on the one hand and the Danes and West Greenlanders on the other. When the West Greenlandic missionary Gustav Olsen moved his mission station to Kangerlussuaq in 1917, he built himself "a brand new house, a wooden house with two rooms of the same type as those generally seen among the best placed families in Danish West Greenland" (Rasmussen 1918: 22). The neat and comfortable wooden houses of Rasmussen, Freuchen, and the other Danes along the shore of North Star Bay were in striking contrast to the timber and turf houses of the Inuhuit settlement of Uummannaq less than a mile away across the low-lying shingle peninsula that culminated in the heart-shaped hill Uummannaq (Fig. 3). This differential was transferred in 1953–54 to Qaanaaq along with the inhabitants, both Inuhuit and Danish. Just as there had been two separate settlements at Uummannaq–North Star Bay, the Inuhuit village of Uummannaq and the Danish–West Greenlandic administrative center of Thule, so too in the new Qaanaaq (Fig. 15) there were two separate precincts. The humble Inuhuit houses, which were heated by coal kitchen ranges, lacked sanitary arrangements. Water was obtained from a neighboring hose in the summer and by melting ice or snow in the winter. The Danish–West Greenlandic houses, grouped together on higher ground to the east, were larger and were serviced by a power station and central heating plant: cooking and lighting were electric and every house had hot and cold running water (Fristrup 1960b, Gilberg 1977b). In spite of its evident shortcomings, within a very few years of its foundation the new Qaanaaq was idealized by Danish visitors, who found it a thriving and successful venture; their simple message was that the Inuhuit had never had it so good (Povlsen 1955, Christensen 1956).

The West Greenlandic religious and administrative presence in Avanersuaq is being reinforced by the spontaneous West Greenlandic colonization of southern Avanersuaq, which began around 1960. When Thule's first missionary, the West Greenlander Gustav Olsen, delivered a speech in Copenhagen on 1 June 1922 making a progress report on his work, he urged the Danish authorities to settle some West Greenlanders in Avanersuaq and asserted that these colonists would be made welcome by the native inhabitants. His idea was not taken up, but some years after the evacuation of Uummannaq to Qaanaaq in 1953 a spontaneous process of colonization began, starting with occasional marriages and an increase in the traditional spring sledge journeying northward of the Upernavik Eskimos (mainly from Kullorsuaq and Nuussuaq (Kraulshavn) in the north of that district) to visit the more southerly Inuhuit settlements at Savissivik and Moriusaq. At Savissivik its effects were clear in the distribution of nuclear families there in 1975 and 1980: roughly three-quarters of them were based on West Greenlandic–West Greenlandic or mixed West Greenlandic–Inuhuit marriages and only one-quarter were based on Inuhuit–Inuhuit marriages (Søby 1979 and 1985). About half of Savissivik's population was West Greenlandic. This colonization from the south has naturally been accompanied by the spread of the West Greenlandic Upernavik dialect among the Inuhuit, whose own language, Inuhuatut, has so far existed only in the spoken word, West Greenlandic or Kalaallisut doing duty among them for virtually all their reading. Since West Greenlandic was from the first the language used in the Christianization and education of the Inuhuit, it is not surprising that the West Greenlandic kinship terminology has been adopted to the complete exclusion of the original Inuhuit system (Søby 1977–78).

Will the Inuhuit succeed in maintaining their identity and original culture while at the same time being subsumed into a Greenlandic identity? The coming of such a general Greenlandic identity is made inevitable not only by these West Greenlandic influences and incursions but also by the current development of a centralized national Inuit state in Greenland (Dahl 1986). The proportions of the three ethnic groups to form this state are approximately fifty West Greenlanders to four East Greenlanders and one Inuhuit or rather Inuhuaq (Fægteborg 1986). One fears that only a loose federal arrangement, unlikely to be forthcoming, could save the two dwarfs from domination by the giant. Though peering into Greenland's political future is idle speculation, it may be that the recent increasing contacts between the Inuhuit and their close relatives the Canadian Inuit may prove of significance. Their own identity has been remarkably buoyant in the past, and one may note that the newcomers from the Upernavik district have adopted bearskin trousers, tea drinking on sledge trips, the *kiviaq* or feast of fermented little auks, and other Inuhuit traditions.

The Danes currently compose about one-fifth of the population of Greenland. Their share in shaping the destiny of the Inuhuit has been paramount but has often been impugned, even in the present work. They have been accused of destroying Inuhuit beliefs and practices by introducing Christianity among them, but there are plenty of people alive today who think that these Eskimos gladly exchanged a bad old religion for a good new one. They have been accused of encouraging the Inuhuit to drink, of introducing among them a money economy that had the effect of making them more dependent than ever on the outside world, of ruining their teeth by selling them sweets, and of allowing a huge military base to be built on their traditional hunting grounds. But these real or imaginary evils have at least partly been offset by the establishment of a rationing system to control liquor consumption, by the maintenance of hunting through the sustained purchase of its products at reasonable prices, by the installation of a dental clinic, and by the severe limitation of

Inuhuit contacts with Thule Air Base. Thus in a gentle and controlled manner, it may be argued, Inuhuit society has been brought into the industrialized world of the twentieth century, which in any case would have impinged on it and transformed it.

The annexation of Avanersuaq, inhabited by people normally described the world over in the nineteenth century as heathen savages, first privately by a group of Danish citizens led by Knud Rasmussen (1910–37) and then by the Danish state, was among the last of a long series of similar episodes in the history of European expansion. Many of these colonial episodes ended in tragedy. One of the first such disasters was the total obliteration of the aboriginal inhabitants of the Canary Islands at the close of the Middle Ages; one of the last was the extinction, probably by an epidemic, of the Sallirmiut Eskimos of Southampton Island in 1902–3. The Inuhuit were more fortunate; they benefited from the lessons learned by earlier white colonists. The Danes contrived to protect them from the worst ravages of "European" diseases. They have improved the Inuhuit standard of living and removed the specters of infanticide and cannibalism, which were formerly the only alternatives to starvation. They have given them the means of regular communication with the rest of the world. More important, the Inuhuit population has greatly increased under Danish rule. This increase, from a fluctuating total that averaged about 250 in the years from 1891 until about 1938, began just at the time when the Danish state took over Avanersuaq from the Cape York Thule Station Committee in 1937. The rate of increase soon accelerated from around 1 percent per year to 4 percent per year in the 1960s, making the Inuhuit population one of the fastest growing in the world. This remarkable population growth had little to do with immigration, though Gilberg (1976) notes that nineteen West Greenlandic women married Inuhuit hunters between 1950 and 1973. Nor was it apparently stimulated by the move to Qaanaaq and the construction of the new town there in 1953–54, events that occurred long after it was already under way. If the value of the products of the hunt increased substantially in the period 1920–50, then the cause of the population explosion must surely be sought in the improvements in health and material comforts this new-found wealth enabled the Thule Station Committee to bring about, especially around 1930, when the first permanent doctor was appointed and a twelve-bed hospital built, enabling the committee to run an efficient free medical service for the local inhabitants, and a new shop was built at Thule Trading Station and the two new ones were opened at Siorapaluk in the north of the district and Savissivik in the south (Sand 1935 and Gilberg 1977a). Having promoted this upward demographic surge, the Danes restrained it in about 1970 by introducing a family planning program based on the use of contraceptives, arguing that neither Avanersuaq nor the Inuhuit life-style could support unlimited population growth (Gilberg 1976b, 1985).

In the final analysis, one has to credit the almost miraculous preservation to this day of the traditional life-style of the Inuhuit Eskimos of northwest Greenland in large measure to the Danes. Their colonial policies were reasonably enlightened, and the Thule Trading Station, followed in 1937 by the Royal Greenland Trade Department, now taken over by the government of Greenland and called Greenland Trade (Kalaallit Niuerfiat, KNI), provided them with a cash income through the purchase of the products of their hunting and trapping. The determination and spirit of independence of the Inuhuit themselves have done the rest. The essence of their life-style was and still is the hunt. This hunting is no longer for subsistence only and is no longer entirely nomadic; the element in it that is crucial for survival of the Inuhuit way of life is the sledge pulled by a team of dogs. These teams have increased in size during this century: Whitney's data (1910) give an average of eleven dogs per team for eight teams, but the present-day dog team averages thirteen in number (Born 1987, which is the source for what follows). In 1984, the 100 or so occupational hunters in a total population of around 750 probably owned nearly twice as many dogs as there were human inhabitants. These dogs (Fig. 16) are fed largely on the meat of walruses and other marine animals caught mainly in the summer months. The Inuhuit have restricted the use of snowmobiles or motorized sledges (Taagholt and Hansen 1977), and the dogsled remains their only effective form of winter transport and of conducting hunting and trapping activities in that season. It is the retention of the dogsled, and thus the role of the dog, that seems to have been decisive in enabling the Inuhuit to maintain their traditional subsistence hunting society. Danish biologist Erik Born has calculated that the average Avanersuaq hunter obtains about 11,025 pounds (5,000 kg) of edible products annually. About 7,050 pounds (3,200 kg) of this is used to feed his dogs and the bulk of the remainder, about 3,530 pounds (1,600 kg), is available for human consumption, providing up to 2 pounds or a kilo daily of meat and blubber per head for him and his family. Although it is true that the Inuhuit hunters, with their need for imported motorboats and fuel for them and rifles with ammunition and for much imported clothing and equipment, are very dependent on the outside world, it is also true that they still rely for subsistence and for cash on an annual kill of 7,500 seals of four species, 250 walrus, 150 narwhal, 60 white whales, some 20 polar bears, and some thousands of dovekies, not to mention the annual harvest of Arctic foxes, caught in traps. Though rifles and other firearms have been in universal use, the Inuhuit hunter still brings the polar bear to bay with dogs before shooting it, still has to harpoon the walrus and narwhal from a kayak to prevent them from sinking when they are killed with the rifle, and still catches dovekies in nets (Herbert 1981, Born 1987, Alexander and Alexander 1989).

Whatever the future may have in store for the Inuhuit, one can be sure that they will continue to be the victims of pressures from outside. New ones are emerging all the time. Because of the progressive poisoning of the seas by the rest of mankind, their diet of marine mammals has already caused unusually high concentrations of mercury and selenium in their bodies (Hansen and Pedersen 1986). In 1985, two years after the sampling of their blood, hair, and plasma that led to this conclusion, the first tourists arrived in Avanersuaq in the guise of a scientific expedition. Other groups followed, and doubtless more will come. In 1984 the local paper published a plan, drawn up by the owner of the modest café there, for a hotel in Qaanaaq (*Hainang,* 30 March 1984). Admittedly it was to contain only thirteen rooms, but would-be hotelier Henry Hansen somewhat ominously pointed out that his proposed new building could bring happiness to the entire population of Qaanaaq by providing a market among the tourists for the products of local craftsmen and artists. In recent years, too, the market for the products of hunting has been placed in jeopardy by campaigns against the sale of sealskin products in Europe, which have led to restrictions on imports and a decline in prices. Thus whether they like it or not, the Inuhuit remain innocent victims of events far away from Avanersuaq.

11

Epilogue

*A*vanersuaq, the land farthest north, most remote, or Ultima Thule, has been relatively untouched by man. I have recounted its history; there remains to be described only the permanent imprints that man has left on the landscape. For even here humans have marked the land indelibly and have wrought destruction. During their intermittent occupations of the area native peoples lived off the land, but they husbanded its resources and seem not to have overexploited them. The numbers of their principal prey animals, both marine and terrestrial, seem not to have been diminished by their predatory activities. They did not destroy their environment. Their summer dwellings left only circles of rocks on the ground called tent-rings; their winter houses, partly concealed underground, were insignificant structures of natural materials available on the spot: stones and turves. These, together with piles of stones that were here and there heaped up over a grave or a meat cache, scarcely altered the landscape. Today the permanent wooden houses of the Inuhuit are clustered in a handful of settlements, but they and the refuse that surrounds them form mere pinpoints of man-made wasteland in the tundra. The half-dozen or so wooden hunters' huts are scattered over so wide an area as to be almost unfindable, and the refuse left by the Inuhuit along these remote shores is nothing compared to the flotsam and jetsam thrown up nearly everywhere else in the world.

Though the whalers and explorers who visited Avanersuaq in the nineteenth and early twentieth centuries had no compunction in leaving their marks on the landscape, these too were insubstantial and widely scattered. The remains of the wooden buildings the explorers sometimes wintered in have long since disappeared. Only stone cairns on the highest points of islands and headlands and an occasional gravestone or other monument survive as a tangible record of these early visitors.

The raising of cairns and the depositing of records within them became a regular craze in the second half of the nineteenth century. Their purpose was to provide positive proof of the spot reached and explored and to give information about ice and weather or about the identity, physical condition, and destination of the party. The tragic history of the Franklin Expedition had much to do with this. On 14 August 1854, in Rensselaer Bay, E. K. Kane (1856a: 345) erected a cairn and deposited a record of his expedition's achievements and intentions specifically to avoid the potentially disastrous error made by Franklin, who had omitted to leave such a record when abandoning his winter quarters at Beechey Island in Barrow Strait in 1846. When the cairn and record subsequently left by the Franklin Expedition at Victory Point on the north coast of King William Island in April 1848, which explained its fate, was found ten years later by Lieutenant W. R. Hobson, R.N., of Captain M'Clintock's expedition, the importance of leaving such a record was again underlined. No wonder that cairns sprang up in profusion on the headlands and islands of Avanersuaq. Following Kane's example, on 19 May 1861 Hayes (1867: 351) built a cairn to mark the most northerly point of his explorations and deposited a record beneath it "in proof of our presence," which was enclosed in a "small glass vial, which I brought for the purpose." Twenty years later, in August 1881, A. W. Greely (1886a: 63–64) searched Littleton Island for the mail for the Nares Expedition, which had been landed there in 1876 by Allen Young, and reported that "some fifty cairns, great and small, were found." The custom of building cairns was taken up by whalers as well as explorers. Among the fifty cairns on Littleton Island in 1881 was one built by Captain Walker of the Dundee whaler *Erik* on the remarkably early date of 20 June 1878. On 18 August 1875, when the crew of Allen Young's *Pandora* landed on the most northwesterly of the Cary Islands, they discovered a cairn erected by a Dundee whaleship in July 1867. It contained a record stating that absolutely no ice was visible at that time from the summit. The thoughtful whaler had deposited in the cairn some chewing tobacco and half a bottle of rum with which the finders toasted him (Beynen 1876: 50). Food depots were left by explorers from time to time against an emergency or for possible future use. The famous one left by George Nares on the most easterly of the Cary Islands in July 1875 was still partly usable nine years later. On 28 April 1917 two of Knud Rasmussen's companions on the Second Thule Expedition found another depot left by the Nares Expedition on 23 August 1875 at Cape Morton on the coast of Washington Land (Nares 1878a: 107–8; Rasmussen 1921a: 70–71 and 1928: 40–41). Although a barrel of sugar had been smashed open and the contents eaten by a bear, the fortunate Danes found 24 nine-pound tins of New Zealand mutton, "fresh and delicious as if it had been left only the previous day" instead of forty-two years before. The tins were labeled "Meat Preserving Co. Ltd., Agents, Witherspoon and Co. Works, Winton, Southland, N.Z." Rasmussen comments (1921a: 71): "For a long time we were thus able to live grandly on food originally meant for Arctic colleagues who had travelled here before any of us were born. Our thanks to the brave Englishmen who left it here; our compliments to the excellent firm which prepared this durable article!"

When the obsession with raising cairns and depositing records within them subsided in the early twentieth century, people began to take pleasure in searching for cairns and recovering the records. The American explorer Donald MacMillan (1918b) made a hobby of it and wrote an article for *Harpers Magazine* entitled "Record-Hunting in the Arctic." His wife proudly recorded that he had "brought back twenty-four records left by explorers" (MacMillan 1948: 287), including those of Kane, Nares, and Peary. Peary deposited records in cairns on headlands along the coast of northern Greenland and Canada, in many of which the names of fifteen or eighteen members of his fan club, the Peary Arctic Club of New York (see, for example, Peary 1907: 329), were written out in full on a scrap of paper.

In contrast to the numerous cairns constructed in Avanersuaq, only a handful of tombs and other monuments have been set up on these lonely shores. The grave of one of the British sailors who died during the overwintering of HMS *North Star* in 1849–50 is still to be seen near what is now Thule Air Base. On the coast not far from Iita, south of Foulke Fjord, is the tombstone erected early in 1861 over the grave of August Sonntag, a scientist accompanying the Hayes Expedition, who died of exposure after accidentally falling through thin ice. Curiously, were it not for a photograph taken by MacMillan (1918a: 120) in about 1914 we should be uncertain of the exact wording of the inscription chiseled into the stone, though Hayes himself and two others at least took the trouble to write it down. The second of these, Jean Malaurie, claimed in 1951 that he "could still read the inscription fairly well" but gave a second faulty reading in a later edition of his book. The different versions are as follows:

IN MEMORY OF AUGUST SONNTAG DIED, Dec. 1860 AGED 29 Yrs (MacMillan's photograph)

AUGUST SONNTAG. Died December, 1860, AGED 28 YEARS (Hayes 1867: 275)

August Sonntag. Died December 29, 1860 (Whitney 1910: 48)

August Sonntag Died in December 1860 aged 29 years (Malaurie 1956: 168)

AUGUST SONNTAG died December 1860 aged 28 years (Malaurie 1982: 301)

Farther north, in the land named after him, is the grave of C. F. Hall, who died in 1871 while leading the United States expedition to the North Pole. Rumors were that Hall was poisoned. After his body was exhumed in 1968, concentrations of arsenic were found which had apparently been ingested in the last few weeks of his life. Even so, his biographer could not be sure that he had been murdered; arsenic was used for medicinal purposes at the time and Hall might inadvertently have poisoned himself while attempting to treat a stroke (Loomis 1972).

The two greatest explorers of Avanersuaq are both commemorated there. In 1932 a slender column of rough-hewn stone with a large P at the top was erected on the mountain above Cape York as a monument to Peary (Bartlett 1934: 251−80). In 1935, when the twenty-fifth anniversary of the foundation of the Thule Trading Station was being celebrated, a stone slab with the following inscription in Danish and Greenlandic was unveiled there: "Knud Rasmussen founded Thule 19.8.1910 and administered the Cape York District until his death 21.12.1933."

The cairns and monuments mentioned thus far are minor compared to the massive impact on Avanersuaq's landscape brought about by the construction of Thule Air Base and the ancillary installations around it in the years after 1951. At least 30 square miles (50 km^2) of low-lying marsh and dry, stony tundra have been more or less transformed into wasteland or built over. The delicately balanced tundra ecosystem has virtually disappeared from this area. Only the snow bunting is at home in the base itself; some other birds still survive in the neighborhood. The ground has been disturbed everywhere, and only certain plants seem able to colonize these wastes, among them the yellow Arctic poppy, which thrives on disused roads, and the purple saxifrage, which makes a magnificent display on heaps of discarded earth. Nowhere in all this area is there a view where man-made objects do not intrude; everywhere a road, a ruined building, an abandoned rocket site, pieces of discarded wire, or other metal objects meet the eye. Pituffik Valley has been devastated. It seems to have been one of only three extensive low-lying marshy areas in the whole of northwest Greenland where bird and plant life could flourish in a sheltered, fertile environment. Let us hope that the lakes and marshes at the head of McCormick Fjord and those on the coast south of Booth Sound, the other two such sites in Avanersuaq, will remain forever, as they still are now, undisturbed and unaltered.

Though the country itself remains for the most part unspoiled, the white man's map of northwest Greenland has been literally plastered with names, reflecting the egoism, folly, sycophancy, ignorance, or nationalism of different explorers or, in more recent times, of the Danish authorities. This book may perhaps fittingly be concluded with some consideration of these curious historical monuments.

Giving names to lands not previously visited by whites and to prominent geographical features in them, regardless of whether they already had native names, was for long considered a prerogative of the explorer. Thus northwest Greenland was sprinkled first with British, then with American names (see

Laursen 1972, which is crucial for this section). Islands, headlands, glaciers, and fjords were the main victims of this quaint game; Eskimo names for Eskimo settlements were respected, albeit in a garbled form.

William Baffin has been complimented on refraining "from scattering the names of all the great men of his day and of all his friends and acquaintances round the head" of Baffin Bay (Markham 1866). On the Greenland side of the bay he bestowed only six names. One, Whale Sound, was descriptive but turned out to be somewhat inappropriate because no whales have been seen there since his visit in 1616. Another, Hakluyt Island, commemorated Richard Hakluyt, the famous Elizabethan geographer. "Carys Islands" were named after Alwyn Cary, his ship's husband or housekeeper (Markham 1881: 146 and n.). The remaining two, Cape Dudley Digges and Wolstenholme Fjord, were named after two of the four prominent entrepreneurs who had financed the voyage: Sir Dudley Digges and Sir John Wolstenholme. The less picturesque names of the other two, Smith and Jones, were reserved by Baffin for the inlets discovered later on his voyage. Two hundred years after Baffin, Sir John Ross scattered some twenty-seven British names along the Avanersuaq coast, commemorating shipmates (Bushnan's Island, Capes Hoppner and Parry) and others, among them Felix Booth (Booth Sound) a wealthy London distiller, who funded one of Ross's later expeditions. Ross's (1819: 116) map of the coast of Avanersuaq south of Whale Sound is notable for its inclusion of three Inuhuit names: the Petowaak Glacier (Pituffik), Inmelick (Imilik), and Sowallick (Savissivik). The wintering of HMS *North Star* in 1849–50 provided a name for the bay where that ship wintered, as well as for the flat-topped mountain that overlooks it, named Mount Dundas after Sir David Dundas, member of the council of the Royal Geographical Society, and for the large island offshore, which was named Saunders Island after the ship's master.

After the British names, which included Edward Inglefield's (1853: 54) fanciful one for the three islets in the mouth of Granville Fjord, the "Three Sister Bees," "after the three industrious young ladies who had supplied me with the dolls for the Greenland children," and some thirty or more others, Avanersuaq began to receive American names, given in the first place by Kane and Hayes: Cape Constitution and Washington Land, Academy Bay after the Philadelphia Academy, and the Harvard Islands. Hayes (1867: 430) writes of the last, "A cluster of islands at the farther end of the gulf I called Harvard Islands, in remembrance of the University at Cambridge, to members of whose faculty I am indebted for many courteous attentions while fitting out at Boston."

In spite of all this naming activity, there were still plenty of glaciers and a few other features in Avanersuaq left for Peary to name. In 1891–92 alone he named forty-two different glaciers, many of them after companions, friends, and patrons or potential patrons. Later, in the far north of Greenland, he immortalized "the armchair explorers of the Peary Arctic Club by writing their names across the map" (Horwood 1977: 71; Laursen 1972: 101): Cape Morris K. Jesup, Cape Bridgman, Frederick E. Hyde Fjord, G. B. Schley Fjord. Even so, there were still unnamed glaciers in a land of glaciers like Avanersuaq. In the extreme south of the region along the northern shores of Melville Bay, Peary's Norwegian colleague Eivind Astrup was able in 1894 to write the first Scandinavian names on the map, calling glaciers after King Oscar II of Norway-Sweden, Norwegian meteorologist Henrik Mohn, the Swedish explorer A. E. Nordenskiöld, the Danish Greenland expert H. J. Rink, and the Norwegian explorers Fridtjof Nansen and Otto Sverdrup. Subsequent explorers had to go farther and farther afield to play the naming game. W. Elmer Ekblaw (1918: 353) played it in remote Ellesmere Island, where he confessed that "naming the new capes and bays and mountains and glaciers and islands was some of the best fun I had on my lonely trip."

Two of the unwritten rules of the naming game prohibited the renaming of features that had already been named and the naming of features after oneself, which, at least in the English-speaking world, was considered bad form. But the Danes who arrived in Avanersuaq in 1903 in the shape of the Literary Greenland Expedition thought otherwise. After displaying an imaginative touch by naming two glaciers after Danish newspapers that were supporting their expedition by printing and paying for their dispatches (the Politiken and Berlingske Glaciers after *Politiken* and *Berlingske Tidende*), Knud Rasmussen and Harold Moltke chose two out of three fine glaciers that debouch into the sea at the head of Wolstenholme Fjord to commemorate themselves, apparently unaware that these three glaciers had already been named by Peary for Charles A. Moore, T. C. Chamberlin, and Rollin D. Salisbury (Peary 1898a: 455, Wright 1939: 15, Gilberg 1984b: 51–52).

The haphazard system of naming by individual explorers was replaced in Greenland in the heyday of Danish colonialist nationalism by a disciplined system of officially approved Danish naming of Greenlandic places and geographical features. From 1933, a few years before Avanersuaq was appropriated by the Danish state, a place name committee for Greenland composed exclusively of Danes was empowered to decide on the official "correct" spelling of all Greenlandic places. Naturally, English geographical terms like bay, sound, cape, and island, hitherto used, were replaced by their Danish equivalents *bugt, sund, kap,* and *ø.* Thus Saunders Island became Saunders Ø, Bowdoin Glacier became Bowdoin Gletscher, and Cape Robertson, Kap Robertson. At the same time the English components of some names, no longer understood by the authorities, were garbled: the Cary Islands became Carey Øer, McCormick Fjord became Mac Cormick Fjord, and the Harvard Islands are now officially the Harward Øer.

This nonsense may soon be a thing of the past. As early as 1902 Robert Stein (1902a) drew attention to the existence of Eskimo names for geographical features and published a list of Inuhuit place names spelled, as he claimed, phonetically and not in corrupt Anglicized versions. Thus his allegedly improved renderings, Ita, Kana, Akpan, and Umana were to replace Etah, Karnah, Akbat, and Umanak. The substitution of artificial modern names for the original Eskimo ones became increasingly unpopular. The difficulty was well expressed in 1934 by the American ornithologist George M. Sutton, who began his book *Eskimo Year* as follows:

> There is a nineteen-thousand-square-mile heap of rock that sprawls almost across the mouth of Hudson Bay. The Eskimos that inhabit this vast heap of rock call it Shugliak: The Island-Pup That Is Suckling the Continent Mother-Dog. They never call it Southampton Island, for to them Southampton Island is simply not its name. They cannot read the proud words on the White Man's charts; and when they hear the White Man talking about Southampton it does not occur to them that Shugliak and Southampton can be one and the same place.
>
> I am one of the few white men that have lived on Shugliak. The Island-Pup That Is Suckling the Continent Mother-Dog was my home for a year. I am obliged to call the place Southampton Island rather than Shugliak most of the time because I wish not to be misunderstood by cartographers, zoögeographers, and casual acquaintances. But you will understand me when I say that it was Shugliak, rather than Southampton Island, that was my home; that it is to Shugliak, not to Southampton Island, that I wish to return. I am not sure, myself, that Southampton Island and Shugliak are precisely one and the same. Shugliak is a place where interesting and friendly human beings live; Southampton Island is part of a map.

In Canada at any rate, Sutton is having his way. On 12 January 1987 an article in the *Daily Telegraph* headed "British Names Vanishing from Map" explained that from 1 January 1987, Eskimo names would be substituted for those of certain British explorers. Thus Baffin Island has been replaced by Qikirtaluk, the "island," and Frobisher Bay by Iqaluit, "salmon" or "the place where there is an abundance of salmon or trout." Perhaps within a few years the Cary Islands or Carey Øer will receive back their original name Kitsigsut, "those that lie far out at sea towards the west" (Vahl 1929: 453), Saunders Island will once more become Appat or Agpat, "the place where there is a bird cliff with thick-billed murres," and Littleton Island, Pikiutdlek, "the place which is low and at highwater is apt to be washed over in a gale."

Perhaps at some future date the Inuhuit will be in a position to choose their own spellings of names for their own places, in which case one can surmise that the current official spellings of Eskimo place names in Avanersuaq (used in this book)—for example, Iita, Qaanaaq, Uummannaq—which, being approved by the government of Greenland in Nuuk, are naturally transcribed in

West Greenlandic, will be modified once again by being rendered in Inuhuit. The name Thule, except in Thule Air Base, has already disappeared, for the attempt to rename Qaanaaq Thule, when the population of Uummannaq was evacuated there in 1953, has been a failure (Gilberg 1974). With the closing down and abandonment in 1985–86 of the buildings and installations grouped round the old Thule Trading Station on the shore of North Star Bay, the name Dundas, given to the place in 1953 after the name Thule was officially transferred to Qaanaaq, will also disappear.

It is fortunate indeed that changing the names on the map makes no difference to the land itself. But just how long will Avanersuaq remain, as it has been so far, one of the least human-altered places on earth? The Inuhuit seem determined to maintain their own way of life and their own distinctive culture, welcoming change only when it helps them to do this. So long as they preserve the subsistence hunting element in their economy their life-style can be perpetuated, and they seem set to remain in their traditional home. Their future and the future of their so far almost unspoiled hunting territories, just as has their past, depend on pressures from outside and their reactions to them. In the coming decade the most immediate problems requiring solution will probably be political interventions from Inuit neighbors, namely the new Greenlandic state and the Canadian Inuit; the need to defend subsistence hunting against conservationist ideologies and policies or find alternatives; and, not least in importance, the repercussions of the worldwide search for oil and gas.

Bibliography

Manuscript Sources Consulted

Cambridge, England. Scott Polar Research Institute. Wordie Collection of whalers' logbooks.

Hull, England. Local Studies Library. Whalers' logbooks, local newspapers, and miscellaneous items.

_____. Town Docks Museum. Whalers' logbooks, transcript of C. E. Smith's diary of his voyage in the *Diana*.

New York City. American Museum of Natural History, Archives and Reference Library. Miscellaneous papers.

Books and Articles Referenced

Adler, C. 1979. *Polareskimo-Verhalten. Von den Verhaltensweisen eines altertümlichen Jägervolkes. Ein monographie zur Humanethologie.* Argelsried.

Ahlman, A. 1957. *Fra Øresund til Thule.* Copenhagen.

Alexander, B. and C. 1989. "Polar Eskimos: The Northernmost People." *World Magazine* 22: 26–35.

Allen, E. S. 1962. *Arctic Odyssey: The Life of Rear Admiral Donald B. MacMillan.* New York.

Alt, B. T., R. M. Koerner, D. A. Fisher, and J. C. Bourgeois. 1986. "Arctic Climate during the Franklin Era as Deduced from Ice Cores." In Sutherland 1985: 69–92.

Amundsen, R. 1907. *Nordvest-passagen. Beretning om* Gjøa-*Ekspeditionen, 1903–1907.* Kristiania (Oslo). English translation, *The Northwest Passage, Being the Record of a Voyage of Exploration of the Ship* Gjøa, *1903–1907.* New York, 1928.

Ancker, P. E. 1977. "Thule Air Base." *Tidsskrift for Søvæsen* 148: 449–96.

Andreasen, J. 1984. *Nye slædespor. Dagbogsblade fra den Litterære Grønlandsekspedition 1902–04.* Copenhagen.

Andreassen, C. 1982. "Nipaitsoq og Vesterbygden." *Grønland* 30: 177–88.

Anonymous. 1852. *Arctic Miscellanies: A Souvenir of the Late Polar Search by the Officers and Seamen of the Expedition.* London.

177

Astrup, E. 1895. *Blandt Nordpolens naboer.* Kristiania (Oslo). English translation, *With Peary Near the Pole.* London, 1908.

Balchen, B. 1958. *Kom nord med meg.* Oslo. English translation, *Come North with Me.* New York, 1958.

Balchen, B., C. Ford, and O. La Forge. 1945. *War below Zero: The Battle for Greenland.* London.

Barr, W. 1982. "Robert Stein's Expedition to Ellesmere Island, 1899–1901." *Polar Record* 21: 253–74.

———. 1985. *The Expeditions of the First International Polar Year, 1882–3.* Calgary.

Barron, W. 1890. *An Apprentice's Reminiscenses of Whaling in Davis's Straits: Narrative of the Voyages of the Hull Barque* Truelove, *from 1848 to 1854.* Hull.

———. 1895. *Old Whaling Days.* Hull.

Barrow, J. 1846. *Voyages of Discovery and Research within the Arctic Regions from the Year 1818 to the Present Time.* New York.

Bartlett, R. A. 1928. *The Log of Bob Bartlett.* New York.

———. 1934. *Sails over Ice.* New York.

Beck, A. G. 1946. *Nakorsak—Læge på Inlandsisen.* Copenhagen.

Belcher, E. 1855a and b. *The Last of the Arctic Voyages; Being a Narrative of the Expedition in H.M.S.* Assistance *during the Years 1852–4.* 2 vols. London.

Bernier, J. E. 1910. *Report on the Dominion of Canada Government Expedition to the Arctic Islands and Hudson Strait on Board the D.G.S.* Arctic. Ottawa.

Berton, P. 1988. *The Arctic Grail: The Quest for the Northwest Passage and the North Pole, 1818–1909.* New York.

Bessels, E. 1875. "Einige Worte über die Inuit (Eskimo) des Smith-Sundes, nebst Bemerkungen über Inuit-Schädel." *Archiv für Anthropologie* 8: 107–22.

———. 1879. *Die amerikanische Nordpol-Expedition.* Leipzig.

———. 1884. "The Northernmost Inhabitants of the Earth: An Ethnographic Sketch." *American Naturalist* 18: 861–82.

Beynen, L. R. K. 1876. *De Reis der* Pandora *naar de Noordpoolgewesten in den Zomer van 1875.* Amsterdam.

———. 1877. *De Tweede Reis der* Pandora. Amsterdam.

Birket-Smith, K. 1936. *Knud Rasmussens Saga.* Copenhagen.

Birket-Smith, K., E. Mentze, and M. F. Møller, eds. 1950 a and b. *Grønlands Bogen.* 2 vols. Copenhagen.

Bjøl, E. 1977. "Den politiske Baggrund for Oprettelsen af Thule Air Base. Den Kolde Krig." *Grønland* 25: 255–60.

Blake, E. V., ed. 1874. *Arctic Experiences: Containing Capt. George E. Tyson's Wonderful Drift on the Ice-Floe, a History of the* Polaris *Expedition, the Cruise of the* Tigress, *and Rescue of the* Polaris *Survivors.* New York.

Born, E. W. 1986. "Observations of Narwhals (*Monodon monoceros*) in the Thule Area (NW Greenland), August 1984." *Report of the International Whaling Commission* 36: 387–92.

———. 1987. "Aspects of Present-Day Maritime Subsistence Hunting in the Thule Area, Northwest Greenland." In Hacqebord and Vaughan 1987: 109–32.

Born, E. W., and T. Kristensen. 1981. "Hvalrossen i Thule." *Naturens Verden* 132–43.

Born, E. W., and L. R. Olesen. 1986. "Er Narhvalen Truet?" *Naturens Verden* 65–80.

Borup, G. 1911. *A Tenderfoot with Peary*. New York.

Brandt, H. 1943. *Alaska Bird Trails*. Cleveland, Ohio.

Brill, A. A. 1913. "Piblokto or Hysteria among Peary's Eskimos." *Journal of Nervous and Mental Disease* 40(8): 514–20.

Brun, E. 1950. "Grønland under den Anden Verdenskrig." In Birket-Smith et al. 1950a: 305–18.

————. 1966a. "Thule-Qanaq. Nogle Oplysninger for at Undgå, at Myter Bliver til Historie." *Grønland* 14: 109–10.

————. 1966b. "Flytningen af Thule: Eske Bruns Kommentar Hertil." *Grønland* 14: 399–400.

————. 1985. *Mit Grønlandsliv*. Copenhagen.

Bryant, H. G. 1895. *The Peary Auxiliary Expedition of 1894*. Philadelphia.

Bræstrup, F. W. 1941. "A Study of the Arctic Fox in Greenland." *Meddelelser om Grønland* 131(4): 1–101.

Brøsted, J. 1986. "Territorial Rights in Greenland: Some Preliminary Notes." *Arctic Anthropology* 23: 325–38.

————. 1988. "Danish Accession to the Thule District." *Nordic Journal of International Law* 57: 259–65.

Brøsted, J., and M. Fægteborg. 1985. *Thule—Fangerfolk og Militæranlæg*. Copenhagen.

Buchwald, V. F. 1964. "Meteorit- og Jernfund i Grønland fra John Ross' Rejse for at Opsøge Nordvestpassagen 1818 til Vore Dage." *Naturens Verden:* 33–64.

————. 1988. "The Cape York Iron Meteorite Shower." *Newsletter from the Commission for Scientific Research in Greenland* 17: 37–39.

Buchwald, V. F., and G. Mosdal. 1985. "Meteoritic Iron, Telluric Iron and Wrought Iron in Greenland." *Meddelelser om Grønland. Man and Society* 9: 1–49.

Bugge, Å. 1965. "Kallihirua. Polareskimoen i Canterbury." *Grønland* 13: 161–75.

Bøggild, O. B. 1927. "The Meteoric Iron from Savik Near Cape York, North Greenland." *Meddelelser om Grønland* 74(2): 9–32.

Carlson, W. S. 1962. *Lifelines through the Arctic*. New York.

Chamberlin, T. C. 1895, 1896, 1897. "Glacial Studies in Greenland." *Journal of Geology* 3: 469–80, 565–82, 668–81, 833–43; 4: 582–92; 5: 229–40.

Christensen, F. 1986. "'Jeg er Hadet af Missionen og Elsket af Eskimoerne. Kan jeg Forlange Mere': Peter Freuchens Kritik af Missionen i Thule." *Grønland* 34: 63–74.

Christensen, H. 1956. "Fra det nye Thule." *Grønland* 5: 289–94.

Clæsson, P., ed. 1983. *Grønland, Middelhavets Perle. Et Indblik i amerikansk Atomkrigsforberedelse*. Copenhagen.

Cook, F. A. 1894. "Medical Observations among the Eskimo." *New York Journal of Gynecology and Obstetrics* 4: 282–89.

————. 1911. *My Attainment of the Pole, Being a Record of the Expedition Which First Reached the Boreal Center, 1907–1909*. New York.

Corner, G. W. 1972. *Doctor Kane of the Arctic Seas*. Philadelphia.

Counter, S. A. 1988. "The Henson family." *National Geographic*, Sept., pp. 422–29.

Dahl, J. 1986. "Greenland: Political Structure of Self-Government." *Arctic Anthropology* 23: 315–24.

Damas, D., ed. 1984. *Handbook of North American Indians, 5. Arctic.* Smithsonian Institution. Washington.

Dansgård, W., S. J. Johnsen, and H. B. Clausen. 1970. "Grønlands Klima—før, nu og 50 År Frem." *Grønland* 18: 161–72.

Daugherty, C. M. 1963. *City under the Ice: The Story of Camp Century.* New York.

Davies, T. D. 1990. "New Evidence Places Peary at the Pole." *National Geographic* 177: 44–61.

Davies, W. E., D. B. Krinsley, and A. H. Nicol. 1963. "Geology of the North Star Bay Area, Northwest Greenland." *Meddelelser om Grønland* 162(12): 1–68.

Davis, C. H., ed. 1876. *Narrative of the North Polar Expedition: U.S. Ship Polaris.* Washington, D.C.

Dawes, P. R. 1986. "Hans Hendrik og Familie på Fotografier og Graveringer." *Grønland* 34: 141–51.

Dawes, P. R., M. Elander, and M. Ericson. 1986. "The Wolf (*Canis lupus*) in Greenland: A Historical Review and Present Status." *Arctic* 39: 119–32.

Dodge, E. S. 1973. *The Polar Rosses: John and James Clark Ross and Their Explorations.* London.

Doerflinger, W. M. 1972. *Songs of the Sailor and Lumberman.* New York.

Dumond, D. E. 1977. *The Eskimos and Aleuts.* London.

Eames, H. 1973. *Winner Lose All: Dr. Cook and the Theft of the North Pole.* Boston.

Ekblaw, W. E. 1919. "The Food Birds of the Smith Sound Eskimos." *Wilson Bulletin* 31: 1–5.

Elder, W. 1858. *Biography of Elisha Kent Kane.* Philadelphia.

Erichsen, M. 1943. "Knud Rasmussen og Polareskimoerne." *Nordisk Tidsskrift* 19: 474–90.

Erngaard, E. 1973. *Grønland i Tusinde År.* Copenhagen.

Fabricius, O. 1929. *Fauna Groenlandica. Pattedyr og Fugle.* Translated by O. Helms. Det Grønlandske Selskabs Skrifter, 6. Copenhagen.

[Fisher, A.] [1819]. *Journal of a Voyage of Discovery to the Arctic Regions Performed between 4 April and 18 November 1818 in H.M.S.* Alexander. London.

Fisher, A. 1821. *A Journal of a Voyage of Discovery to the Arctic Regions in H.M. Ships* Hecla *and* Griper *in the Years 1819 and 1820.* London.

Fitzhugh, W. W. 1984. "Palaeo-Eskimo Cultures of Greenland." In Damas 1984: 528–39.

Fogelson, N. J. 1985. "Robert E. Peary and American Exploration in the Arctic, 1886–1910: A Period of Progress and Modernization." *Fram: The Journal of Polar Studies* 2: 130–40.

Franke, R. 1914. *Erlebnisse eines Deutschen im hohen Norden. Auf Zeichnungen und Berichte Rudolph Frankes.* Ed. Ed. Volckmann. Hamburg.

Fredskild, B. 1985. "The Holocene Vegetational Development of Tugtuligssuaq and Qeqertat, Northwest Greenland." *Meddelelser om Grønland, Geoscience* 14: 1–20.

Freeman, A. A. 1961. *The Case for Doctor Cook.* New York.

Freuchen, D., ed. 1961. *Peter Freuchen's Book of the Eskimos.* Cleveland, Ohio.

Freuchen, P. 1936. *Arctic Adventure: My Life in the Frozen North.* London.

———. 1954. *Vagrant Viking: My Life and Adventures.* London.

———. 1959. *Min Grønlandske Ungdom.* Copenhagen. 1st ed. 1936.

Freuchen, P., and F. Salomonsen. 1958. *The Arctic Year.* New York.

Fristrup, B. 1960a. "Nogle Amerikanske Undersøgelser på Grønlands Inlandsis." *Grønland* 8: 281–94.

———. 1960b. "Thule, 50 år siden Knud Rasmussen grundlagde Thule." *Naturens Verden* 44: 232–45.

———. 1966. *The Greenland Ice Cap.* Copenhagen.

———. 1977. "Thulebasens Bagland: Inlandsisen." *Grønland* 25: 292–306.

———. 1978. "Geografi." In Petersen and Staffeldt 1978: 5–21.

Furnas, C. C., et al. 1966. *The Engineer.* Amsterdam.

Fægteborg, M. 1986. "Lille Sprog, hvad Nu?" *Grønland* 34: 306–9.

Gad, F. 1984. *Grønland.* Copenhagen.

Garboe, A. 1961. "Meteoriter fra Grønland. Lidt om Fund og Hjemtransport." *Grønland* 9: 41–48.

———. 1964. "En Dansk Meteoritekspedition i 1843." *Grønland* 12: 185–94.

Gibson, L. 1922. "Bird Notes from North Greenland." *Auk* 39: 350–63.

Gilberg, L., and Å. Gilberg. 1986. "Antropologiske, Arvebiologiske og Genealogiske Undersøgelser af Polareskimoerne." *Grønland* 34: 5–24.

Gilberg, R. 1969–70. "Uisåkavsak, 'The big liar.'" *Folk* 11–12: 83–95.

———. 1970. "'Den storre løgner'"—Polareskimoen Uisåkavsak." *Grønland* 18: 204–19.

———. 1974. "Thule." *Grønland* 22: 297–99.

———. 1976a. "En canadisk Eskimoindvandrings Indflydelse på Polareskimoernes Tilværelse in 1860erne i Thule Distriktet, Nordgrønland." *Grønland* 24: 45–57.

———. 1976b. "The Polar Eskimo Population, Thule District, North Greenland." *Meddelelser om Grønland* 203(3): 1–87.

———. 1977a. "En Arktisk Handelstation i 'Ingenmandsland.'" *Grønland* 25: 247–54.

———. 1977b. "Fra Umánaq til Qânâq. Flytningen af en By i 1953." *Grønland* 25: 307–20.

———. 1984a. "Polar Eskimo." In Damas 1984: 577–94.

———. 1984b. "Helte Opkalder man Steder efter: Knud Rasmussen på Kortet." *Grønland* 32: 51–58.

———. 1984c. "Missionen iblandt Inuhuit." *Meddelelser om Den Grønlandske Kirkesag* 120: 18–27.

———. 1985. "Inuhuit (the Polar Eskimos): A Greenland Minority." In K. de La Barre, ed., *Proceedings of the International Workshop on Population Issues in Arctic Societies,* 295–310. Montreal.

———. 1988. "Inughuit, Knud Rasmussen and Thule." *Etudes/Inuit/Studies* 12: 45–55.

———. 1990. "Kyo—åndemaneren som vidste for meget!" *Grønland* 38: 235–47.

Gilberg, Å. 1948. *Eskimo Doctor.* New York. Translated from *Verdens nordligste Læge.* Copenhagen, 1940.

Gilberg, Å., L. Gilberg, R. Gilberg, and M. Holm. 1978. "Polar Eskimo Genealogy." *Meddelelser om Grønland* 203(4): 1–196.

Godfrey, W. C. 1857. *Narrative of the Last Grinnell Arctic Exploring Expedition in Search of Sir John Franklin, 1853–4–5.* Philadelphia.

Goldschmidt, V. 1950. "Kriminalitet i Thule." *Nordisk Tidsskrift for Kriminalvidenskab* 38: 12–22.

Goodsell, J. W. 1983. *On Polar Trails: The Peary Expedition to the North Pole, 1908–1909.* Austin, Texas.

Goodsir, R. A. 1850. *An Arctic Voyage to Baffin's Bay and Lancaster Sound, in Search of Friends with Sir John Franklin.* London.

Greely, A. W. 1886a and b. *Three Years of Arctic Service: An Account of the Lady Franklin Bay Expedition of 1881–4.* 2 vols. New York.

Green, F. 1926. *Peary: The Man Who Refused to Fail.* New York.

Gulløv, H. C. 1982a. "Eskimoens Syn på Europæeren." *Grønland* 30: 226–34. English translation 1983: "The Eskimo's View of the European: The So-Called Norse Dolls and Other Questionable Carvings." *Arctic Anthropology* 20: 121–29.

———. 1982b. "Migration et Diffusion—Peuplement Inuit de l'Ouest du Groenland à l'Époque post-médiévale." *Etudes/Inuit/Studies* 6: 3–20.

———. 1986. "Introduction." *Arctic Anthropology* 23: 1–18.

Gussow, Z. 1960. "Piblokto (hysteria) among the Polar Eskimo: An Ethnopsychiatric Study." *Psychoanalytic Study of Society* 1: 218–36.

Hacquebord, L., and R. Vaughan, eds. 1987. *Between Greenland and America: Cross-Cultural Contacts and the Environment in the Baffin Bay Area.* Arctic Centre. Groningen.

Haig-Thomas, D. 1939. *Tracks in the Snow.* London.

Hansen, J. C., and H. Pedersen. 1986. "Environmental Exposure to Heavy Metals in North Greenland." *Arctic Medical Research* 41: 21–34.

Hansen, K. 1969–70. "The People of the Far North." *Folk* 11–12: 97–108.

———. 1988. "Kiliffak—lidt om Mammutten i Grønland." *Grønland* 36: 174–81.

Harington, C. R. 1989. "Arctic Profiles: Nookapingwa (1893–1956)." *Arctic* 42: 163–65.

Harper, K. 1986. *Give Me My Father's Body. The Life of Minik, the New York Eskimo.* Frobisher Bay.

Hart, H. C. 1880. "Notes on the Ornithology of the British Polar Expedition, 1875–6." *Zoologist* (3)4: 121–29, 204–14.

Harwood, D. M. 1986. "Do Diatoms Beneath the Greenland Ice Sheet Indicate Interglacials Warmer Than Present?" *Arctic* 39: 304–8.

Hauser, M. 1986. "Traditional and Acculturated Greenlandic Music." *Arctic Anthropology* 23: 359–86.

Hayes, I. I. 1860. *An Arctic Boat Journey in the Autumn of 1854.* Boston.

———. 1862. "On a Meteorite from Savissivik." *Proceedings of the Academy of Natural Sciences of Philadelphia,* p. 520.

———. 1867. *The Open Polar Sea: A Narrative of a Voyage of Discovery towards the North Pole in the Schooner* United States. New York.

Heilprin, A. 1891. "Report on the Operations of the West Greenland Expedition." *Proceedings of the Academy of Natural Sciences of Philadelphia,* pp. 494–96.

———. 1893. *The Arctic Problem and Narrative of the Peary Relief Expedition of the Academy of Natural Sciences of Philadelphia.* Philadelphia.

Heinbecker, P., and R. H. Pauli. 1927. "Blood Groupings of the Polar Eskimo." *Journal of Immunology* 13: 279–83.

Hendrik, H. 1878. *Memoirs of Hans Hendrik the Arctic Traveller, Serving under Kane, Hayes, Hall and Nares, 1853–1876.* Translated from the Eskimo by Dr. Henry Rink. London.

Henson, M. 1912. *A Negro Explorer at the North Pole.* New York.

———. 1969. *A Black Explorer at the North Pole.* New York.

Herbert, M. 1974. *The Snow People.* London.

Herbert, W. 1981. *Hunters of the Polar North: The Eskimos.* Amsterdam.

———. 1989. *The Noose of Laurels: The Discovery of the North Pole.* London.

Hobbs, W. H. 1930. *Exploring about the North Pole of the Winds.* New York.

———. 1936. *Peary.* New York.

Hobson, W. 1972. "The Breeding Biology of the Knot." *Proceedings of the Western Foundation of Vertebrate Zoology* 2: 5–26.

Holmes, C. D., and R. B. Colton. 1960. "Patterned Ground Near Dundas (Thule Air Force Base), Greenland." *Meddelelser om Grønland* 158(6): 1–15.

Holtved, E. 1938a. "Foreløbig Beretning om den Arkæologisk-Etnografiske Expedition til Thule Distriktet. 1935–37." *Geografisk Tidsskrift* 41: 1–24.

———. 1938b. "Arbejder og Indtryk under to Års uphold blandt Polareskimoerne, 1935–37. *Det Grønlandske Selskabs Årsskrift,* 60–78. Reprinted 1981 in *Grønland* 29: 186–204.

———. 1942. *Polareskimoer.* Copenhagen.

———. 1944a and b. "Archaeological Investigations in the Thule District." *Meddelelser om Grønland* 141(1 and 2): 1–308, 1–184.

———. 1945. "Har Nordboerne været i Thule Distriktet?" *Fra Nationalmuseets Arbejdsmark,* 79–84.

———. 1950. "Thule Distriktet." In Birket-Smith et al. 1950b: 269–90.

———. 1951. "The Polar Eskimos: Language and Folklore." *Meddelelser om Grønland* 152(1 and 2): 1–367, 1–153.

———. 1954a. "Nûgdlît, en Forhistorisk Boplads i Thule Distriktet." *Grønland* 3: 89–94.

———. 1954b. "Archaeological Investigations in the Thule District, 3. Nûgdlît and Comer's Midden." *Meddelelser om Grønland* 146(3): 1–135.

———. 1960. "Omkring Thulestationens Grundlæggelse." *Grønland* 8: 241–48.

———. 1967. "Contributions to Polar Eskimo Ethnography." *Meddelelser om Grønland* 182(2): 1–180.

Hoppin, B. [1897]. *A Diary Kept While with the Peary Arctic Expedition of 1896.* N.p.

Horwood, H. 1977. *Bartlett: The Great Canadian Explorer.* New York.

House, E. J. 1909. *A Hunter's Camp-Fires.* New York.

Hrdlička, A. 1901. "An Eskimo Brain." *American Anthropologist* 3: 454–500.

———. 1910. "Contribution to the Anthropology of Central and Smith Sound Eskimo." *Anthropology Papers of the American Museum of Natural History* 5: 177–280.

Hunt, H. J., and R. H. Thompson. 1980. *North to the Horizon: Searching for Peary's Crocker Land.* Camden, Maine.

Hunt, W. R. 1981. *To Stand at the Pole: The Dr. Cook–Admiral Peary North Pole Controversy.* New York.

Inglefield, E. A. 1853. *A Summer Search for Sir John Franklin; with a Peep into the Polar Basin.* London.

Ito, H. 1982. "Sea Ice Atlas of Northern Baffin Bay." *Zürcher Geographischen Schriften* 7: 1–142.

Jacobsen, N. K., et al. 1980. "The Knud Rasmussen Memorial Expedition." *Geografisk Tidsskrift* 80: 29–44.

Jensen, F. 1960. "Sommerlæge i Grønland." *Grønland* 8: 41–48.

Jones, T. R., ed. 1875. *Manual of the Natural History, Geology and Physics of Greenland . . . Together with Instructions . . . for the Use of the Arctic Expedition of 1875.* London.

Jordan, R. H. 1984. "Neo-Eskimo Prehistory of Greenland." In Damas 1984: 540–48.

Kallstenius, A. 1967. *Tragedin i Smiths Sund. Björling-Kallstenius Expeditionen 1892.* Stockholm.

Kampen, A. van 1953. *Groenland. Continent der eenzamen.* Amsterdam.

Kane, E. K. 1856a and b. *Arctic Explorations: The Second Grinnell Expedition in Search of Sir John Franklin, 1853, 1854, 1855.* 2 vols. Philadelphia.

————. 1856c. *The United States Grinnell Expedition in Search of Sir John Franklin.* New ed. Philadelphia. 1st ed. 1853.

Keely, R. N., and G. G. Davis. 1893. *In Arctic Seas: The Voyage of the* Kite *with the Peary Expedition.* Philadelphia.

Kersting, R., ed. 1902. *The White World.* New York.

King, J. C. H. 1982. "A Preliminary Description of a Polar Eskimo Sledge Collected by Sir John Ross." *Inter-Nord* 16: 278–81.

Kjems, R. 1921. *Horisonter af Is. Erobringen af den grønlandske Inlandsis.* Copenhagen.

Kleivan, I., and B. Sonne. 1985. *Iconography of Religions* 8(2). *Eskimos. Greenland and Canada.* Leiden.

Knudsen, A. 1974. "Selvbyggerhuse." *Grønland* 22: 126–29.

Knudsen, H. 1964. "Status for Flytningerne fra Upernavik." *Grønland* 12: 121–34.

Knuth, E. 1977–78. "The 'Old Nûgdlît Culture' site at Nûgdlît Peninsula, Thule District, and the 'Mesoeskimo' Site Below It." *Folk* 19–20: 15–47.

Koch, L. 1928. "Contributions to the Glaciology of North Greenland." *Meddelelser om Grønland* 65: 181–464.

Krabbe, T. N. 1930. *Greenland: Its Nature, Inhabitants and History.* London and Copenhagen.

Kroeber, A. L. 1899a. "The Eskimo of Smith Sound." *Bulletin of the American Museum of Natural History* 12: 265–327.

————. 1899b. "Animal Tales of the Eskimo." *Journal of American Folklore* 12(44): 17–23.

————. 1899c. "Tales of the Smith Sound Eskimo." *Journal of American Folklore* 12(46): 166–82.

Laguna, F. de 1977. *Voyage to Greenland: A Personal Initiation into Anthropology.* New York.

Lanman, C. 1885. *Farthest North; or the Life and Explorations of Lt. J. B. Lockwood of the Greely Arctic Expedition.* New York.

Larsen, O. 1955. "Sommertandlæge i Grønland." *Grønland* 4: 57–65.

Larsen, W. 1972. *Kirken under Polarstjernen. Fra den grønlandske Kirke.* Copenhagen.

Lauritzen, P. 1983. *Thule. En Avis om Verdens nordligste Kommune.* Atuagagdliutit/ Grønlandsposten. Godthaab/Nuuk.

———. 1987. *Myten om Minik.* Copenhagen.

Laursen, D. 1955. "Grønlændere i Forskningens Tjeneste. Hans Zakæeus med Ross 1818." *Grønland* 4: 397–400.

———. 1956. "Grønlændere i Forskningens Tjeneste, 2. Hans Hendrik fra Fiskenæsset." *Grønland* 5: 144–49.

———. 1965. "Björling-Mysteriet." *Grønland* 13: 354–68.

———. 1972. "The Place Names of North Greenland." *Meddelelser om Grønland.* 180(2): 1–443.

Leden, C. 1910. "Kurzer Bericht über meine Grönlandreise 1909." *Globus* 97(13): 197–202.

———. 1952. "Über die Musik der Smith Sund Eskimos." *Meddelelser om Grønland.* 152(3): 1–92.

Leslie, A. 1879. *The Arctic Voyages of Adolf Erik Nordenskiöld, 1858–1879.* London.

Lewin, W. H. 1935. *The Great North Pole Fraud.* London.

Lidegaard, M. 1985. *Hans—en Eskimo.* Copenhagen.

Lillingston, F. G. I. 1876. *The Land of the White Bear: Being a Short Account of the Pandora's Voyage during the Summer of 1875.* Portsmouth and London.

Lindskog, K. 1959. "Grønlands Frimærker." *Grønland* 8: 1–24.

Lithner, K. 1973. "Mordet på Ross Marvin—ett Problem i Internationell Straffrätt." *Nordisk Tidsskrift for Kriminalvidenskab* 61: 293–300.

Loomis, C. C. 1972. *Weird and Tragic Shores: The Story of Charles Francis Hall, Explorer.* London.

Low, A. P. 1906. *Report on the Dominion Government Expedition to Hudson Bay and the Arctic Islands on Board the D.G.S. Neptune, 1903–1904.* Ottawa.

Lubbock, B. 1937. *The Arctic Whalers.* Glasgow.

Lufkin, D. 1977. "Forberedelserne til Oprettelse af Thule Air Base." *Grønland* 25: 261–67.

Lundbak, A. 1956. "Det Internationale Geofysiske År. 1957–1958." *Grønland* 5: 428–40.

Lund-Drosvad, A. 1961. "En gammel Udstedsbestyrer Fortæller." *Grønland* 9: 169–76.

Lundsteen, P. H. 1954. "Befolkningsflytninger i Grønland." *Grønland* 3: 129–42.

Lynge, H. 1955. "Inegpait eller Fornemme Mennesker, som Melville Bugtens Eskimoer kalder sig selv." *Meddelelser om Grønland* 90(2): 1–187.

MacGahan, J. A. 1876. *Under the Northern Lights.* London.

MacGregor, C. J. 1939. "The MacGregor Arctic Expedition to Etah, Greenland, July 1, 1937 to October 4, 1938." *U.S. Weather Bureau Monthly Review* 67: 366–82.

Mackersey, I. 1954. *Rescue below Zero*. London.

MacKintosh, Dr. 1884. *A Whaling Cruise in the Arctic Regions*. London.

MacMillan, D. B. 1918a. *Four Years in the White North*. New York.

————. 1918b. "Record Hunting in the Arctic." *Harper's Magazine* 137: 549–62.

————. 1927. *Etah and Beyond*. Boston.

————. 1930. "Geographical Report of the Crocker Land Expedition, 1913–1917." *Bulletin of the American Museum of Natural History* 56: 379–435.

————. 1934. *How Peary Reached the Pole*. Boston.

MacMillan, M. 1948. *Green Seas and White Ice*. New York.

Malaurie, J. 1956. *The Last Kings of Thule: A Year among the Polar Eskimos of Greenland*. London. Translated from *Les deniers rois de Thulé*. Paris, 1955.

————. 1968. *Thèmes de Recherche géomorphologique dans le Nord-ouest du Groenland*. Université de Paris Thèse Principale, 1962. Centre Nationale de la Recherche Scientifique. Paris.

————. 1973. "Du Droit des Minorités Esquimaudes Nord-Americaines et de la Population Groenlandaise. Notions implicites au Diagnostic de Sous-développement." In J. Malaurie, ed., *Le peuple Esquimau Aujourd'hui et Demain. Quatrième Congrés International de la Fondation Française d'Etudes Nordiques*, 27–49. Paris.

————. 1976. "Les Changements du Climat dans le Nord-ouest du Groenland pendant le Postglaciaire récent: Nouvelles Conclusions Palynologiques, Géomorphologiques et Ethnogénétiques." In R. Boyer, ed., *Les Vikings et leur civilisation: Problèmes actuels*, 89–101. Paris.

————. 1982. *The Last Kings of Thule: With the Polar Eskimos as They Face Their Destiny*. New York. Translated from *Les derniers rois de Thulé*. Paris, 1976.

Malaurie, J., et al. 1972. "Preliminary Remarks on Holocene Paleoclimates in the Region of Thule and Inglefield Land, Above All since the Beginning of Our Own Era." In Y. Vasari et al., eds., *Climatic Changes in Arctic Areas during the Last Ten Thousand Years: A Symposium Held at Oulanka and Kevo, 4–10 October 1971*, 105–36.

Markham, A. H. 1875. *A Whaling Cruise to Baffin's Bay and the Gulf of Boothia, and an Account of the Rescue of the Crew of the* Polaris. 2d ed. London.

————. 1878. *The Great Frozen Sea: A Personal Narrative of the Voyage of the* Alert *during the Arctic Expedition of 1875–6*. London.

Markham, C. R. 1865. "On the Origin and Migrations of the Greenland Esquimaux." *Journal of the Royal Geographical Society* 35: 87–99.

————. 1866. "The Arctic Highlanders." *Transactions of the Ethnological Society of London*, n.s. 4: 125–37.

————, ed. 1881. *The Voyages of William Baffin, 1612–1622*. Hakluyt Society. London.

Mary-Rousselière, G. 1980. *Qitdlarssuaq: L'histoire d'une migration polaire*. Montreal.

Mathiassen, T. 1934. "Knud Rasmussen's Sledge Expeditions and the Founding of the Thule Trading Station." *Geografisk Tidsskrift* 37: 16–30.

————. 1945. "The Archaeology of the Thule District." *Geografisk Tidsskrift* 47: 43–71.

McGhee, R. 1984. "Contact between Native North Americans and the Medieval Norse: A Review of the Evidence." *American Antiquity* 49: 4–26.

————. 1987. "The Relationship between the Medieval Norse and Eskimos." In Hacquebord and Vaughan 1987: 51–60.

M'Clintock, F. L. 1859. *The Voyage of the* Fox *in the Arctic Seas: A Narrative of the Discovery of the Fate of Sir John Franklin and His Companions.* London.

———. 1869. *The Voyage of the* Fox *in the Arctic Seas in Search of Franklin and His Companions.* 3d ed. London.

M'Dougall, G. F. 1857. *The Eventful Voyage of H. M. Discovery Ship Resolute to the Arctic Regeions in Search of Sir John Franklin . . . in 1852, 1853, 1854.* London.

Meldgaard, M. 1986. "The Greenland Caribou—Zoogeography, Taxonomy, and Population Dynamics." *Meddelelser on Grønland. Bioscience* 20: 1–88.

Melville, G. W. 1896. *In the Lena Delta. A Narrative of the Search for Lieut.-Commander De Long and his Companions.* Boston.

Ministeriet for Grønland, ed. 1985. *Grønland. Årsberetning.* Copenhagen.

Mirsky, J. 1954. *Elisha Kent Kane and the Seafaring Frontier.* Boston.

Moltke, H. 1964. *Livsrejsen.* Copenhagen. 1st ed. 1936.

Monzino, G. 1971. "Polo Nord." *Tempo* 33 (29): 32–40; 33 (30): 29–37; 33 (31): 28–35.

Moss, E. L. 1978. *Shores of the Polar Sea: A Narrative of the Arctic Expedition of 1875–6.* London.

Müller, F., A. Ohmura, and R. Braithwate. 1977. "The North Water Project." *Polar Geography* 1: 75–85.

Munck, S. 1941. "Geological Observations from the Thule District in the Summer of 1936." *Meddelelser om Grønland* 124(4): 1–38.

Muus, B., F. Salomonsen, and C. Vibe. 1981. *Grønlands Fauna. Fisk. Fugle. Pattedyr.* Copenhagen.

Mylius-Erichsen, L. 1905. *Kap York. Foredrag ved det Private Møde i Bethesda den 3. maj 1905.* Copenhagen.

Mylius-Erichsen, L., and H. Moltke. 1906. *Grønland.* Copenhagen.

Møller, V. 1961. "Af Knud Rasmussens Oplevelser i Grønland, maj 1907–februar 1908." *Grønland* 9: 237–40.

Nanton, P. 1971. *Arctic Breakthrough: Franklin's Expeditions, 1819–1847.* London.

Nares, G. 1878a and b. *Narrative of a Voyage to the Polar Sea during 1875–6.* 2 vols. London.

Neatby, L. H. 1970. *The Search for Franklin.* London.

Nichols, R. L. 1953. "Geomorphologic Observations at Thule, Greenland and Resolute Bay, Cornwallis Island, N.W.T." *American Journal of Science* 251: 268–75.

———. 1969. "Geomorphology of Inglefield Land, North Greenland." *Meddelelser om Grønland* 188(1): 1–109.

Nielsen, E. 1960. "Oprettelsen af Station Nord." *Grønland* 8: 339–51.

Nordenskiöld, A. E. 1885. *Den andra Dicksonska Expeditionen till Grönland.* Stockholm.

Nordenskiöld, G. 1894. "Om Björlings och Kallstenii Expedition till Trakten af Smith Sound." *Ymer* 14: 1–16.

Ohlin, A. 1895a. *På Forskningsfärd efter Björling och Kallstenius. Strödda Dagboksanteckningar från en Färd till Nordgrönland Sommaren 1894.* Stockholm.

———. 1895b. "Appendix B: Zoology, Birds." In Bryant 1895: 63–69.

Oldendow, K. 1960. "Kunúnguaq." *Grønland* 8: 261–72.

Olsen, G. 1910. "Til Samfundet, som har Udsendt Missionærer til Kap York." *Meddelelser om Den Grønlandske Kirkesag* 17: 1–16.

————. 1911. "Uddrag af et Brev fra Missionspræst G. Olsen." *Meddelelser om Den Grønlandske Kirkesag* 21: 1–14.

————. 1913a. "Brev fra Kap York." *Meddelelser om Den Grønlandske Kirkesag* 25: 3–5.

————. 1913b. "Den Grønlandske Kirkesag og Kap York Missionen." *Meddelelser om Den Grønlandske Kirkesag* 26: 1–7.

————. 1914. "I 'Midmørket.'" *Meddelelser om Den Grønlandske Kirkesag* 31: 1–5.

————. 1922. "Foredrag i København 1. juni." *Meddelelser om Den Grønlandske Kirkesag* 46: 4–10.

Operti, A. 1902. "An Artist in the Frozen Zone." In Kersting 1902: 293–304.

Orvig, S. 1981. "A Century of Arctic Meteorology: From Discovery to Science." In M. Zaslow, ed., *A Century of Canada's Arctic Islands, 1880–1980*, 131–40. Ottawa.

Osborn, S. 1865. *Stray Leaves from an Arctic Journal*. Edinburgh.

Oswalt, W. H. 1987. "Technological Complexity: The Polar Eskimos and the Tareumiut." *Arctic Anthropology* 24: 82–98.

Peary, J. D. 1893. *My Arctic Journal: A Year among Icefields and Eskimos*. London.

Peary, R. E. 1892. "Report on the Operations of the North Greenland Expedition of 1891–1892." *Proceedings of the Academy of Natural Sciences of Philadelphia*, 342–49.

————. 1894. "The Cape York Ironstone." *Journal of the American Geographical Society* 26: 447–88.

————. 1898a and b. *Northward over the "Great Ice."* 2 vols. New York.

————. 1904a. "North Polar Exploration: Field Work of the Peary Arctic Club, 1898–1902." *Annual Report of the Smithsonian Institution*, 1903, pp. 427–57. Reprinted in Peary 1907: 293–352.

————. 1904b. *Snowland Folk*. New York.

————. 1907. *Nearest the Pole: A Narrative of the Polar Expedition of the Peary Arctic Club in the S.S. Roosevelt, 1905–1906*. London.

————. 1910. *The North Pole: Its Discovery in 1909 under the Auspices of the Peary Arctic Club*. New York.

Petersen, H., and E. Staffeldt, eds. 1978. *Bogen om Grønland. Fortid, nutid og fremtid*. Copenhagen.

Petersen, J. C. C. 1857. *Erindringer fra Polarlandene Optegnede af Carl Petersen, Tolk ved Pennys og Kanes Nordexpeditioner, 1850–1855*, ed. L. B. Deichmann. Copenhagen.

————. 1860. *Den Sidste Franklin-Expedition med Fox, Capt. M'Clintock*. Copenhagen.

Petersen, R. 1964. "Eskimoernes Sidste Indvandring fra Canada til Grønland." *Grønland* 12: 373–87. Translation of "The Last Eskimo Immigration into Greenland." *Folk* 4: 95–110. 1962.

Petersen, S. 1922. "Kap York Missionen." *Meddelelser om Den Grønlandske Kirkesag* 46: 1–4.

Petrow, R. 1967. *Across the Top of Russia: The Cruise of the U.S.C.G.C. Northwind into the Polar Seas North of Siberia*. London.

Phillips, C. G. 1851. "Commander Phillips, R.N. to Captain Ross. Enclosure No. 2." *Arctic Expeditions. Blue Book 2*. No. 9(B), pp. 87–88. London.

Pommier, R. 1953. *Au-dela de Thulé sur la Route des Glaces*. Paris.

Povlsen, E. 1955. "Jul i Thule." *Grønland* 4: 441–51.

Powell, T. 1961. *The Long Rescue*. London.

Preston, D. J. 1986. *Dinosaurs in the Attic: An Excursion into the American Museum of Natural History*. New York.

Putnam, D. B. 1926. *David Goes to Greenland*. New York and London.

Putnam, G. P. 1947. *Mariner of the North. The Life of Captain Bob Bartlett*. New York.

Rasmussen, K. 1908. *The People of the Polar North*. London. Translation of *Nye mennesker*. Copenhagen, 1905.

———. 1915. "Report of the First Thule Expedition 1912." *Meddelelser om Grønland* 51(8): 283–340.

———. 1918. *Fra Verdens Ende*. Copenhagen.

———. 1921a. *Greenland by the Polar Sea: The Story of the [Second] Thule Expedition from Melville Bay to Cape Morris Jesup*. London. Translation of *Grønland langs Polhavet*. Copenhagen, 1919.

———. 1921b. "Beskrivelse af Thule Distrikt." In G. C. Amdrup et al., *Grønland i Tohundredaaret for Hans Egedes Landing*, 1. *Meddelelser om Grønland* 60: 517–67.

———. 1925. *Myter og Sagn fra Grønland, 3. Kap York-Distriktet og Nordgrønland*. Copenhagen.

———. 1928. "Report on the Second Thule Expedition for the Exploration of Greenland from Melville Bay to De Long Fjord, 1916–1918." *Meddelelser om Grønland* 65: 1–181.

———. 1935. "Foran Dagens Øje." In P. Freuchen et al., eds. *Mindeudgave* 3: 173–218. Copenhagen. 1st ed. Copenhagen, 1915.

———. 1957. *Min Rejsedagbog. Skildringer fra den Første Thule-Ekspedition*. Copenhagen. 1st ed. Copenhagen, 1915.

[———.] 1961. "Knud Rasmussen og Thule." *Grønland* 9: 24–26.

Raven, H. C. 1927. "Northward for Narwhal." *Natural History* 33–44.

Rawlins, D. 1973. *Peary at the North Pole. Fact or Fiction?* Washington.

Rawson, K. L. 1927. *A Boy's-Eye View of the Arctic*. New York.

Richards, R. L. 1985. *Dr. John Rae*. Whitby.

Rickard, T. A. 1941. "The Use of Meteoric Iron." *Journal of the Anthropological Institute of Great Britain and Ireland* 71: 55–65.

Rink, H. 1875. *Tales and Traditions of the Eskimo*. London.

Roby, D. D., H. Thing, and K. L. Brink. 1984. "History, Status and Taxonomic Identity of Caribou (*Rangifer tarandus*) in Northwest Greenland." *Arctic* 37: 23–30.

Rockwell, T. O. 1984. "Ross Gilmore Marvin (1880–1909): Explorer and Teacher." *Fram: The Journal of Polar Studies* 1: 374–78.

Rodahl, K. 1953. *North: The Nature and Drama of the Polar World*. New York.

Rosbach, S. 1910a. "Uddrag af et Brev fra Overkateket Sechmann Rosbach." *Meddelelser om Den Grønlandske Kirkesag* 18: 9–11.

———. 1910b. "Beretning fra Missionær Sechmann Rosbach." *Meddelelser om Den Grønlandske Kirkesag* 20: 1–7.

Ross, C. 1934. *Mit Kind und Kegel in die Arktis*. Leipzig.

Ross, F. S., and P. E. Ancker. 1977. "Thule Air Base." *Grønland* 25: 268–78.

Ross, J. 1819. *A Voyage of Discovery, Made under the Orders of the Admiralty, in H.M. Ships* Isabella *and* Alexander, *for the Purpose of Exploring Baffin's Bay, and Enquiring into the Probability of a North-West Passage.* London.

Ross, W. G. 1975. *Whaling and Eskimos: Hudson Bay, 1860–1915.* Ottawa.

———. 1983. "George Comer (1858–1937)." *Arctic* 36: 294–95.

Sabine, E. 1819. "An Account of the Esquimaux Who Inhabit the West Coast of Greenland above the Latitude 76°." *Quarterly Journal of Literature, Science and the Arts* 7: 72–94.

Sabine, J. 1818. "An Account of a New Species of Gull Lately Discovered on the West Coast of Greenland." *Transactions of the Linnaean Society of London* 12: 520–23.

Salomonsen, F. 1943. "Report on the Natural History Expedition to Northwest Greenland 1936." *Meddelelser om Grønland* 124(1): 1–38.

Sand, R. 1935. "Knud Rasmussens Virke i og for Thule-Distriktet." In P. Freuchen et al., eds., *Mindeudgave* 3: 381–92. Copenhagen.

———. 1936. "Nogle Træk af Thules Historie." *Det Grønlandske Selskab Årsskrift,* 43–59.

Sandgreen, O. 1989. "Avangnâta uvdloriâ"—"Nordstjernen." *Fra Thulemissionens første dage.* Godhavn.

Saunders, J. 1851. "Proceedings of H.M.S. *North Star,* Mr. James Saunders Master-Commanding of an expedition to Barrow Straits, with stores and provisions, in 1849 and 1850." *Arctic Expeditions. Blue Book 2.* No. 6, pp. 56–66. London.

Savours, A., ed. 1960. "Journal of a Whaling Voyage from Dundee to Davis Strait, 1894." *Polar Record* 10: 26–37.

Schledermann, P. 1979. "Norse Artefacts on Ellesmere Island." *Polar Record* 19: 493–94.

———. 1980. "Notes on Norse Finds from the East Coast of Ellesmere Island, N.W.T." *Arctic* 33: 454–63.

———. 1982. "Nordbogenstande fra Arktisk Canada." *Grønland* 30: 218–25.

———. 1990. *Crossroads to Greenland. Three Thousand Years of Prehistory in the Eastern High Arctic.* Calgary.

Schley, W. S. 1887. *Report of Winfield S. Schley, Commander, U.S. Navy, Commanding Greely Relief Expedition of 1884.* Washington.

Schley, W. S., and J. R. Soley. 1889. *The Rescue of Greely.* New York.

Schultz-Lorentzen, C. 1913. "Forbindelsen med Missionsstationerne." *Meddelelser om Den Grønlandske Kirkesag* 27: 1–6.

Schultz-Lorentzen, H. 1990. "Nye Overførsler fra Nationalmuseet til Grønland." *Grønland* 38: 113–20.

Senn, N. 1907. *In the Heart of the Arctics.* Chicago.

Shackleton, E. 1937. *Arctic Journeys: The Story of the Oxford University Ellesmere Land Expedition, 1934–5.* London.

Silis, I. 1968. "Fedsten i Thule. En Usædvanlig Rejseoplevelse med Thule-eskimoerne i 1965–67." *Grønland* 16: 50–54.

———. 1970. *Slædesporene Fyger Til.* Copenhagen.

———. 1984. "Narwhal Hunters of Greenland." *National Geographic* 165: 520–39.

Simmonds, P. L. 1852. *Sir John Franklin and the Arctic Regions: With Detailed Notices of the Expeditions in Search of the Missing Vessels under Sir John Franklin.* Buffalo.

Simpson, C. J. W. 1957. *North Ice: The British North Greenland Expedition.* London.

Skeie, J. 1931. *Grønlandssaken.* Oslo.

Skov, O. 1966a. "Det Ydersts Øde." *Grønland* 14: 49–54.

———. 1966b. "Flytningen af Thule. Svar til Fhv. Departementschef Eske Brun." *Grønland* 14: 397–99.

Smith, C. E. 1923. *From the Deep of the Sea: Being the Diary of the Late Charles Edward Smith, Surgeon of the Whaleship* Diana *of Hull.* New York. 1st ed. London, 1922.

Snow, W. P. 1851. *Voyage of the* Prince Albert *in Search of Sir John Franklin.* London.

Spitzka, E. A. 1902. "Contributions to the Encephalic Anatomy of the Races: Three Eskimo Brains from Smith's Sound." *American Journal of Anatomy* 2: 25–71.

Stahlschmidt, N., and J. Tommerup. 1978. *Vandringsfolk ved Nordpolen.* Copenhagen.

Steensby, H. P. 1909. "The Polar Eskimos and the Polar Expeditions." *Fortnightly Review* 92: 891–902.

———. 1910. "Contributions to the Ethnology and Anthropogeography of the Polar Eskimos." *Meddelelser om Grønland* 34: 253–407.

Stefansson, V. 1943. *Greenland.* London.

Stein, R. 1902a. "Geographische Nomenklatur bei den Eskimos des Smith-Sundes." *Petermanns Geographische Mitteilungen* 48: 195–201.

———. 1902b. "Eskimo Music." In Kersting 1902: 333–56.

Streeter, D. W. 1929. *An Arctic Rodeo.* New York.

Sutherland, P. C. 1852a and b. *Journal of a Voyage in Baffin's Bay and Barrow Straits, in the Years 1850–1851, Performed by H.M. Ships* Lady Franklin *and* Sofia. 2 vols. London.

Sutherland, P. D., ed. 1985. *The Franklin Era in Canadian Arctic History, 1845–1859.* Ottawa.

Sutton, G. M. 1985. *Eskimo Year.* Norman, Okla. 1st ed. New York, 1934.

Sverdrup, O. 1903. *Nyt land, Fire aar i Arktiske Egne.* 2 vols. Kristiania (Oslo). English translation, *New Land: Four Years in Arctic Regions.* 2 vols. London and New York, 1904.

Søby, R. M. 1977–78. "The Kinship Terminology in Thule." *Folk* 19–20: 49–84.

———. 1979. "Sprog og Identitet i Thule." In B. Basse and K. Jensen, eds., *Eskimosprogenes vilkår i dag,* 143–52. Arkona.

———. 1985. "Savigsivik—Vestgrønlandsk Indflydelse i en Bygd i Thule." *Grønland* 33: 245–64.

Sørensen, A. K. 1983. *Danmark-Grønland i det 20 Århundrede—en Historisk Oversigt.* Copenhagen.

Taagholt, J. 1977. "Den Videnskabelige Aktivitet Omkring Thule Air Base." *Grønland* 25: 279–91.

Taagholt, J., and G. Andersen. 1981. "Amerikansk Forskning i Grønland." *Forskning i Grønland* 1: 24–28 and 2: 29–33.

Taagholt, J., and K. Hansen. 1977. "Thule." *Grønland* 25: 245–46.

Thing, H. 1976. "Field Notes on Birds in Thule District, Greenland, 1975." *Dansk Ornithologisk Forenings Tidsskrift* 70: 141–43.

Thorén, R. 1979. *Svenska Arktiska Expeditioner under 1800-talet.* Stockholm.

Thür, H. 1958. *Unternehmen Thule. Eskimosiedlung wird Grossflughafen.* Graz.

Troelsen, J. C. 1950. "Contributions to the Geology of Northwest Greenland, Ellesmere Island and Axel Heiberg Island." *Meddelelser om Grønland* 149(7): 1–86.

Ulloriaq, I. 1984. "Hvad Man har Hørt om de To Første Nordpolsfarere." *Grønland* 32: 61–88.

———. 1985. *Beretningen om Qillarsuaq og hans Lange Rejse fra Canada til Nordgrønland i 1860erne.* Copenhagen.

Vahl, M., G. C. Amdrup, L. Bobé, and A. S. Jensen, eds. 1928a and b, 1929. *Greenland.* 3 vols. Copenhagen and London.

VanStone, J. W. 1972a. "The First Peary Collection of Polar Eskimo Material Culture." *Fieldiana Anthropology* 63: 31–80.

———. 1972b. "New Evidence Concerning Polar Eskimo Isolation." *American Anthropologist* 74: 1062–65.

Vaughan, R. 1982. "The Arctic in the Middle Ages." *Journal of Medieval History* 8: 313–42.

———. 1986. "Bowhead Whaling in Davis Strait and Baffin Bay during the Eighteenth and Nineteenth Centuries." *Polar Record* 23: 289–99.

———. 1987. "How Isolated Were the Polar Eskimos in the Nineteenth Century?" In Hacquebord and Vaughan 1987: 95–107.

Vibe, C. 1938. *Fangerfolk og Fuglefjelde.* Copenhagen.

———. 1946. *Ene ligger Grønland. Livet i Grønland under de 6 Lange Adskillelsens Aar 1939–45.* Copenhagen.

———. 1948. *Langthen og Nordpaa.* Copenhagen.

———. 1950. "The Marine Mammals and the Marine Fauna in the Thule District, with Observations on Ice Conditions in 1939–41." *Meddelelser on Grønland* 150(6): 1–117.

———. 1967. "Arctic Mammals in Relation to Climatic Fluctuations." *Meddelelser om Grønland* 170(5): 1–227.

———. 1968. "Thule-eskimoernes Isbjørnejagter." *Grønland* 16: 175–80.

———. 1981. "Pattedyr." In Muus et al. 1981: 363–459.

———. 1986. "The Musk Ox Project 1986." *Newsletter from the Commission for Scientific Research in Greenland* 14: 25.

Vigh, G. 1970. "B-52 Nedstyrtningen ved Thule i januar 1968." *Grønland* 18: 193–203.

Villarejo, O. M. 1965. *Dr. Kane's Voyage to the Polar Lands.* Philadelphia.

Wager, W. 1962. *Camp Century: City under the Ice.* New York.

Walker, A. B. 1909. *The Cruise of the Esquimaux to Davis Straits and Baffin Bay, April–October 1899.* Liverpool.

Wallace, A. F. C., and R. E. Ackerman. 1960. "An Interdisciplinary Approach to Mental Disorder among the Polar Eskimos of Northwest Greenland." *Anthropologica* 2: 249–60.

Wamberg, P. 1961. "Knud Rasmussen og Anlæggelsen af Handelstationen Thule, 1910". *Handels- og Søfartsmuseets på Kronborg, Årbog*, pp. 23–48.

Weems, J. E. 1967. *Peary: The Explorer and the Man*. London.

Weidick, A., et al. 1970. "Thule Kommune." In J. P. Trap, ed., *Danmark*, 14: *Grønland*, pp. 600–613. Copenhagen.

Whitney, H. P. 1910. *Hunting with the Eskimos*. New York.

Wissler, C. 1918. "Archaeology of the Polar Eskimo." *Anthropological Papers of the American Museum of Natural History* 22: 103–67.

Wordie, J. M. 1938. "An Expedition to Northwest Greenland and the Canadian Arctic in 1937." *Geographical Journal* 92: 385–421.

Wright, J. W. 1939. "Contributions to the Glaciology of Northwest Greenland." *Meddelelser om Grønland* 125(3); 1–43.

Wright, N. 1959. *Quest for Franklin*. London.

Young, A. 1879. *The Two Voyages of the Pandora in 1875 and 1876*. London.

Index

Aamma, 54
Aapilarsuaq, 117
Aasiaat. *See* Egedesminde
Aberdeen, 42; ships from: *see Bon Accord;
Elizabeth*
Academy Bay, 173
Ackerman, R. E., 120
Active, the (Dundee whaler), 68, 82
Adak, the (icebreaker), 137–38
Adams, William, Jr., 44, 46–47, 77, 156
Adams, William, Sr., 77
Adler, Christian, 60, 160
Admiralty, British, 29, 30–32, 35–36,
    93–94, 97, 100
Advance, the (brig), 33–34, 55–57, 64
Advice, the (Dundee whaler), 92
Akilineq, 17
Akpohon meteorite, 108
Akuunaarmiut, 8
Alaska, 12, 74, 75, 135
Alcoholic drinks, 65, 76, 141, 159–60
Aleqasina, 124
Aleqatsiaq, 43, 101
Alert, Ellesmere Island, 135, 148, 149
Alert, HMS, 36
Alexander, HMS, 41, 67, 79, 96
Alexander, the (Dundee whaler), 43
Amaannalik, 116, 159
America, 13, 14, 41, 63, 130
American Museum of Natural History,
    New York, 40–41, 61, 70, 71, 78, 132;
    and the Cape York meteorites, 103, 104,
    106, 108, 109, 121, Fig. 12; *Anthropol-
    ogy Papers* of, 125; Greenland Expedi-
    tion of (1926), 87–88, 117, 126; Inuhuit

housed at, 123–24; Peary collects for,
    113–14, 127; *piblocto* photographs in,
    119; West Greenland Expedition of
    (1891), 37, 101, 113, 126–27. *See also*
    Crocker Land Expedition
American Philosophical Society, 29
American public, 57, 105
American Red Cross, 134
Ammassalik, 74, 144
Amundsen, Roald, 38, 46–47
Anaakkaq, 54
Angakkoq or shaman, 16, 24, 52, 64, 156,
    157–59
"Aniutark," 52
Anniversary Lodge, Bowdoin Fjord, 38, 64,
    82, 101, 102
Anoritooq, 13, 20, 27, 39–40; Rudolph
    Franke at, 54, 70; John Murphy at, 69
Antarctica, 148
Appalilik, 108
Appat. *See* Saunders Island
Arctic, the DGS, 39
Arctic, the USS, 34
Arctic Circle, 142
Arctic Highlanders, 12, 14, 24, 30–31, 96,
    112
Arctic Ocean, 39
Ariel, the (Hull whaler), 42
Armed Forces Day, 140–41
Arnaaluk, 52, 53
Arrutaq, 28
Asiajuk, 72–73
Asivaq, 125
Assistance, HMS, 32, 51, 93
Associated Press (AP), 162

Astrup, Eivind, 38, 85, 114, 115, 174;
crosses the Inland Ice with Peary, 37, 58,
112
Atangana, 123, 125
Aurora, the (Dundee whaler), 45
Austin, H. T., 32
Avannarliit, 9
Avens, mountain (*Dryas integrifolia*), 6
Aviaq, 123, 124, 125
Axel Heiberg Island, 59

Baffin Bay, 5, 6, 29–30, 31, 35, 68; William
Baffin in, 173; ice-pack in, 80; whales
and whalers in, 42, 78–79
Baffin Island (Qikirtaluk), 27–28, 29, 42, 53,
151, 175
Baffin, William, 16, 29, 41, 79, 173
Baku, 73
Balaena, the (Dundee whaler), 47
Balchen, Bernt, 134, 137, 145
Ballistic Missile Early Warning System
(BMEWS), 139, 142–44
Banks, Joseph, 97
Barron, William, 92
Barrow, John, 30–31
Bartlett, John, 122
Bartlett, Robert, 40, 41
Bear, the, 36, 67
Bear, polar (*Ursus maritimus*), 40, 84–85,
95, 167
Bearskin, 23–24, 53, 70–72, 84, 157
Beck, A. G., 119
Beebe, William M., 44
Beechey Island, Barrow Strait, 170
Belcher, Edward, 22, 32, 67, 93
Beluga or white whale, *Delphinapterus leu-
cas,* 86, 167
Bement, L. C., 62
Beothic, the (sealer), 40, 41
Berlin, 136; University of, 98
Berlingske Glacier, 174
Bernier, J. E., 39
Bessels, Emil, 27, 48, 57–58, 114, 116; col-
lects skulls, 126, 128
Beynen, L. R. Koolemans, 36
Biering, Adam, 73
Bird, Junius, 109
Birds, 7, 14, 18. *See also names of individ-
ual species*

Bird-skin clothing, 23–24, 92, 162
Björling, Alfred, 44–45
Björling Island, Cary Islands, 44–45
Boas, Franz, 120, 123
Bon Accord, the (Aberdeen whaler), 79
Booth, Felix, 173
Booth Sound, 18, 55, 91, 172, 173
Born, Erik, 87–88, 89, 92, 167
Borup, George, 44, 89
Boston, Mass., 173; School of Technology,
103
Bow and arrow, 14, 15, 18, 27, 81–82
Bowdoin, the (schooner), 41
Bowdoin Fjord, 38, 101
Bowdoin Glacier, 174
Bowhead or Greenland right whale (*Ba-
laena mysticetus*), 9, 14, 78–79
Bradley, John R., 39
Brezina, A., 105
Bridgman, H. L., 38
Brill, A. A., 119–20
Britain, 134
British Arctic Expedition (1875–76), 35–36,
44–45, 90, 93, 100, 105; depots left by,
170; mail, 170
British Museum, 21, 94, 99, 105, 109, 111
British North Greenland Expedition, 150
Broberg, Daniel, 66
Brun, Eske, 134
Brønland, Jørgen, 59
Buchanan Bay, Ellesmere Island, 15
Buchwald, Vagn F., 97–98, 108, 110
Bunting, snow (*Plectrophenax nivalis*), 114
Burials, 25, 31, 171–72
Bushnan Island, 30, 32, 107, 127, 173

Caches, 44–45, 46–47
Cairns, 36, 169–71
Cambridge University, 128
Camp Century, 146–47
Camp Lloyd, 134
Camp Tuto (Thule Take Off), 145, 146, 148
Campion, moss (*Silene acaulis*), 6
Canada, 10, 12, 16, 17, 74, 134; adopts
Inuit names, 175; annexes Ellesmere
Island, 133; meteoritic iron in, 110. *See
also* Inuit
Canadian Arctic Islands, the, 13, 31, 34, 38,
134–35; Cook in, 40, 50; whalers in, 42

Canary Islands, 166
Cape Alexander, 9, 18, 36
Cape Atholl, 18, 33, 42, 81, 92, 101; Loran
  Station at, 149
Cape Bridgman, 174
Cape Cleveland, 8, 11, 37
Cape Constitution, 173
Cape Dorset, Baffin Island, 14
Cape Dudley Digges, 42, 82, 93, 173, Fig. 2
Cape George Russell, Inglefield Land, 80
Cape Hatteras, 143
Cape Hecla, Ellesmere Island, 48–49
Cape Hoppner, 173
Cape Isabella, Ellesmere Island, 35, 133
Cape Morris K. Jesup, 174
Cape Morton, Washington Land, 170
Cape Parry, 8, 43, 55, 82, 101, 173
Cape Robertson, 174
Cape Sabine, Ellesmere Island, 27
Cape Seddon, Melville Bay, 110, 129
Cape Sparbo, Devon Island, 39
Cape Thomas Hubbard, Axel Heiberg
  Island, 59
Cape York (Ivnanganeq), 8, 18, 50, 132,
  157; bartering at, 63; bear shooting off,
  85; Cook at, 70; Danes at, 51, 99, 132;
  dovekies at, 90, 93; Eskimos at, 20, 25,
  32–33, 51, 53, 104, 114; explorers off,
  32–35, 51; gifts distributed at, 66;
  Heilprin and colleagues at, 113;
  monument to Peary at, 41, 172; Peary at,
  39, 44, 68, 121, 123; Ross's expedition at,
  30, 67, 79–80, 90–91, 96–97; whales and
  whalers off, 29, 35, 42–44, 53, 68, 87
Cape York district, 5
Cape York meteorites, 15–16, 18, 96–110,
  121, Fig. 12. *See also* Peary
Caribou or reindeer (*Rangifer tarandus*), 7,
  13, 18, 27–28, 51, 81–84; close season
  for, 95; meat of, 52; shooting of, 37, 50,
  82–84; skins of, 50–51, 162
Cary, Alwyn, 173
Cary Islands (Kitsigsut), 9, 35–36, 42–43,
  128; Björling at, 44–45; British Arctic
  Expedition at, 35, 44–45, 93; named, 173,
  174, 175
Caspian Sea, 73
Chamberlin, T. C., 38, 174
"Cheepchow," 51
Chester, Colby M., 69

Chicago, 112–13; Field Museum of Natural
  History in, 114; University of, 38, 127,
  135
Chladni, E. F. F., 98
Christian VIII, king of Denmark, 98
Christian IX, king of Denmark, 132
Christianity, 155, 165. *See also* North Star
  Mission
Christianshåb (Qasigiannguit), 100, 115
Christophersen, G. M. Q., 98–99
Civil War (U.S.), 72
Claushavn (Ilimanaq), 115
Clavering, Douglas C., 13
Clements Markham Glacier, 49, 132
Climate, 10–11, 16
Coal, 1, 55, 157
Cold War, 144
Comer, George, 6, 128, 130, 131
Comer's Midden, 6, 15, 109, 129–30, Fig.
  13
Conical Rock, 8, 32, 43, Fig. 2
Conservation, 95, 154
Cook, Frederick A., 24, 61, 70–71, 105,
  118, 122; censuses the Inuhuit, 116–17;
  ethnologist on North Greenland
  Expedition, 37, 58, 113, 120; North Pole
  expedition of, 39–40, 48, 50, 51
Copenhagen, 75, 115, 125, 126, 142, 157;
  Danish National Museum in, 15, 114,
  117–18, 131; G. Olsen in, 158, 164; Royal
  Dockyard at, 107; travel to, 40, 163
Copenhagen University: Mineralogical
  Museum, 106–7, 108; Zoological
  Museum, 94, 99
Cornell University (Ithaca, N.Y.), 60, 103
Cramer, Parker, 144
Crimson Cliffs, 8
Crocker Land Expedition, 40–41, 50, 54,
  59, 92, 119; and the Cape York
  meteorites, 106, 108, 109; at Iita, 71, 83,
  133; collects artifacts, 128; excavates
  Comer's Midden, 130
Crowberry, *Empetrum nigrum*, 7
Cruikshank, George, 8, 30, 94
Cryolite, 1, 134
Cullamore, J., 32, 64
Cumberland Sound, 53, 68

Dallas Bay, Inglefield Land, 83

Dalrymple Rock, 38, 43, 46–47, 63, 93
Danes, 9, 16, 151, 165; and the Inuhuit, 49–50, 66, 117, 166–67; at Thule Air Base, 140, 142–43, 148–50. *See also* Literary Greenland Expedition
Danish Arctic Contractors, 143
Danish Atomic Energy Commission, 143
Danish Foreign Office, 45, 132
Danish Geodetic Institute, 149
Danish Ministry of Ecclesiastical Affairs, 159
Danish Mission Society, 156
Danish Natural History Expedition to Northwest Greenland (1936), 94, 95
Danish West Indies (now Virgin Islands), 133
Danmark, the, 41
Danmark Expedition (1907), 73
Danmark Fjord, 145
Dannebrog, the Danish flag, 9, 74, 132, 133, 154
Dansgård, W., 147
Daugaard-Jensen, Jens, 46
Daugherty, C. M., 146
Davis Strait, 29–30, 31, 35
Denmark, 98, 133, 134, 135, 158; and the annexation of Avanersuaq, 95, 132, 133, 151–52
Devon Island, 17, 27, 39
Diana, the, 38, 89
Diana, the (Dundee whaler), 46–47, 53, 93
Diana, the (Hull whaler), 84–85, 87, 92
Diebitsch, Emil, 102
Digges, Dudley, 173
Discouerie, the, 79
Discovery, HMS, 36, 93
Disko, 41, 42, 98, 99
Disko Bay, 115
Dogs, 9, 14, 22–23, 52, 72, 167, Fig. 16; barter for, 67; used by explorers, 48–49
Dorset People, 14
Dovekie or little auk (*Alle alle*), 7, 18, 23–24, 31, 90–93, 95, Figs. 2, 11; as food, 53, 56, 90–91, 93
Drown Bay, 18
Drum song, 28, 52, 114–16, 159
Dundas, 176
Dundas, David, 173
Dundas Dining Hall, Thule Air Base, 86, 141, 142–43

Dundee, Scotland, 69; ships from: *See names of individual ships*
Dunn, Gilbert, 44
DYE 2 and 3 (radar stations), 146

Eclipse, the (Dundee whaler), 43, 45, 46–47, 53
Edward VII, king of England, 133
Effie M. Morrissey, the (schooner), 41, 87
Egedesminde (Aasiaat), 115
Eider, common (*Somateria mollissima*), 43, 91–93, 95; king (*Somateria spectabilis*), 7, 95, 135
Eider Duck Islands, 46
Ekblaw, W. Elmer, 6, 74–75, 92, 106–7, 108
Elizabeth, the (Aberdeen whaler), 42
Ellesmere Island, 6, 16, 17, 27, 33, 44–45; Christian Adler in, 60; air photography of, 135, 137; annexed by Canada, 133; bear hunting in, 84; ice shelf, 149; Inuhuit in, 28; meteoritic iron in, 108, 109; musk-oxen in, 81, 156; names given by Ekblaw in, 174; Nukappiannguaq in, 158; Oxford University Expedition to, 128; Peary in, 38, 40, 49; Robert Stein in, 114; J. M. Wordie in, 128
Emma, the (Hull whaler), 43
Enterprise, the (Peterhead whaler), 31
Eqariusaq, 123
Eric the Red, 14
Erik, the, 38, 39–40, 69
Erik, the (Dundee whaler), 170
"Ervick," 26
Eskimo, 12, 13
Esquimaux, the (Dundee whaler), 43, 82, 127
Ethnographical Society of London, 16
Eureka, Ellesmere Island, 135
Everthorpe, the (Hull whaler), 42, 79
Expéditions Polaires Françaises, 144

Fabricius, Otto, 80
Falcon, the (St. John's whaler), 38, 85, 102
Faroes, 133–34
Feilden, H. W., 90
Fire, 21
Fish, 18, 28

Fisher, Alexander, 17, 22, 25, 41–42, 67, 90–91; on meteoritic iron, 96–97
FitzClarence Rock, Booth Sound, 56
Fletcher, Joseph, 149
Fletcher, Lazarus, 105
Florida, 138
Flowering plants, 6. *See also names of individual species*
Foulke Fjord, 9, 36, 38, 39, 45, 171; Hayes in, 71, 83, 89, 144; MacGregor Expedition in, 132
Fox (yacht), 34, 35, 65, 66, 72, 80
Fox, Arctic (*Alopex lagopus*), 53, 74, 85–86, 95, Fig. 10; trapping the, 18, 74, 77, 85, 162, 163
Fox skins: for clothing, 23–24, 51, 85, 162, Fig. 5; trade in, 69, 70–72, 74–77
Franke, Rudolph, 39–40, 54, 69, 70, 73; on Ellesmere Island, 28, 39, 133
Franklin Expedition, the, 31, 32, 33, 51, 151, 170
Franklin, Jane, 32–33, 34
Franklin, John, 29, 31, 33, 34
Frederick E. Hyde Fjord, 174
Frederikshåb (Paamiut), 80
Freuchen, Peter, 1, 40, 45, 48, 84, 156; and Comer's Midden, 130; and the Cape York meteorites, 106–7; and the Cape York mission, 158; manages Thule Station, 73, 74–76; on thick-billed murres, 91–92; on Uisaakassak, 124. *See also* Thule expeditions
Friendship, the (Hull whaler), 42
Fristrup, Børge, 144
Frobisher Bay (Iqaluit), 175

Garlington, E. A., 44
G. B. Schley Fjord, 174
General A. W. Greely (schooner), 132
George B. Cluett (auxiliary schooner), 40
Gerzah, Egypt, 98
Gibson, Langdon, 37, 92
Giddings, James L., 131
Gilberg, Lisbet, 118, 126
Gilberg, Rolf, 27–28, 113, 117, 124, 162, 166; researches the Inuhuit, 117–18, 126
Gilberg, Åge, 118, 119, 126
Gjøa, the, 38, 46–47, Fig. 7
Gladan, the, brig, 99

Godfrey, William, 16, 24, 56–57
Godhavn (Qeqertarsuaq), 44, 51, 100, 101, 151
Godthåb (Nuuk), 15, 110, 154; American consulate in, 134; National Museum of Greenland in, 108, 131
Godthåb, the, 115
Goldsmith, Oliver: *The Vicar of Wakefield,* 34
Goodsell, John W., 61, 118
Goodsir, R. A., 92
Goose, snow (*Chen caerulescens*), 7, 95, 135
Granville Fjord, 173
Gravill, John, 85, 87
Greely, Adolphus W., 36, 45, 170
Greely relief expeditions, 36, 44–45, 67
Green, Fitzhugh, 59–60, 122
Greenland, 154, 165
Greenland Church Cause, 156, 157, 158
Greenland Geological Survey, the, 149
Greenland government or Home Rule Authorities, 111, 139, 141, 154–55
Greenlandair, 141
Greer, J. A., 35
Grinnell, Henry, 33
Guillard, Robert, 145
Gull, Sabine's (*Xema sabini*), 30, 94
Gussow, Zachary, 120

Hainang, North Greenland's Newspaper, 136, 159, 160
Hakluyt, Richard, 5, 173
Hakluyt Island, 7, 93, 173
Hall, Charles F., 35, 57, 63, 87, 132, 171–72
Hall Land, 13
Hans Egede, the, 115
Hansen, Henry, 168
Hansen, Holger B., 107
Hare, Arctic (*Lepus arcticus*), 18, 51, 86
Harlow, Charles H., 67
Harper, Ken, 123
Hart, H. C., 93
Hartstene, Henry J., 34, 36
Harvard Islands, 87, 173, 174
Harvard University, 120, 173; Peabody Museum of American Archaeology and Ethnology at, 112

Hauser, Michael, 116
Haven, Edwin J. De, 33
Hayes, Isaac I., 16, 19, 21–23, 24, 48; and
    the Inuhuit, 54–57, 60; builds a cairn,
    170; expedition of 1860–61 of, 34–35,
    171; given iron flakes, 99; his collections
    unpublished, 94; hunts walrus, 89;
    investigates the Inland Ice, 33–34, 144;
    leads withdrawal party from Kane's
    expedition, 34, 55–57; names given by,
    173; on catching and eating dovekies, 91;
    on musk-oxen, 80, 81; on the Inuhuit
    population, 27, 116, 151; plans a trading
    post, 71–72; proposes North Pole
    expedition, 29; robs graves, 126; shoots
    and watches caribou, 82–83
Heather, Arctic bell (*Cassiope tetragona*), 7
Hecla, HMS, 42
Heilprin, Angelo, 37, 43, 66, 101, 116–17,
    126–27
Helsinki Botanical Garden, 99
Hendrik, Hans, or Suersaq, 16, 17, 28, 57,
    100, 155
Henson, Matthew, 49, 54, 58, 69, 73, 102
Herbert, Wally, 159–60
Herbert Island (Qeqertarsuaq), 5, 61, 161
Hiroshima, 137
Hoba, Namibia, 108
Hobbs, William H., 104, 134
Hobson, W. R., 94–95, 170
Holm, Mogens, 118, 119
Holtved, Erik, 12, 28, 83, 130, 162;
    excavates house ruins, 14–15, 129, 130;
    finds meteoritic iron, 108–9; transcribes
    Inuhuit fables, 116
Hope, the 103–4, 121, 123, 124, Fig. 12
Hoppin, Benjamin, 103
House, Edward J., 89
Houston, Edwin J., 66
Hovey, Edmund Otis, 71
Hrdlička, Ales, 118, 125
Hudson Bay, 68, 109, 130
Hull, Cordell, 134
Hull, England: ships from, 42–43. *See also*
    names of individual ships
Humboldt Glacier, 3, 6, 9, 13, 21, 34: bear
    hunting near, 84
Hunt, Harrison J., 54, 71, 83, 106, 130
Hunt, W. R., 61
Hunters' Council, the, 95, 153–55

Ice "islands," 149–50
Iceland, 133–34
Iggia, 114
Iita, 9, 11, 20, 34, 35, 57; *Beothic* at, 40;
    Cook at, 39, 70; Crocker Land
    Expedition at, 40–41, 71, 106, 133;
    dovekies at, 90, 93; Hayes at, 21, 27,
    34–35, 82, 99, 126; in 1908–9, 39–40;
    John Murphy at, 69; Kane at, 25, 92;
    MacMillan at, 41, 83; named, 175, 176;
    Oxford University Ellesmere Island
    Expedition at, 83, 128–29; Peary at, 38,
    62
Ilimanaq. *See* Claushavn
Illuluarssuit, 20
Illuminerssuit, 110, 129
Ilulissat. *See* Jakobshavn
Imilik, 173
Inaalliaq, 119
Independence Fjord, 37
Independence People, 14
Ingegerd, the (gunboat), 99
Inglefield, Edward A., 25, 27, 32–33, 173
Inglefield Gulf, 8, 38, 82, 83, 124, 162–63,
    Fig. 1; narwhals in, 86–87
Inglefield Land, 3, 9, 18, 33, 34, 119;
    caribou in, 82–84; Holtved excavates in,
    109, 129; musk-oxen in, 80
Ingnerit, 18
Inland Ice, the, 3, 5, 6, 10, 13, 121; Danes
    on, 49–50; flights over, 144, 150; Hayes
    on, 33–34, 144; Peary on, 37–38, 50, 58,
    93, 101, 105; radar stations on, 139–40,
    145, 146; retreat of, 10, 108, 147; study
    of, 144–48; Swedes on, 100
International Court of Justice at The
    Hague, 154
International Geophysical Year (1957–58),
    148, 150
International Polar Year (1882–83), 36
Intrepid, HMS, 32
Inuarfissuaq, Inglefield Land, 15, 83
Inuhuatut, 165
Inuhuit (singular Inuhuaq), the, 12; diet of,
    27–28, 167; fur clothing of, 16, 23–24,
    112, 162; health of, 24, 118–19, 160–61,
    165; houses of, 19–21, 25, 28, 79,
    112–13, 161–64; photographs of, 120–21;
    plaster casts of, 121–22; population of,
    166

Inuit, 12; of Canada, 21, 26, 27, 28, 82, 151, 165, 176
Inukitsoq, 50
Inukitsupaluk (Inighito), 60–62
Inussuk culture, 16, 18
Inuutersuaq, 75, 81, 154, 160
Iron, 32, 63–64, 66, 67, 72, 84; meteoritic, 18, 96–110; wrought, 96–97
Iron pyrites, 18
Ironstone Fjeld, 101
Isabel, the (schooner), 27, 32
Isabella, HMS, 79, 94, 96
Isbjörn Island, Cary Islands, 128
Issuvissooq, 100, 112
Iterlak, Fig. 11
Itilleq, Inglefield Gulf, 20, 66, 127
Ittukusuk, 27, 50, 59
Ittukusunguaq, 158
Ivalo, 53
Ivittuut, 134
Ivnanganeq. *See* Cape York

Jakobshavn (Ilulissat), 110, 115
Jakobshavn Glacier, 115
Jeanie, the, 40
Jensen, F., 159
Jesup, Morris K., 70, 103, 105
Jesup, Mrs. Morris K., 106
John R. Bradley, the, 39, 70
Jones, Francis, 173
Jones Sound, 173

Kallstenius, Evald G., 44–45
Kane, Elisha Kent, 16, 21–22, 23, 24, 25, 170; and Inuhuit drum songs, 114; and the Inuhuit, 54–57; birds and eggs eaten by him and his men, 93; expedition of 1853–55, 33–34, 132, 155; finds musk-ox remains, 80; his *Arctic Explorations,* 34, 65, 127; names given by, 173; on birds and bird eating, 91–92; on the Inuhuit population, 27, 116, 151; robs Eskimo graves, 126, 127; shoots caribou, 82; loses his specimens, 94
Kane Basin, 3, 6
Kangerlussuaq, 109, 161, 164
Kann, Karl, 44

Kap York, the, 74, 157
Kauffmann, Henrik, 134
Kayaks, 14, 17, 25–26, 46, 66, 81; Baffin Island type introduced in 1862, 27–28, 88, 90, 91; lack of, 16, 79; West Greenlandic, 25, 28, 161
Keely, Robert N., Jr., 51
Kennedy Channel, 34
Kiatak. *See* Northumberland Island
Kiliffak. See Mammoth
King William Island, 170
Kingigtorssuaq, 14
"Kingiktok," 56
Kite, the 51, 68, 69, 101, 104; in summer 1892, 37, 43, 58–59, 69; in summer 1895, 38, 102, 123
Kittiwake, black-legged (*Rissa tridactyla*), 93
Kiviaq, 91, 165
Knot (*Calidris canutus*), 94, 95
Knud Rasmussen Memorial Expedition, 110, 129
Knud Rasmussen Recreation Center, Thule Air Base, 141
Knuth, Eigil, 12, 131
Koch, Lauge, 5, 45, 130
Korean War, 136
Krabbe, T. N., 115
Kraulshavn (Nuussuaq), 132, 164
Kristensen, T., 89
Kristiansen, Knud, 61
Kroeber, A. L., 113–14, 116, 125
Kullorsuaq, West Greenland, 103, 163, 164
Kyoahpadu, 58, 64

Labrador, 35
Lady Franklin, the, 32
Lady Franklin Bay Expedition, 36, 67
Laguna, Frederica de, 14
Lake Alida, 83
Lake Taserssuaq, 83
Lancaster Sound, 27, 29, 31, 33, 42–43
Lappland, 162
Larkins, the (Leith whaler), 41–42
Larsen, O., 160
Lavoisier, Antoine-Laurent, 98
Leask, Mr., 32
Leden, Christian, 115–16
Lee, Hugh J., 101, 102, 117

Leith, Scotland, 63; ships from, 42. *See also Larkins*

Leningrad (St. Petersburg), 98

Lethbridge, T. C., 128

Lifeboat Cover, 36, 64, 126

Literary Greenland Expedition, 29, 39, 46–47, 116, 119, 128; and Eqariusaq, 123; and the Inuhuit, 51, 52, 59; anthropological work, 125–26; encounters caribou, 82; encounters whales, 79; information obtained by, 53, 68, 69, 82; names given by, 174; opens new trade route, 28, 71, 99; plans trading station, 72; robs graves, 127–28

Little Ice Age, 10, 16

Littleton Island (Pikiutdlek), 9, 35, 36, 92, 170, 175

London, 8, 30, 42, 97. *See also* British Museum

Lorenzen, Johannes, 110

Low, A. P., 39, 133

Lubbock, Basil, 42

Lufkin, Daniel, 136

Lynge, Christian, 98–99

MacGregor Arctic Expedition (1937–38), 132

MacKintosh, Dr., 68–69

MacMillan, Donald B., 40–41, 50, 54, 59–60, 83, 132; and the Cape York meteorites, 106; barters for fox skins, 71; describes and photographs *piblocto,* 119; hunts for records, 171; on Danes in Avanersuaq, 133, 155; on Marvin's death, 62; photographs Sonntag's grave, 171. *See also* Crocker Land Expedition

Majaq (in 1818), 25–26, 67

Majaq (in 1903), 46, 59; wife of, 51

Malaurie, Jean, 53, 54, 60, 83, 117; on alcohol, 159; on Inuhuit clothing, 84; on Inuhuit diet, 84; on Inuhuit fables, 116; on Inuhuit teeth, 160–61; on *piblocto,* 119; on Rasmussen, 153; on Sonntag's grave, 171; on the evacuation of Uummannaq, 162; on the fox skin trade, 74–75; on walrus, 88; on whales, 79

Mammoth, wooly, or *kiliffak,* 78

Mannik, 119

Markham, Albert H., 42, 48

Markham, Clements R., 12, 13, 16, 27, 37

Marshall Bay, Inglefield Land, 14, 15, 83

Marshall Plan, the, 136

Martin, Robert, 31

Marvin, Ross G., 49, 60–62, 106, 117

Massachusetts Institute of Technology, 136

Mathiassen, Therkel, 14, 16, 127, 129, 130

Mattak, 86

McCormick Fjord, 8, 10, 37, 93, 172, 174; musk-oxen at, 81; Peary in, 65; the *Kite* at, 58–59, 123. *See also* Red Cliff House

McDonald, Herbert, 44

McGary, James, 55

McGary Rock, Littleton Island, 92

McGuire Air Force Base, New Jersey, 142

McKay, Captain, 45

M'Clintock, F. L., 27, 35, 65, 93, 151; beset in Baffin Bay, 80; recovers Franklin relics, 34, 170

M'Dougall, George F., 25, 32

Meddelelser om Grønland, 116

Meeham, William E., 65–66

Meldgaard, Morten, 84

Melville Bay, 3, 6, 12, 16, 33; bear hunts in, 84; coast, 132, 157; excavations in, 129; explorers in, 38, 44, 46; glaciers named by Astrup in, 174; ice in, 100, 102, 103, 138; sledging across, 13, 28, 71, 156; Uisaakassak in, 124; whalers and whales in, 31, 41–42, 46, 47, 64 79

Meqo, 124

Meteorite Island, 102–4, 108, 122

Michigan, University of, 134

Milne, W. F., 43, 45, 46–47, 82

Minik or Mene, 122, 123

Miteq or Metek, 80

Miuk, 55

Mohn, Henrik, 174

Moltke, Harald, 1, 39, 59, 127, 174; designs stamps, 154; draws an Inuhuit house, 128, Fig. 4; paints Inuhuit portraits, 126; sick in 1903, 46–47, 52, 156. *See also* Literary Greenland Expedition

Monroe Doctrine, 134

Monzino, Guido, 149

Moore, Charles A., 174

Morgan, "Blowtorch," 147–48

Moriusaq, 141, 161, 164

Morning, the (Dundee whaler), 44, 47, 156
Moscow, 137
Mosdal, G., 97–98, 110
Mount Dundas. *See* Uummannaq
Mount Washington, New Hampshire, 144
Munich, Bavarian Institute of Minerals in, 105
Murchison Sound, Fig. 15
Murphy, John, 40, 69
Murre, thick-billed, or Brünnich's guillemot (*Uria lomvia*), 91, 92
Musk-ox (*Ovibos muschatus*), 13, 14, 40, 78–81
Mylius-Erichsen, Ludwig, 39, 46–47, 52, 53, 72, 156; and Majaq, 59; claims Avanersuaq for Denmark, 132, 152; measures Inuhuit, 125–26; robs graves, 127–28; studies Inuhuit genealogy, 117; urges Danish colonization of Avanersuaq, 72–73

Naalagaq, 24
Nagasaki, 137
Names and naming, 172–76
Nansen, Fridtjof, 174
Nares, George, 35, 36, 44, 64. *See also* British Arctic Expedition
Narsaarsuk, 20
Narsarsuaq, 134, 137
Narwhal (*Monodon monoceros*), 18, 69, 86–88, 167; tusks of, 86–87, 112; tusks of, as artifacts, 84, 90, 94, 96; tusks of, for trade, 67, 68–71, 74
Nathorst, A. G., 100, 112
National Geographic Society, 41, 61
Natsilivik, 20, 25, 33, 35, 55–57, 109; Allen Young at, 36, 63, 67; the *Kite* at, 68, 113
Neptune, the DGS (Newfoundland sealer), 36, 40, 41, 133
Neqi, 20, 49, 90
Newfoundland, 103
New Hampshire, 124
New Haven, Connecticut, 103
New York, 33, 113, 121, 137; Bellevue Hospital in, 123, 125; Brooklyn Naval Shipyard at, 104, 106; Columbia University in, 125; Inuhuit in, 116, 122–25; Neurological Society of, 120;

Obstetrical Society of, 118. *See also* American Museum of Natural History
Nielsen, Edmund, 147
Nielsen, Hans, 61, 95, 107, 161
Nigerliit, 8
Nilsson, Elias, 45
Nipaitsoq, West Greenland, 15, 110
Nordenskiöld, Adolf E., 47, 99, 100, 101, 105, 112; glacier named after, 174
Nordenskiöld, Gustaf, 45
Norfolk, Virginia, 137–38
North Atlantic, 133
North Atlantic Contractors, 137
North Atlantic Treaty Organization (NATO), 136
Northeast Passage, 47
Northice, 150
North Mountain, plateau between Uummannaq and Thule Air Base, 95, 139 148, 149, Fig. 14
North Pole, the 12, 29, 35, 132, 137, 149–50. *See also* Cook, Frederick A.; Peary, Robert E.
North Star, HMS, 31–32, 34, 51–52, 64, 104–5, 171; names resulting from her overwintering, 173
North Star Bay, 10, 20, 31–32, 72, 157, 176; Cook barters at, 70; sporting activities in, 140–41; U.S. military activities in, 134–35, 137–38; visitors at, 39–41. *See also* Thule Air Base; Thule Trading Station
North Star Inn, Thule Air Base, 141
North Star Mission, 51, 72–73, 115, 133, 155–62
Northumberland Island (Kiatak), 5, 20, 56, 87, 91, 108; North Greenland Expedition at, 113
North Water, the, 6, 7, 11, 31, 79, 90, Fig. 2; whalers in, 41–43
Northwest Passage, 29–30, 31, 33, 35–36, 46, 134
Northwind, the (icebreaker), 141–42
Nova Zembla, the (Dundee whaler), 43
Nukappianguaq, 158
Nuktaq, 123, 125
Nunatarsuaq Peninsula, 145
Nuuk. *See* Godthåb
Nuulliit, 14, 15, 109, 129

Nuussuaq. *See* Kraulshavn
Nyeboe, Ib, 73, 76

Ohlin, Axel, 38, 85
Oldsquaw or long-tailed duck (*Clangula hyemalis*), 7, 93
Olesen, Lars, 87–88
Olrik Fjord, 82–83
Olsen, Gustav, 117, 155–58, 163, 164
Olsen, Jens, 61, 87–88, 158, 161, 163
Ommanney, Erasmus, 32, 51
Oodaaq, 124, 136, 156
"Ootinah," 52
Operation Blue Jay, 137, 144
Operti, Albert, 121–22
Oqqorliit, 8
Osborn, Henry Fairfield, 78
Oscar II, king of Norway-Sweden, 174
Otter, Frederik W. von, 99
Owl, snowy (*Nyctea scandiaca*), 92
Oxford University Ellesmere Land Expedition (1934–35), 128

Paakitsoq, 8
Paamiut. *See* Frederikshåb
Pallas, P. S., 98
Palloq, 159
Pandora, the, 35–36, 63, 170
Pandora Harbour, 36
Paris, 125
Parker Snow Bay, 8, 39–40, 41, 87, 128; Swedes in, 36, 100, 112
Parry, William E., 42, Fig. 6
Peary, Josephine D., 37, 58, 65, 68, 102, 118–19, Fig. 9; and Eqariusaq, 123; and the Cape York meteorites, 106; shoots game, 82, 93
Peary, Robert E., 5, 8, 28, 43, 48, 77; acquires ethnological material, 112–14, 128, 131; and Christianity, 155; and Inuhuit women, 50–51, 54; and Qilluttooq, 62; and the Cape York meteorites, 36, 38, 101–6, 109; and the North Pole, 36, 38, 39, 105; barters for furs and ivory, 69–70; Greenland expeditions of, 29, 36–39, 50–51, 65, 101–2, 112–13, 132; his *Northward over the "Great Ice,"* 50–51, 118, 120; in

North Star Bay, 155–56; inspired by Nordenskiöld, 101; makes plaster-casts of Inuhuit, 121–22; monument to, 41, 172; names given by, 173–74; North Pole expeditions of, 48–49, 60, 62, 70, 71, 124, 136; on Inuhuit health, 118; on *piblocto,* 118–19; on the bowhead, 79; organizes censuses of the Inuhuit, 49, 116–17; photographs the Inuhuit, 120–21; raids Hakluyt Island bird cliffs, 93; said to have planned trading post, 73; shoots caribou, 82; takes Inuhuit to New York, 116, 122–25; urges purchase of Greenland by U.S.A., 133
Peary Arctic Club, 69–70, 171, 173–74
Peary Land, 14
Penny, William, 51
Permafrost, 6
Peterhead, Scotland, ships from: *See Enterprise*
Petersen, Carl, 16, 34, 56, 80–81
Philadelphia, 33, 66, 113; Geographical Club of, 38
Philadelphia Academy of Natural Sciences, 43, 65–66, 173; museum collections of, 101, 113, 114, 126; Peary and, 37, 101, 112–13, 120
Phillips, C. G., 32
Phillips, Jeffrey, 43
Phoenix, HMS, 27
Piblocto or *perlerorpoq,* 118–20
Pingorssuit or P-mountain, 139, 143
Pioneer, HMS, 85
Pitoraarfik, 16, 18, 20, 24
Pituffik Glacier, 18, 43, 173
Pituffik River and Valley, 134–36, 162, 172. *See also* Thule Air Base
Piuaatsoq, 59–60
Point Barrow, Alaska, 149
Polar Eskimo, 12
Polaris, the USS, 35, 64, 132
Polaris Bay, 58
Polaris House, 35, 57–58, 64
"Polar Sea," 33, 34
Politiken Glacier, 174
Polynia, the (Dundee whaler), 43
Pommier, Robert, 147
Poppy, Arctic (*Papaver radicatum*), 7, 172
Post or mail, 36, 43–44, 46, 51
Pritchard, Billy, 40

Project Icicle, 149
Project Mint Julep, 144
Project Snowman, 144
Proteus, the, 36
Protococcus nivalis, 8
Pualorsuaq, 116
Putnam, David Binney, 152–53
Putnam, Frederick Ward, 112–13
Putnam, George Palmer, 41, 61, 78, 87

Qaanaaq, 3, 11, 49, 58, 79, 141, Figs. 1, 15,
  16; alcoholism at, 159–60; hotel at, 168;
  inhabitants of, 130, 162–63, 164; local
  council (Avanersuup Kommunia), 1, 136,
  155; mission at, 158, 161, 163; named,
  175, 176; narwhal hunt at, 87–88;
  population of, 161, 163; renamed Thule,
  176; scientific research at, 148–49
Qaavigarsuaq, 107–8
Qalasersuaq, 16, 19, 32, 82
Qasigiannguit. *See* Christianshåb
Qavanngarnitsat, 17
Qeqertarsuaq, Avanersuaq. *See* Herbert
  Island
Qeqertarsuaq, West Greenland. *See*
  Godhavn
Qeqertat, Harvard Islands, 87–88, 161
Qilluttooq (Kudlooktoo), 60–62, 106
Qisuk (1), 17
Qisuk (2), 55
Qisuk (3), 123, 125
Qisuk, Miteq, 140–41
Qitlaq, 27–28
Qulutana, 21, 56–57, 81, 123
Qulutannguaq, 54, 58

Rae, James, 52
Rae, John, 34
Rasmussen, Dagmar, 73
Rasmussen, Knud, 1, 9, 28, 39, 46, 76–77;
  administers the Thule Station, 95, 118,
  152–53, 161, 166; and Marvin's death,
  61–62; and the Cape York meteorites,
  106, 107, 108; at Uummannaq in 1909,
  73, 115; founds the Thule Station, 72–74,
  133, 156; hunts caribou, 82–83; hunts
  walrus, 74; monument to, 172; names a
  glacier, 174; on Uisaakassak, 124;

recommends airfield at Pituffik, 134; sets
  up Hunters' Council, 95, 153–54; trades
  in fox skins and ivory, 70, 72, 74;
  transcribes Inuhuit tales, 115–16, 126;
  urges Danish annexation of Avanersuaq,
  73, 132. *See* Literary Greenland
  Expedition; Thule expeditions
Ravenscraig, the (Scottish whaler), 35
Red Cliff House, McCormick Fjord, 37, 43,
  50, 64, 82; gifts distributed at, 66, Fig. 9;
  Inuhuit at, 58, 113; Pearys overwinter at,
  62, 68, 101, 112
Release, the USS, 34
Rensselaer Bay, Inglefield Land, 11, 33, 81,
  128, 132; Kane at, 57, 64 170
Resolute, Cornwallis Island, 135
Resolute, HMS, 25, 32
Rickard, T. A., 98
Rink Henrik J., 116, 174
Ripple, the (schooner), 44–45
Robertson Fjord, 8, 117
Roosevelt, Franklin D., 134
Roosevelt, the, Peary's expedition ship,
  39–40, 41, 49, 60
Rosbach, Sechmann, 119, 155–56, 156–57
Ross, John, 8, 16, 21, 23, 24, 92; and
  meteoritic iron, 96–97, 104, 109; and the
  Inuhuit, 55, 111–12, 116; and the musk-
  ox, 79–80; barters for artifacts, 66–67,
  111, Fig. 6; describes an Inuhuaq, 26; de-
  scribes drum song, 111, 114; distributes
  gifts, 64–65; encounters whales, 79;
  inspires ethnic studies, 111, 120; names
  given by, 173; on Inuhuit food, 91; on
  Inuhuit health and hygiene, 25, 112, 118;
  on Inuhuit hunting methods, 86; on
  objects of natural history, 94; voyage of
  1818, 29–31, 94, 98
Ross, W. Gillies, 68
Rothrock, Joseph T., 65–66
Royal Canadian Mounted Police, 158
Royal Danish Scientific Society, 98
Royal Geographical Society, 13, 36, 37, 173
Royal Greenland Trade Department
  (KGH), now Greenland Trade (KNI), 66,
  136, 151, 154, 167; monopoly of, 76, 141
Royal Navy, 13, 29, 31–32, 67, 85, 93. *See
  also names of individual ships*
Royal Society, 93, 94
Ruin Island, Inglefield Land, 15

Sabine, Edward, 17, 24, 30, 67, 79;
appointed by Royal Society, 93–94; on
Eskimo boats, 25–26; on meteoritic iron,
96; on musk-oxen, 80
Sabine Islands, Melville Bay, 79
Sacheuse, John, 25, 28, 30, 96–97, Fig. 6
St. John's, Newfoundland, 38, 43, 44
Salisbury, Rollin D., 174
Sallirmiut, 166
Salomonsen, Finn, 94
Sand, Rudolf, 154
Satdloq, 52
Saunders Island (Appat), 38, 53, 67, 73, 91,
132; Danes on, 46–47, 51–52, 59, 117,
123, 127–28; Eskimos on, 20, 55, 63;
named, 173, 174, 175; whales near, 79
Saunders, James, 5, 18, 31
Saveqaafik, 106
Savik meteorite, the, 106–8
Savissivik, 101, 108, 161, 163, 166, 173;
children's playground at, 141; dovekies at,
90; iron from, 18, 97, 99, 100; population
of, 161, 164–65
Saxifrage, purple (*Saxifraga oppositifolia*),
6, 172
Scandinavian Airlines System (SAS), 142
Scurvy, 31–32, 93
Seal, bearded (*Erignathus barbatus*), 86, 88,
90
Seal, harp (*Pagophilus groenlandicus*), 86,
90
Seal, ringed (*Phoca hispida*), 86, 90
Seals, 13, 18, 86, 89–90, 167; meat of, 52,
90
Sealskin, 24, 53, 68, 90; buoys of, 88; coat
of, 23, 92, Fig. 5; nets of, 18, 90; ropes
of, 82, 88, 90
Seasons, 25
Senn, Nicholas, 127, 135–36
Shackleton, Edward, 83, 160
Sharp, William, 31
Shipwrecks, 15, 63
Shugliak. *See* Southampton Island
Siberia, 98, 141
Silis, Ivars, 18
Silluk, 71, 124
Siorapaluk, 9, 141, 159–60, 161, 166;
dovekies at, 90, 92
"Sipsu," 56

Skulls, 25, 126–28
Smith, C. E., 84–85, 92
Smith, "Iceberg," 134
Smith Sound, 3, 6, 28, 29, 30, 54; American
explorers in, 33–35; lands on either side
of, 13, 15 17, 27, 110, 132–33; whalers in,
42
Smith, Thomas, 173
Snow, W. Parker, 51
Soapstone, 18, 19, 67, 112
Sofia, the, 36, 100, 112
Somerset Island, 109–10
Sonntag, August, 55–56, 57, 171
Sophia, the, 32
Soqqaq, 52, 156
Southampton Island (Shugliak), 166, 175
Soviet Union, 136, 137, 138, 144, 145
Spitsbergen, 44, 45
Spitzka, E. A., 125
Station Centrale, 147
Station Nord, 147–48, 150
Stauning, Thorvald, 74
Steensby, Hans P., 18, 81–82, 114, 115, 119
Steensby Land, 8, 14, 109
Stein, Robert, 17, 28, 114, 174–75
Stockholm, 99; Royal Academy in, 99
Streeter, Daniel W., 87–88, 152, 155, 159,
160
Suersaq. *See* Hendrik
Suersaq, Augo, 108
Sutherland Island, 36
Sutton, George M., 175
Sverdrup, Otto, 38, 73, 174
Sweden, 98
Swedes, 44–45, 99, 112
Sydney, Nova Scotia, 121
Søkongen, the, 74, 107
Søndre Strømfjord, 81, 134, 137, 142, 144,
163

Taagholt, Jørgen, 148
Taateraaq, 68, 82
Tanquary, M. C., 75
Tasiusaq, West Greenland, 71, 99, 157
"Tcheitchenguak," 21
Terra Nova, the (Dundee whaler), 43
Theft, 24, 55, 57, 154
Thetis, the, 36, 67

Thing, Henning, 92, 95
Thomas, the (Hull whaler), 42
Thomsen, Thomas, 114
Three Sister Bees, Granville Fjord, 173
Thule, 1, 11, 176
Thule Air Base, 7, 9, 10, 31, 136–50,
165–66, Fig. 14; and the evacuation of
Uummannaq, 162; Arctic foxes at, 86,
Fig. 10; damages the environment, 172.
See also Pituffik
Thule Country Club, 143
Thule district, 1, 12, 16
Thule expeditions, 49–50, 74, 83, 115, 130,
171
Thule Law, 153–55
Thule people, 14
Thule Port Authority, 142–43
Thule Times, 139–42
Thule Trading Station, 40, 95, 130, 134,
153–55, 172; abandoned, 176; and the
Inuhuit, 159–67; and the Savik
meteorite, 106–7; coinage, 76; committee
(the Cape York Station Thule
Committee), 152–53, 158, 166;
established in 1910, 1, 72–74, 106, 156;
trade in fox skins at, 71, 74–76
Thür, Hans, 137
Tigress, the USS, 35
Torngi, 54, 82, 83, 133
Tornginnguaq, 54
Tourists, 41, 127, 168
Trade and barter, 15, 17–18, 63–77
Truelove, the (Hull whaler), 42
Truman Doctrine, 136
Tugto Valley, 8
Tuluvaq, 16, 24
Tunorput meteorite, 108
Tupeq, 21
Tuttulissuaq, 84, 124, 129
Tyson, George, 35

Uisaakassak, 123, 124–5
Uivfaq, 99–100, 101, 107
Ulloriaq, 50, 157
Umiaq or women's boat, 14, 16–17, 79,
101, 115
United States of America, the, 33, 38, 40,
49, 62, 126; flag of, 36, 132–33; and

Greenland, 132–50; Inuhuit in, 123;
president of, 33, 132–33, 134
United States Air Force, 135, 138, 139, 148,
149–50
United States Army Corps of Engineers,
134, 137, 138, 144, 145
United States Army Signal Corps, 148
United States Coast Guard, 10, 134,
141–42, 149
United States National Academy of
Sciences, 87
United States Navy, 33, 67, 100, 103, 104,
134–35. *See also names of individual
ships*
United States Weather Bureau, 135
United States, the (schooner), 34, 71
Upernallit, 43
Upernavik, 16, 34, 40, 46, 98–99
Upernavik district, the, 16, 17, 39, 71, 98,
165. *See also* Kullorsuaq
Ur of the Chaldees, 98
Utiniaq, 28
Uummannaq, Avanersuaq, 1, 32–33, 50,
72, 115, 141; artifacts and clothing
acquired at, 114; barter at, 69; Danish
flag unfurled at, 74; descriptions of, 136,
164; evacuation of the inhabitants of, in
1953, 153, 162–63, 164, 176; excavations
at, 14, 129, 130; Franke at, 69; gifts
distributed at, 66; grave robbed at, 127;
mountain of, called Mount Dundas, 31,
129, 143, 154, 173, Fig. 3; musk-oxen
near, 81; named, 175, 176; population of,
157, 161, 163; Rasmussen monument at,
172; Steensby at, 119; *See also* Comer's
Midden; North Star Mission; Thule
Trading Station
Uummannaq, West Greenland, 103, 126
Uusaqqaq, 126, 159

VanStone, James W., 109, 114
Vega, the (Dundee whaler), 47
Verhoeff, John M., 10, 37
Vibe, Christian, 84, 107–8
Victor, Paul-Emile, 144–45
Victory Point, King William Island, 170
Vienna: Museum of Natural History of,
97–98, 105

Vikings, 14–16, 110

Wallace, A. F. C., 120
Wallace, William, 124
Walrus (*Odobenus rosmarus*), 1, 40, 52, 86, 88–89, 95; hunting, 18, 88–89, 162–63, 167; ivory of, 15, 17–18, 70–72, 74, 88, 112; meat of, 49, 52, 55–56, 74, 88; shooting, 37
Wanderers' Home, the, 55–57, 91, Fig. 8
Washington Land, 13, 33, 173
Weather stations, 134–35, 137, 145, 147–48, 150
Weinschenk, E. A., 105
West Greenland, 1, 14, 23, 55, 95; coast of, 16, 42, 46, 78, 80, 85; iron artifacts from, 110; municipal system in, 155; plans to move Inuhuit to, 151
West Greenlanders or Kalaallit, 12, 16, 17–18, 26, 99; in Avanersuaq, 16–17, 28, 164–65; mission to Avanersuaq staffed by, 115, 152, 155–59, 164
West Greenlandic language or Kalaallisut, 24, 155, 157, 159, 165, 175–76
Westover Air Force Base, Massachusetts, 137
Whalers, 29, 41–47, 53, 68–69, 79; caribou shot by, 82
Whales, 1, 9, 13, 29, 41, 79; bones of, 9, 15, 79, 128. *See* Bowhead

Whale Sound, 8, 17, 42, 43, 50, 121; bartering in, 68; named by Baffin, 79, 173; walrus hunts in, 89; whales in, 79
White, Joseph G., 69
Whitney, Harry P., 28, 40, 69, 92, 119, 167; hunts caribou, 83; hunts narwhal, 87
Widmanstätten, Alois von, 98
Wife exchange, 52–53, 54, 117, 156, 159
Willow, Arctic (*Salix arctica*), 7
Windward, the, 38, 124
Wissler, Clark, 109, 130
Wolf (*Canis lupus*), 85
Wolstenholme, John, 41, 173
Wolstenholme Fjord, 8, 10, 14, 15, 46–47, 81; aircraft crashes in, 143; hunting in, affected by Thule Air Base, 162–63; J-site overlooking, 139; named by Baffin, 173; naming of glaciers debouching into, 174; *North Star* in, 31, 34, 105
Wolstenholme Island, 32, 43, 84
Wood, 18, 32, 63–64, 66, 67, 72
Wordie, J. M., 128
World Aeronautical Chart, 135
World's Columbian Exhibition in Chicago, 112–13, 114

Yantic, the USS, 36
Young, Allen, 35–36, 63, 67, 170

NORTHWEST GREENLAND
was composed in 10/12 Times Roman on a Varityper system
by Professional Book Compositors, Inc.;
printed by sheet-fed offset on 55-pound Glatfelter Natural stock,
an acid-free sheet bulking at 360 pages per inch,
with a photo signature printed on 70-pound enamel stock,
notch bound and cased into .088″ binders boards
covered in Holliston Kingston Natural cloth,
with 80-pound Rainbow Antique endpapers,
and wrapped with dust jackets printed in four colors
on 80-pound enamel stock and film laminated
by BookCrafters, Inc.;
designed by Will Underwood;
and published by
THE UNIVERSITY OF MAINE PRESS
Orono, Maine 04469-0150